EXAM✓CRAM

P9-AOO-910

The CCNA Voice Cram Sheet

This Cram Sheet contains the distilled, key facts about the CCNA Voice exam. Review this information as the last step before you enter the testing center, paying special attention to those areas where you feel that you need the most review.

PSTN COMPONENTS AND TECHNOLOGIES

1. The legacy PSTN is the most common mode for voice communications.

PSTN Services

2. The following are the most common connections to legacy PSTN service providers:
   - ▶ Local loop with loop start or ground start signaling
   - ▶ Digital CAS service for T1 or E1
   - ▶ ISDN basic (BRI) or primary (T1/E1) common channel signaling (CCS)

Time-Division and Statistical Multiplexing

3. TDM provides multiple constantly active paths transported over individual isolated subcircuits using a single physical connection (T1/E1).

4. A statistical multiplexing connection provides a single physical connection that can carry one to many conversations, where everyone shares the bandwidth (Ethernet).

Signaling Types

5. The signaling types are as follows:
   - ▶ **Supervisory:** On-hook, off-hook, and ringing
   - ▶ **Informational:** Busy, ringback, reorder, and dial tones
   - ▶ **Addressing:** Pulse or DTMF

Numbering Plans

6. All numbering plans require codes (such as area codes) that are digits that do not always need to be dialed and local numbers that must always be dialed.

Analog Circuits

7. Types of analog circuits include the following:
   - ▶ Local loop with loop or ground start to the CO
   - ▶ E&M to a PBX
   - ▶ DID from a CO

Digital Circuits

8. PSTN digital circuits:
   - ▶ T1 or E1 with CAS signaling
   - ▶ BRI, T1 (PRI), or E1 (PRI) with ISDN signaling (CCS)

PBX, Key Systems, Trunks, and Tie Lines

9. Customer telephone systems and circuits:
   - ▶ **Key systems:** 50 or fewer users, all lines on all phones
   - ▶ **PBX:** More features, extensions, multiple DID numbers multiplexed over fewer CO connections
   - ▶ **Trunk:** CO connection
   - ▶ **Tie line:** Point-to-point private connection

VOIP COMPONENTS AND TECHNOLOGIES

Voice Packetization

10. Voice packetization is the conversion of analog signals to a digital format.

11. Sequence of operations is sampling the analog signal into 8 bits of information, quantization to identify waveform instance, encoding the quantized voice, and compression.

12. Enough samples are gathered to create 10ms of voice and handed to RTP for packetization.

13. The most commonly used VoIP codec is G.711, which operates with u-law in North America and Japan and a-law in the rest of the world.

RTP and RTCP

14. RTP takes 10ms voice samples and puts together one, two, or three 10ms samples with an RTP header that describes the media type, and provides sequence numbers for the media stream with time stamps.

15. RTCP records any issues, such as jitter and dropped packets, and periodically sends the statistics to the sender.

Codec Functions and Differences

16. A codec is a standards-based definition that describes the format of the 10ms voice samples created during the packetization process.

17. The G.711 codec is the simplest to understand: 1 byte in is the same as 1 byte out.

18. G.729a is the second most common codec used in VoIP environments. This codec predicts the upcoming signal and only measures the variation from the prediction, saving bandwidth. This results in an 8-to-1 compression ratio that reduces IP network bandwidth requirements.

H.323, MGCP, SIP and SCCP Signaling Protocols

19. H.323 is a peer-to-peer, ITU-standard protocol that is based on the ISDN Q.931 protocol.

20. SIP is a peer-to-peer, IETF-standard protocol that handles signaling for voice, video, instant messaging, and presence.

21. The Media Gateway Control Protocol (MGCP) is an IETF-standard client/server protocol.

22. SCCP is a client/server, Cisco-proprietary protocol that is used primarily with Cisco IP phones.

GATEWAYS, VOICE PORTS, AND DIAL PEERS

23. Gateways are used to connect a CME solution to the PSTN (or another PBX).

Voice Gateways

24. Two types of gateways convert the incoming voice to VoIP packets and the outgoing VoIP packets to voice:

   ▶ Analog gateways have FXS, FXO, and/or E&M ports.

   ▶ Digital gateways have T1, E1, or BRI ports.

Voice Ports

25. Two types of voice ports exist: analog and digital.

26. Digital port types are BRI, PRI (T1 has 23 voice channels, E1 has 30), and CAS.

27. The destination of a POTS dial peer is a voice port.

Call Legs

28. A call leg is a logical connection between two end devices.

29. A call between two devices typically uses two call legs per router hop.

Voice Dial Peers

30. A dial peer is used to route a call.

31. The two types of dial peers are POTS and VoIP.

32. POTS dial peers point to voice ports.

33. VoIP dial peers point to an IP address.

34. A sample POTS dial peer follows:

```
dial-peer voice 20 pots
destination-pattern 2000
port 0/0/1
```

35. A sample VoIP dial peer follows:

```
dial-peer voice 30 voip
destination-pattern 3...
session target ipv4:10.10.11.1
```

CONFIGURE A CISCO NETWORK TO SUPPORT VOIP

36. IP is the transport mechanism for VoIP traffic.

VLANs in a VoIP Environment

37. The typical configuration of a Catalyst switch port to support VoIP creates a native or access data VLAN for the PC and an 802.1Q portal for a single voice VLAN.

38. The voice VLAN is used for security and QoS.

Configure Voice and Data VLANs

39. A standard VoIP interface implementation follows:

```
interface fa0/1
 switchport mode access
 switchport access vlan 10
 switchport voice vlan 110
 spanning-tree portfast
```

PoE

40. Power over Ethernet (PoE) provides power for the IP phones connected to the switch. If the power goes out, the UPS backing up the switch also keeps the IP phone operating.

Voice Quality

41. The three network issues that lead to poor voice quality are delay, both end-to-end and hop-by-hop; bandwidth requirements; and dropped packets.

QoS

42. The Cisco AutoQoS feature simplifies the implementation of QoS for Cisco IP networks.

CISCO CONFIGURATION ASSISTANT (CCA) FOR UC500

43. CCA is a GUI that allows you to monitor and configure the UC500. It offers two graphical views, topology and UC500 front panel.

Cisco Configuration Assistant

44. Choose **Configure** > **Telephony** > **Voice** to configure the telephony features of the UC500 from CCA. From here you can access the configuration screens.

Device Tab

45. From the Device tab, you can view the following fields:

   ▶ **Router Platform:** Displays the UC500 model information

   ▶ **Built In:** Displays built-in devices such as Unity Express, FXO, and FXS ports

   ▶ **VIC:** Displays what is displayed in the VIC slot

   ▶ **Wireless:** Displays whether a built-in WAP exists

CCNA Voice

David Bateman and William Burton, CCIE No. 1119

About the Authors

David J. Bateman is a certified Cisco instructor with more than 20 years of inter-networking experience. In addition to teaching, he is involved in authoring courses and books, including *Configuring Cisco CallManager and Unity: A Step-by-Step Guide*, published by Cisco Press. David currently is the director of curriculum development for Skyline-ATS. His years of real-world technical and business knowledge allow him to bring a unique perspective to the classroom, where he not only delivers critical technical knowledge but also explains how technologies can be used to address various business needs.

William E. Burton, CCSI, CCIE No. 1119, CCVP, CCNP, CCVA, CCNA, is an author, instructor, and IT implementer with more than 35 years of experience. Mr. Burton's experience includes small to global network architecture and deployments for federal agencies, state and local governments, corporations, and educational institutions. He also has extensive programming experience in the telephony arena at AT&T Long Lines and Bell Labs.

About the Contributing Author

Dave Schultz has more than 25 years of experience with various technologies, ranging from routing and switching to security and voice technologies. Dave currently teaches voice technology classes at Skyline Advanced Technology Services, including CCMSA, AUM, and CIPT. Before joining the Skyline ATS, he was involved in network engineering and consulting, project management, and oversight of engineering and maintenance activities for a reseller in the Midwest. He has taught various technologies to customers and engineers and created various process and procedure methodologies, service pricing, and documentation. Dave has created a technical assistance center, while being a manager and director of professional services and performing installation, support, and consulting in various customer environments. He also has had contracting responsibilities at a large global enterprise-level corporation, where duties included routing, switching, security, wireless, and project management. Dave resides in Cincinnati, Ohio, with his wife and three daughters, Amy, Ericka, and Tiffany.

About the Reviewers

Toby Sauer is the lead voice instructor at Skyline Advanced Technology Services, a Cisco Learning Solutions Partner. Toby has more than 25 years of experience in traditional voice installations with companies such as Qwest, Norstan Communications (now part of Black Box), and the United States Marine Corps. Toby has been installing Cisco Communications Manager systems since Cisco started selling the product. He has spent the last eight years as an instructor with Skyline ATS, teaching all voice-related courses. Toby was recently given the additional responsibility of all voice lab development with his assignment to his new title of voice curriculum manager.

Ted Trentler has been in the IT field for 13 years, focusing on implementation and design, with the last several years primarily concentrated in Unified Communications consulting. He is currently a lead instructor for Global Knowledge and is webmaster for UC500.com, an IOS voice support website. He also is a technical contributor to Global Knowledge's Cisco IOS voice labs. Some of his certifications include CCDA, CCVP Cisco IP Communications Express Specialist, and Cisco IP Telephony Design Specialist. He also is a certified Cisco instructor. Ted lives in the Tampa Bay area of Florida with his wife Denise and daughter Madison.

Dedication

To Nikki, my wife, my love, my soulmate. She is the one
who makes all of life's joys even sweeter.
—David Bateman

To Barbara, my better half, who put up with
the long hours tying up our home computer.
—William Burton

Acknowledgments

From David Bateman:

I'd like to thank the Academy . . . oh wait, that's the wrong speech. Seriously, I want to start off by thanking my unofficial editor, my wife. The hours she spends reading my work are greatly appreciated. I also want to thank Bill Burton for taking on the challenge of writing this book when we were both already too busy with other projects. I'd like to thank my coworkers at Skyline-ATS who have challenged and inspired me to learn and teach. And of course, I thank the good folks at Pearson Education, who gave us the opportunity to write this book.

From William Burton:

Thanks to Dave Bateman for sharing this writing experience and bringing me back to the joy of writing books. Thanks to Dayna Isley and the team from Pearson Education for making sure I didn't wander too far from the beaten path.

We Want to Hear from You!

As the reader of this book, *you* are our most important critic and commentator. We value your opinion and want to know what we're doing right, what we could do better, what areas you'd like to see us publish in, and any other words of wisdom you're willing to pass our way.

As an associate publisher for Que Publishing, I welcome your comments. You can email or write me directly to let me know what you did or didn't like about this book—as well as what we can do to make our books better.

Please note that I cannot help you with technical problems related to the topic of this book. We do have a User Services group, however, where I will forward specific technical questions related to the book.

When you write, please be sure to include this book's title and authors as well as your name, email address, and phone number. I will carefully review your comments and share them with the authors and editors who worked on the book.

Email: feedback@quepublishing.com

Mail: Dave Dusthimer
             Associate Publisher
             Que Publishing
             800 East 96th Street
             Indianapolis, IN 46240 USA

Reader Services

Visit our website and register this book at informit.com/register for convenient access to any updates, downloads, or errata that might be available for this book.

Introduction

Welcome to *CCNA Voice Exam Cram*. Whether this book is your first or your fifteenth *Exam Cram* series book, you'll find information here that will help ensure your success as you pursue knowledge, experience, and certification. This book aims to help you get ready to take and pass the Cisco CCNA Voice exam number 640-460.

This introduction explains the Cisco certification programs in general and talks about how the *Exam Cram* series can help you prepare for the Cisco CCNA Voice exam. Chapters 1 through 15 are designed to remind you of everything you'll need to know to pass the 640-460 certification exam. The two practice exams at the end of the book should give you a reasonably accurate assessment of your knowledge, and we've provided the answers and their explanations for these practice exams. Read the book and understand the material, and you'll stand a very good chance of passing the real test.

Exam Cram books help you understand and appreciate the subjects and materials you need to know to pass Cisco certification exams. *Exam Cram* books are aimed strictly at test preparation and review. They do not teach you everything you need to know about a subject. Instead, the authors streamline and highlight the pertinent information by presenting and dissecting the questions and problems they've discovered that you're likely to encounter on a Cisco test.

Nevertheless, to completely prepare yourself for any Cisco test, we recommend that you begin by taking the "Self Assessment" that immediately follows this introduction. The self-assessment tool will help you evaluate your knowledge base against the requirements for the Cisco CCVA exam under both ideal and real circumstances. This can also be the first step in earning more advanced voice certifications.

Based on what you learn from the self-assessment, you might decide to begin your studies with classroom training or some background reading. On the other hand, you might decide to pick up and read one of the many study guides available from Que or a third-party vendor.

We also strongly recommend that you spend some time installing, configuring, and working with Cisco Unified Communications Manager Express, Cisco Unity Express, and the UC500 Smart Business Communications System, because the CCNA Voice exam is focused on these products and the knowledge and skills they can provide for you. Nothing beats hands-on experience and familiarity when it comes to understanding the questions you're likely to encounter on a certification test. Book learning is essential, but without a doubt, hands-on experience is the best teacher of all!

Cisco Certifications Overview

The first step in general Cisco career certifications begins either with CCENT as an interim step to Associate level or directly with CCNA for network operations or CCDA for network design. A variety of specialist-focused certifications are also available to show knowledge in specific technologies, solutions, or job roles. The following sections describe the general certification levels and paths.

General Certifications: Three Levels of Certification

The three levels of certification for general certifications are

▶ **Associate:** The first step in Cisco networking begins at the Associate level, which also includes CCENT, an interim step to Associates for those with little job experience. Think of the Associate level as the apprentice or foundation level of networking certification.

▶ **Professional:** This is the advanced or journeyman level of certification.

▶ **Expert:** This is CCIE, the highest level of achievement for network professionals, certifying an individual as an expert or master.

General Certifications: Six Different Paths

The widely respected IT certification programs available through Cisco Career Certifications bring valuable, measurable rewards to networking professionals, their managers, and the organizations that employ them. The following is the list of these six certification technologies:

▶ **Routing and Switching:** This path is for professionals who install and support Cisco technology–based networks in which LAN and WAN routers and switches reside.

▶ **Design:** This path is aimed at professionals who design Cisco technology–based networks in which LAN and WAN routers and switches reside.

▶ **Network Security:** This path is directed toward network professionals who design and implement Cisco Secure networks.

▶ **Service Provider:** This path is aimed at professionals working with infrastructure or access solutions in a Cisco end-to-end environment primarily within the telecommunications arena.

- **Storage Networking:** This path is for professionals who implement storage solutions over extended network infrastructure using multiple transport options.

- **Voice:** This path is directed toward network professionals who install and maintain voice solutions over IP networks.

Taking a Certification Exam

After you prepare for your exam, you need to register with a Pearson VUE testing center. At the time of this writing, the cost to take the CCNA Voice exam is $250 for individuals. If you don't pass, you can take the exam again for the same cost as the first attempt, for each attempt until you pass. In the United States and Canada, tests are administered by Pearson VUE. Here's how you can contact them:

- **Prometric:** You can sign up for a test through the company's website, http://www.2test.com or http://www.prometric.com. Within the United States and Canada, you can register by phone at 800-755-3926. If you live outside this region, you should check the Prometric website for the appropriate phone number.

- **Pearson VUE:** You can contact Virtual University Enterprises (VUE) to locate a nearby center that administers the test and to make an appointment. The sign-up web page address for the exam is http://www.vue.com/cisco. You can also use this web page (click the Contact button, click the View Telephone Directory by Sponsor link, and then click Cisco) to obtain a telephone number for the company, if you can't or don't want to sign up for the exam on the web page.

To sign up for a test, you must provide payment as approved by Pearson VUE.

To schedule an exam, call the appropriate phone number or visit the Pearson Vue website at least one day in advance. To cancel or reschedule an exam in the United States or Canada, you must call before 3 p.m. Eastern time the day before the scheduled test time (or you might be charged, even if you don't show up to take the test). To schedule a test, have the following information ready:

- Your name, organization, and mailing address.

- Your Cisco test ID. (In the United States, this could be your Social Security number; citizens of other countries should call ahead to find out what type of identification is required to register for a test.)

▸ The name and number of the exam you want to take.

▸ A method of payment. (A credit card is the most convenient method, but alternate means can be arranged in advance, if necessary.)

After you sign up for a test, you are told when and where the test is scheduled. You should arrive at least 15 minutes early. You must supply two forms of identification, one of which must be a photo ID, to be admitted into the testing room. Be prepared for a biometric fingerprint scan and the taking of a digital picture each time you take an exam.

Tracking Certification Status

After you pass the exam, you are certified. Official certification is normally granted after six to eight weeks, so you shouldn't expect to get your credentials overnight. The package for official certification that arrives includes a Welcome Kit that contains a number of elements (see the Cisco website for other benefits of specific certifications):

▸ A certificate that is suitable for framing, along with a wallet card.

▸ A license to use the related certification logo. This means you can use the logo in advertisements, promotions, and documents and on letterhead, business cards, and so on. Along with the license comes a logo sheet, which includes camera-ready artwork. (Note that before you use any of the artwork, you must sign and return a licensing agreement that indicates you'll abide by its terms and conditions.)

Many people believe that the benefits of certification go well beyond the perks that Cisco certifications provide to newly anointed members of this elite group. We're starting to see more job listings that request or require applicants to have Cisco and other related certifications, and many individuals who complete Cisco certification programs can qualify for increases in pay and responsibility. As an official recognition of hard work and broad knowledge, a certification credential is a badge of honor in many IT organizations.

About This Book

We've structured the topics in this book to build on one another. Therefore, some topics in later chapters make the most sense after you've read earlier chapters. That's why we suggest that you read this book from front to back for your initial test preparation. If you need to brush up on a topic or if you have to bone up for a second try, you can use the index or table of contents to go straight to the topics and questions that you need to study. Beyond helping you prepare for the test, we think you'll find this book useful as a tightly focused reference to some of the most important aspects of the Cisco CCVA certification.

Chapter Format and Conventions

Each topical *Exam Cram* chapter follows a regular structure and contains graphical cues about important or useful information. Here's the structure of a typical chapter:

▶ **Opening hot lists:** Each chapter begins with a list of the terms, tools, and techniques that you must learn and understand before you can be fully conversant with that chapter's subject matter. The hot lists are followed with one or two introductory paragraphs to set the stage for the rest of the chapter.

▶ **Topical coverage:** After the opening hot lists and introductory text, each chapter covers a series of topics related to the chapter's subject. Throughout that section, we highlight topics or concepts that are likely to appear on a test, using a special element called an Exam Alert:

EXAM ALERT

This is what an Exam Alert looks like. Normally, an alert stresses concepts, terms, software, or activities that are likely to relate to one or more certification-test questions. For that reason, we think any information in an alert is worthy of unusual attentiveness on your part.

You should pay close attention to material flagged in Exam Alerts; although all the information in this book pertains to what you need to know to pass the exam, Exam Alerts contain information that is really important. You'll find what appears in the meat of each chapter to be worth knowing, too, when preparing for the test. Because this book's material is condensed, we recommend that you use this book along with other resources to achieve the maximum benefit.

In addition to the alerts, we provide tips and notes that will help you build a better foundation for security knowledge. Although the tip information might not be on the exam, it is certainly related, and it will help you become a better-informed test taker.

TIP

This is how tips are formatted. Keep your eyes open for these, and you'll become a Cisco Certfied Network Associate - Voice guru in no time!

NOTE

This is how notes are formatted. Notes direct your attention to important pieces of information that relate to the Cisco Certified Network Associate - Voice certification.

▶ **Exam prep questions:** Although we talk about test questions and topics throughout the book, the section at the end of each chapter presents a series of mock test questions and explanations of both correct and incorrect answers.

▶ **Details and resources:** Most chapters end with a section titled "Suggested Reading and Resources" that provides direct pointers to third-party resources that offer more details on the chapter's subject. In addition, that section tries to rank, or at least rate, the quality and thoroughness of the topic's coverage by each resource. If you find a resource you like in that collection, you should use it, but you shouldn't feel compelled to use all the resources. On the other hand, we recommend only resources that we use on a regular basis, so none of our recommendations will be a waste of your time or money (but purchasing them all at once probably represents an expense that many network administrators and certification candidates might find hard to justify).

The bulk of the book follows this chapter structure, but we'd like to point out a few other elements:

▶ "Practice Exam 1" and "Practice Exam 2" and the answer explanations provide good reviews of the material presented throughout the book to ensure that you're ready for the exam.

▶ The Glossary defines important terms used in this book.

▶ The tear-out Cram Sheet attached next to the inside front cover of this book represents a condensed and compiled collection of facts and tips that we think are essential for you to memorize before taking the test. Because you can dump this information out of your head onto a sheet of paper before taking the exam, you can master this information by brute force; you need to remember it only long enough to write it down when you walk into the testing room. You might even want to look at it in the car or in the lobby of the testing center just before you walk in to take the exam.

▶ The MeasureUp Practice Tests CD-ROM that comes with each Exam Cram and Exam Prep title features a powerful, state-of-the-art test engine that prepares you for the actual exam. MeasureUp Practice Tests are developed by certified IT professionals and are trusted by certification students around the world. For more information, visit http://www.measureup.com.

Exam Topics

Table I-1 lists the skills measured by the CCNA Voice 640-460 exam and the chapter in which the topic is discussed. Some topics are covered in multiple chapters.

TABLE I-1   Cisco 640-460 Exam Topics

Exam Topic	Chapter
Describe PSTN Components and Technologies	
Describe the services provided by the PSTN	1, 2, 3
Describe time-division and statistical multiplexing	1, 2, 3
Describe supervisory, informational, and address signaling	1, 2, 3
Describe numbering plans	1, 2, 3
Describe analog circuits	1, 2, 3
Describe digital voice circuits	1, 2, 3
Describe PBX, trunk lines, key systems, and tie lines	1, 2, 3
Describe VoIP Components and Technologies	
Describe the process of voice packetization	4
Describe RTP and RTCP	4
Describe the function of and differences between codecs	4
Describe H.323, MGCP, SIP, and SCCP signaling protocols	4, 5
Describe and Configure Gateways, Voice Ports, and Dial Peers to Connect to the PSTN and Service Provider Networks	
Describe the function and application of a dial plan	6
Describe the function and application of voice gateways	6
Describe the function and application of voice ports in a gateway	6
Describe the function and operation of call legs	6
Describe and configure voice dial peers	6
Describe the differences between PSTN and Internet telephony service provider circuits	6

TABLE I-1 *continued*

Exam Topic	Chapter
Describe and Configure a Cisco Network to Support VoIP	
Describe the purpose of VLANs in a VoIP environment	7
Describe the environmental considerations to support VoIP	7
Configure switched infrastructure to support voice and data VLANs	7
Describe the purpose and operation of PoE	7
Identify the factors that impact voice quality	8
Describe how QoS addresses voice quality issues	8
Identify where QoS is deployed in the UC infrastructure	8
Implement UC500 Using Cisco Configuration Assistant	
Describe the function and operation of Cisco Configuration Assistant	14, 15
Configure UC500 device parameters	14, 15
Configure UC500 network parameters	14, 15
Configure UC500 dial plan and voicemail parameters	14, 15
Configure UC500 SIP trunk parameters	14, 15
Configure UC500 voice system features	14, 15
Configure UC500 user parameters	14, 15
Implement Cisco Unified Communications Manager Express to Support Endpoints Using CLI	
Describe the appropriate software components needed to support endpoints	9, 10, 12
Describe the requirements and correct settings for DHCP, NTP, and TFTP	10, 12
Configure DHCP, NTP, and TFTP	10, 12
Describe the differences between key system and PBX mode	10, 12
Describe the differences between the different types of ephones and ephone-dns	10, 12
Configure Cisco Unified Communications Manager Express endpoints	10, 12, 13
Configure call transfer per design specifications	10, 12
Configure voice productivity features, including hunt groups, call park, call pickup, paging groups, and paging/intercom	10, 12, 13
Configure Music on Hold	10, 12
Implement Voicemail Features Using Cisco Unity Express	
Describe the Cisco Unity Express hardware platforms	11
Configure the foundational elements required for Cisco Unified Communications Manager Express to support Cisco Unity Express	11
Describe the features available in Cisco Unity Express	11
Configure Auto Attendant services using Cisco Unity Express	11
Configure basic voicemail features using Cisco Unity Express	11

TABLE I-1 *continued*

Exam Topic	Chapter
Describe the Components of the Cisco Unified Communications Architecture	
Describe the function of the infrastructure in a UC environment	A
Describe the function of endpoints in a UC environment	A
Describe the function of the call processing agent in a UC environment	A
Describe the function of messaging in a UC environment	A
Describe the function of Auto Attendants and IVRs in a UC environment	A
Describe the function of a contact center in a UC environment	A
Describe the applications available in the UC environment, including Mobility, Presence, and Telepresence	A
Describe how the Unified Communications components work together to create the Cisco Unified Communications Architecture	A

Self-Assessment

So, how do you know when you are ready to take the Cisco IIUC exam (640-460)? You need to consider a number of factors to make that determination. The purpose of this section is to help you to understand these factors before you attempt to achieve your Cisco CCNA Voice certification.

CCNA Voice Certification in the Real World

Cisco certification is one of the most sought-after certifications around. Sure, you can get other certifications, but the Cisco certifications seem to hold a higher value in the eyes of employers and coworkers. One of the most successful Cisco certification programs is the CCNA. This certification proves that an individual has a solid understating of the basic Cisco network components and can successfully configure most common network solutions. The question that most CCNAs ask themselves after passing the CCNA test is, "What's next?" Until recently, the answer was a CCNP, CCVP, CCSP, or CCIP certification. Each of these certifications required the candidate to take and pass three to five tests. Candidates also had to pick an area of specialization. Cisco realized that some individuals wanted to validate their knowledge in certain areas or multiple areas but were not interested or not willing to invest the time and money to pursue the CCxP track. This is why Cisco created the CCNA Voice certification. In addition to the CCNA Voice certifications, Cisco has created a CCNA Security and CCNA Wireless certification.

CCNA Voice is a relatively new certification, and expected demand for individuals with this certification and associate knowledge is very large. This is an excellent certification for a person who has a solid understanding of Cisco Unified Communications Manager Express and wants to be recognized for it.

The following sections take a closer look at the ideal CCNA Voice candidate and give you an opportunity to assess your own readiness.

The Ideal CCNA Voice Certification Candidate

So, what does the ideal CCNA Voice candidate look like? He or she looks like you or the person down the street or the person that works down the hall. In other words, anyone can achieve this certification, that is, anyone with the drive and desire. That being said, there are certain characteristics and background that successful candidates typically have. Let's take a look at a few of them:

- **An honest desire to learn:** The students that excel are those who want to learn more about a topic that they are really interested in and enjoy.

- **Strong studying discipline:** Passing the test is not going to be easy. You are going to need to spend time studying. This is where those who have good studying habits will have an advantage.

- **Solid Cisco networking knowledge:** One of the requirements for a CCNA Voice certification is to already have a CCNA.

- **Telephony background:** Because a portion of the test covers traditional telephony knowledge, a strong telephony background is a plus.

- **Test-taking ability:** Because this certification depends on you passing a test, being a good test taker is helpful. Being a good test taker does not necessarily mean that you are calm and cool and are able to "guess" the correct answers. It merely means that you show up (showing up is a huge help in passing a test), stay focused, and manage your time wisely.

- **Motivation:** This is possibly one of the most important characteristics. Like the saying goes, "It's not the size of the dog in the fight; it's the size of the fight in the dog." With strong motivation and desire, nearly anything is possible.

So let's say you look at this list and you don't feel you have any of these characteristics. Does that mean you can never pass the test? Of course not; this is a description of the "ideal candidate." However, it does mean that you will have a bit of work in front of you.

Put Yourself to the Test

The following series of questions and observations are designed to help you figure out how much work you must do to pursue Cisco certification and what kinds of resources you can consult on your quest. Be absolutely honest in your answers, or you'll end up wasting money on exams that you're not yet ready to take. There are no right or wrong answers—only steps along the path to certification. Only you can decide where you really belong in the broad spectrum of aspiring candidates. Two points should be clear from the outset, however:

- Even a modest background in telephony will be helpful.

- Hands-on experience with Cisco products and technologies is an essential ingredient in certification success.

Educational Background

The following questions concern your level of technical computer experience and training. Depending upon your answers to these questions, you might need to review some additional resources to get your knowledge up to speed for the types of questions that you will encounter on Cisco certification exams:

1. Have you ever taken any computer-related classes?

2. Have you taken any training on telephony technologies?

   This background will help you more quickly understand and digest the many telephony terms and concepts that the test will cover.

3. Have you taken any networking concepts or technologies classes?

   You will probably be able to handle the numerous mentions of networking terminology concepts such as DHCP and VLANs. Because a CCNA is required, it is assumed that you have this knowledge.

4. Have you done any reading on telephony technologies?

   Knowing telephony terms and concepts is good. However, knowing the Cisco take on the telephony world is more important. Students with a very strong telephony background often struggle with Cisco concepts and commands because they are not what they are used to. It is best to have a solid background but an open mind.

5. Have you been involved in a Cisco voice deployment?

   There is simply nothing like hands-on experience. The idea behind any certification is to prove you are capable of successfully completing certain job tasks. This is especially true for the CCNA Voice exam. If you can deploy Cisco Unified Communications Manager Express, you should be able to do quite well on this test.

6. Have you done any reading on Cisco voice solutions?

   The next question is of course "What did you read?" One mistake people make about this test is that they figure because they have been deploying Cisco Unified Communications Manager for years, they should be able to walk in and pass this test. The problem is that this test is focused on the Cisco Unified Communications Manager Express, which is not the same as the Cisco Unified Communications Manager. While the names are very similar, the word *Express* makes a large difference. Even if you have a respectable level of Cisco Unified Communications Manager knowledge, you will need additional study to pass this test.

Hands-On Experience

An important key to success on the CCNA Voice exam lies in obtaining hands-on experience with the Cisco Unified Communications Manager Express solution. There is simply no substitute for time spent installing, configuring, and using the various interfaces for this product.

Have you installed, configured, and worked with the following systems:

▶ Cisco IOS?

Strong experience with the command-line interface (CLI) is essential in completing the simulation questions. Some simulation questions might place you at the CLI of a Cisco device, and you will be expected to configure it based on the criteria supplied. If this is an interface you are not familiar with, you had better find a way to become familiar with it before tackling the exam.

▶ Cisco voice gateways?

Some of the required knowledge can be gained from experience with Cisco H.323 gateways. Concepts such as dial peers are used in voice gateways as well as CME.

▶ Cisco Unified Communications Manager Express?

Because this test is centered around this solution, some hands-on experience is a huge plus.

▶ Cisco UC520?

If you were able to pick one device to use to get hands-on experience, it should be the UC520. With the UC520, you will be able to gain experience with all the appropriate configuration interfaces.

NOTE

You can download objectives, practice exams, and other data about CCNA Voice exams from the Training and Certification page at http://www.cisco.com/web/learning/le3/le2/le0/le3/learning_certification_type_home.html. Because links change from time to time, you can also go to Cisco.com and enter **CCNA voice** in the Search box.

Before you even think about taking any Cisco exam, you should make sure that you've spent enough time studying Cisco voice principles and practices. This time will help you in the exam—and in real life!

How to Prepare for an Exam

Preparing for any Cisco certification test requires you to obtain and study materials designed to provide comprehensive information about the product and its capabilities that will appear on the specific exam for which you are preparing. Because this is a relatively new test, the body of available study material is not as large as it is for the route/switch CCNA. That said, the resources are sure to grow in the near future. In addition to the topics and practice exams included in this book, the following list of materials (available at this writing) can help you study and prepare:

▸ *CCNA Voice Official Exam Certification Guide* (640-460 IIUC), by Jeremy Cioara, Michael J. Cavanaugh, and Kris A. Krake. Cisco Press, 2008. ISBN 1-58720-207-7.

▸ *CCNA Voice Quick Reference* (Digital Short Cut), by Michael Valentine. Cisco Press, 2008. ISBN 1-58705-767-0.

▸ Cisco.com documentation. There is a wealth of information available at Cisco.com, in some cases so much information that you can get lost. Focus on the Cisco Unified Communications Manager Express Command Reference and Cisco Unified Communications Manager Express System Administrator Guide.

▸ The official Cisco IIUC training courseware. This is the courseware that you get when you attend the IIUC course. The only way to get this courseware is to attend the class.

Along with this book, this list of materials represents a comprehensive collection of sources and resources for voice and related topics.

Studying for the Exam

While many websites describe what to study for a particular exam, few sites offer advice about how you should study for an exam. The study process can be broken down into various stages. However, critical to all these stages is the ability to concentrate.

To be able to concentrate, you must remove all distractions. While you should plan for study breaks, it is the unplanned breaks caused by distractions that do not allow you to concentrate on what you need to learn. Therefore, you first need to create an environment that's conducive to studying or seek out an existing environment that meets these criteria, such as a library.

Do not study with the TV on and do not have other people in the room. It is easy for the TV or another person to break your concentration and grab your attention.

There are varying opinions on whether it is better to study with or without music playing. While some people need to have a little white noise in the background to study, if you do choose to have music, you should keep the volume at a low level and you should listen to music without lyrics.

After you find a place to study, you must schedule the time to study. Do not study on an empty stomach, but also do not study on a full stomach because it tends to make people drowsy. You might also consider having a glass of water near to sip on.

In addition, make sure that you are well rested so that you don't doze off when you start studying. Next, make sure that you find a position that is comfortable and that the furniture that you are using is also comfortable. Finally, make sure that your study area is well lit. Natural light is best for fighting fatigue.

When you begin to study, first clear your mind of distractions. Take a minute or two, close your eyes, and empty your mind.

When you prepare for an exam, the best place to start is to take the list of exam objectives and study each objective carefully for its scope. During this time, you then organize your study, keeping these objectives in mind. This will narrow your focus area to an individual topic or subtopic. In addition, you need to understand and visualize the process as a whole. This will help in addressing practical problems in a real environment as well as some unsuspecting questions.

In a multiple-choice-type exam, you do have one advantage: The answer or answers are already there, and you simply have to choose the correct ones. Because the answers are already there, you can start eliminating the incorrect answers by using your knowledge and some logical thinking. One common mistake is to select the first obvious-looking answers without checking the other options, so always examine all the options, and think and choose the right answer. Of course, with multiple-choice questions, you have to be exact and should be able to differentiate between very similar answers. This is where a peaceful place of study without distractions helps so that you can read between the lines and so that you don't miss key points.

Testing Your Exam Readiness

Whether you attend a formal class on a specific topic to get ready for an exam or use written materials to study on your own, some preparation for the CCNA Voice certification exam is essential. At $125 a try pass or fail, you want to do everything you can to pass on your first try. That is where studying comes in.

Included at the end of this book are two practice exams that you can use for self-assessment. While the questions in this book are similar to what is on the test, you need to remember that they are not the actual test questions, so you need to do more then just run through the assessment until you get all the answers right. You have to truly understand the underlying concepts and know why the correct answer is correct. Use this assessment as a tool to determine what areas you need to study in more detail. When you feel you have mastered the material, you might just be ready for the real world!

Because there are two practice exams in this book, if you don't score well on the first test, you can study more and then tackle the second test. If you still don't hit a score of at least 90 percent after these tests, you should spend more time studying before moving forward. There are a number of places that offer practice tests. Before you spend your hard-earned money on these, see what other people are saying about the particular one you are thinking of purchasing.

For any given subject, consider taking a class if you have tackled self-study materials, taken the test, and failed. The opportunity to interact with an instructor and fellow students can make all the difference, if you can afford that privilege. For information about CCNA Voice classes, use your favorite search engine with a string such as "CCNA Voice." Even if you can't afford to spend much, you should still invest in some low-cost practice exams from commercial vendors.

The next question deals with your personal testing experience. Cisco certification exams have their own style and idiosyncrasies. The more acclimated that you become to the Cisco testing environment, the better your chances will be to score well on the exams.

Have you taken a Cisco practice exam? If you scored 90 percent or better, you are probably ready to tackle the real thing. If your score isn't above that threshold, keep at it until you break that barrier.

> **TIP**
>
> When assessing your test readiness, there is no better way than to take a good-quality practice exam and pass with a score of 90 percent or better. When we are preparing ourselves, we shoot for better than 95 percent, just to leave room for the "weirdness factor" that sometimes depresses exam scores when taking the real thing.

Dealing with Test Anxiety

Because a certification exam costs money and requires preparation time and because failing an exam can be a blow to your self-confidence, most people feel a certain amount of anxiety before taking a certification exam. Certain levels of stress can actually help you to raise your level of performance when taking an exam. This anxiety usually serves to help you focus your concentration and think clearly through a problem.

But for some individuals, exam anxiety is more than just a nuisance. For these people, exam anxiety is a debilitating condition that affects their performance with a negative impact on the exam results.

Exam anxiety reduction begins with the preparation process. Ensure that you know the material; you should not be nervous about any topic area. It goes without saying that the better prepared you are for an exam, the less stress you will experience when taking it. Always give yourself plenty of time to prepare for an exam; don't place yourself under unreasonable deadlines. But again, make goals and make every effort to meet those goals. Procrastination and making excuses can be just as bad.

There is no hard-and-fast rule for how long it takes to prepare for an exam. The time required varies from student to student and depends on a number of different factors including reading speed, access to study materials, personal commitments, and so on. In addition, don't compare yourself to peers, especially if doing so has a negative effect on your confidence.

For many students, practice exams are a great way to shed some of the fears that arise in the test center. Practice exams are best used near the end of the exam preparation. Be sure to use them as an assessment of your current knowledge, not as a method to try to memorize key concepts. When reviewing these practice exam questions, be sure that you understand the question and all answers (right and wrong). Finally, set time limits on the practice exams.

If you know the material, don't plan on studying the day of your exam. You should end your studying the evening before the exam. In addition, get a good night's rest before the exam. Of course, you should be studying on a regular basis for at least a few weeks prior to the evening of the exam so that you should not need the last-minute cramming.

Day of the Exam

Before you take an exam, eat something light, even if you have no appetite. If your stomach is actively upset, try mild foods like toast or crackers. Plain saltine crackers are great for settling a cranky stomach. Keep your caffeine and nicotine consumption to a minimum; excessive stimulants aren't conducive to reducing stress. Plan to take a bottle of water or some hard candies with you to combat dry mouth. Be sure to dress comfortably.

Arrive at the testing center early. If you have never been to the testing center before, make sure that you know where it is. You might even consider taking a test drive. If you arrive 15 to 30 minutes early for any certification exam, it gives you time to do the following:

- ▶ Pray, meditate, or breathe deeply.
- ▶ Scan the Cram Sheet at the beginning of this book and the glossary terms before taking the exam so that you can get the intellectual juices flowing and build a little confidence.
- ▶ Practice physical relaxation techniques.
- ▶ Visit the washroom.

But don't arrive too early.

Typically, the testing room is furnished with one to six computers, and each workstation is separated from the others by dividers designed to keep anyone from seeing what's happening on someone else's computer screen. Most testing rooms feature a wall with a large picture window. This layout permits the exam coordinator to monitor the room, to prevent exam takers from talking to one another, and to observe anything out of the ordinary that might go on. The exam coordinator will have preloaded the appropriate Cisco certification exam—for this book, that's Exam 640-460—and you are permitted to start as soon as you're seated at the computer.

TIP

> The testing center's test coordinator is there to assist you in case you encounter some unusual problems, such as a malfunctioning test computer. If you need some assistance not related to the content of the exam itself, feel free to notify one of the test coordinators. After all, he or she is there to make your exam-taking experience as pleasant as possible.

All exams are completely closed book. In fact, you are not permitted to take anything with you into the testing area. You usually receive a blank sheet of paper and a pen or, in some cases, an erasable plastic sheet and an erasable pen. We suggest that you immediately write down on that sheet of paper all the information you've memorized for the test. In *Exam Cram* books, this information appears on the tear-out sheet (Cram Sheet) inside the front cover of each book. You are given some time to compose yourself, record this information, and take a sample orientation exam before you begin the real thing. We suggest that you take the orientation test before taking your first exam, but because all the certification exams are more or less identical in layout, behavior, and controls, you probably don't need to do so more than once.

All Cisco certification exams allow a certain maximum amount of testing time. (This time is indicated on the exam by an on-screen timer, so you can check the time remaining whenever you like.) All Cisco certification exams are computer generated. Most questions are multiple choice, but there will be one or two simulations and a few drag-and-drop questions. Although this format might sound quite simple, the questions are constructed not only to check your mastery of basic facts and figures about Cisco Voice concepts but also to require you to evaluate one or more sets of circumstances or requirements. You are often asked to give more than one answer to a question. Likewise, you might be asked to select the best or most effective solution to a problem from a range of choices, all of which are technically correct. Taking the exam is quite an adventure, and it involves real thinking and concentration. This book shows you what to expect and describes how to deal with the potential problems, puzzles, and predicaments.

PART I

Traditional Telephony

CHAPTER ONE

Traditional Telephony Overview

Terms you need to understand:

✓ Public switched telephone network (PSTN)

✓ Central office (CO)

✓ Private branch exchange (PBX)

✓ European Telephony Numbering Space (ETNS)

✓ North American Numbering Plan (NANP)

✓ Signaling System 7 (SS7)

✓ Dual tone multifrequency (DTMF)

Techniques you need to master:

✓ Know the difference between PBX and key system functionality

✓ Understand the legacy PSTN signaling types: supervisory, addressing, and informational

✓ Know the difference between a numbering plan and a dial plan

✓ Understand E.164 telecommunications addressing

Before implementing Voice over IP (VoIP) technology, you should understand the basics of the current analog and time-division multiplexing (TDM) operation in the public switched telephone network (PSTN). Although VoIP is established for use within an organization, when it is time to communicate outside the organization, the VoIP world needs to interface with the existing PSTN.

Understanding the Legacy PSTN

A legacy public switched telephone network (PSTN) is comprised of the following individual components that provide end-to-end call functionality:

- **Telephones:** Analog telephones are the most common type of phone in a legacy telephony network. Analog phones connect directly to the PSTN.

- **Private or central office (CO) switch:** These switches terminate the local loop and handle signaling, digit collection, call routing, call setup, and call teardown. The CO provides the power to generate call progress signaling such as dial tone, busy, ringing, and ringback.

- **CO trunk:** A CO trunk is a direct connection between a local CO and a PBX that can be analog or digital.

- **Interoffice trunk:** An interoffice trunk is typically a digital circuit that connects the COs of two local telephone companies.

Figure 1.1 illustrates a legacy PSTN.

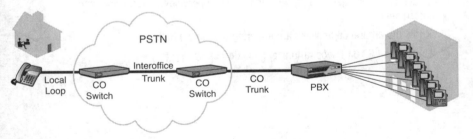

FIGURE 1.1   Legacy PSTN network

Business Phone Systems

The two types of business phone systems are private branch exchanges (PBXs) and key systems.

A PBX provides a common connection to the CO for many users. The sizing of the CO connection depends on the call volume, both incoming to the PBX and outgoing from the PBX. For example, based on call volume, a single T1 circuit that supports up to 24 calls could be used in a PBX environment to support 100 users. The CO routes all calls to the PBX in the customer's Direct Inward Dial (DID) block, such as 773-555-0100 through 773-555-0199, to the T1 connection, and the PBX redirects the incoming calls to the appropriate extension. Typically users dial an access code, such as 9, to gain access to a PSTN circuit.

A key system places all CO connections on everybody's phone. A key system implementation for a small office with 20 people would have 20 phones with eight direct line connections to the CO on each phone. Users select an available line on their phone to access the PSTN directly.

> **EXAM ALERT**
>
> Understand the difference between a key system and a PBX. A key system phone has direct access to PSTN connections; a PBX phone requires an access code to be connected to a shared pool of PSTN connections. Key systems support a limited number of features and users; PBX systems support a larger number of users and have more advanced features.

Call Signaling

Legacy telephony uses the following three types of signaling:

▶ **Supervisory:** Communicates the current state of the telephony device

▶ **Address:** Communicates the digits dialed

▶ **Informational:** Communicates with the people involved about the call status

The following sections describe each signaling type.

Supervisory Signaling

A subscriber and the CO notify each other of the call status using audible tones and electrical current changes. This exchange of information is called *supervisory signaling*. For local loops, the CO end connects one wire to a battery that supplies −48 volts DC with 20 milliamps of current, and the second wire at the CO is connected to ground.

There are three different types of supervisory signaling:

▶ **On-hook:** The handset on the phone controls the local loop, which is a two-wire circuit connected to the CO. When the handset is in the cradle, the circuit is open (broken or on-hook). With an open circuit, there is no electricity flowing.

▶ **Off-hook:** When you pick up the handset, the circuit is closed (off-hook) and the CO detects the current flow, just like turning on a light switch. When the CO detects the current flow, it plays a dial tone on the circuit and waits 15 seconds for you to dial digits. When the CO detects the first digit, it turns off the dial tone.

▶ **Ringing:** When a subscriber receives a call, the CO sends an AC signal at 40 Volts Root Mean Square (Vrms) to the phone ringer to notify the subscriber of an inbound call. In the United States, the signal is 2 seconds on and 4 seconds off. In the U.K., ring timing goes 0.4 second on, 0.2 second off, 0.4 second on, 2 seconds off, and then repeats. The service provider sends a ringback tone (informational signaling) to the caller, alerting the caller that it is sending ringing voltage to the receiver's telephone. The ringback tone sounds similar to ringing, but it is a call-progress or informational tone provided by the caller's CO.

Addressing

There are two types of telephones: a rotary-dial telephone (pulse dialing) and a push-button (DTMF tone) telephone.

Analog telephones use two different types of address signaling to notify the CO which number they are calling:

▶ **Dual tone multifrequency (DTMF):** Each button on the keypad of a touch-tone phone pad is associated with a pair of frequencies, one high and one low. The combination of both tones notifies the CO of the number that is being dialed.

▶ **Pulse:** The large numeric dial wheel on a rotary-dial telephone spins to send digits to place a call. These digits must be produced at a specific rate and within a certain level of tolerance. Each pulse consists of a timed "break" and a "make," to open and close the local loop circuit. The break segment is the time during which the circuit is open. If you dial a 3, three pulses are sent to the CO.

Informational

Tone combinations provide informational signaling that indicates call progress and notifies subscribers of the call status. Each combination of tones represents a different event in the call process. These events include the following:

- **Dial tone:** Indicates that the CO or PBX is ready to receive digits from the user telephone

- **Busy:** Indicates that a call cannot be completed because the telephone at the remote end is already in use

- **Ringback:** Indicates that the CO or PBX is attempting to complete a call on behalf of a subscriber

- **Congestion:** Indicates that congestion in the long-distance telephone network is preventing a telephone call from being processed

- **Reorder tone:** Indicates that all the local telephone circuits are busy, thus preventing a telephone call from being processed

- **Receiver off-hook:** Indicates that a receiver has been off-hook for an extended period of time without placing a call

- **No such number:** Indicates that a subscriber has placed a call to a non-existent number

- **Confirmation tone:** Indicates that the CO or PBX is attempting to complete a call

EXAM ALERT

Understand the three different signaling types and their functionality. The voltages used in supervisory signaling are important. Remember the difference between a supervisory ring signal and an informational ringback signal.

PSTN Call Setup

Call setup in the PSTN requires coordination between the COs involved with the calls, as shown in Figure 1.2.

After the CO collects the subscriber-dialed digits, the CO switch uses SS7 to map the circuit between COs to complete a telephone call across the PSTN. The call usually makes several hops, for example, from the local CO to a long-distance company to the remote CO. At each hop along the way, the CO or service provider telephone switches need to map the incoming call path to the outgoing call path. SS7 is responsible for lining up all the component links to create an end-to-end call.

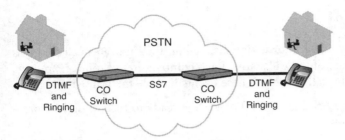

FIGURE 1.2 Call setup in the PSTN

EXAM ALERT

SS7 is the protocol used by the COs over a dedicated signaling network and is used to route end-station calls across the PSTN between COs.

Numbering Plans

A numbering plan is used in telecommunications to allocate telephone number lengths and ranges to countries, regions, areas, and exchanges and to nonfixed telephone networks such as mobile phone networks. The numbering plan defines the rules for assigning numbers to end devices.

A typical dialed telephone number is comprised of two types of digits:

▶ **Codes:** Digits that do not always need to be dialed

▶ **Local number:** Digits that must always be dialed

A standards governing body, such as the North American Numbering Plan organization, typically administers numbering plans. The governing body is responsible for regulating the distribution and formatting of numbers. Many regional and national numbering plans exist, including the following:

▶ North American Numbering Plan (NANP)

▶ U.K. National Numbering Scheme

▶ European Telephony Numbering Space (ETNS)

Using the NANP as our first example, telephone numbers are represented as a standard 10-digit pattern, NXX-NXX-XXXX, where N is a digit from 2 through 9 and X is a digit from 0 through 9. The three sections are typically referred to as area code, exchange, and station or line.

Another example that operates in parallel with the individual European countries, such as the U.K. National Numbering Scheme, is the European Telephony Numbering Space (ETNS). ETNS is a European numbering space that is parallel to the existing national numbering spaces and is used to provision pan-European services, which is an international service that can be invoked from at least two European countries. The main objective is to allow effective numbering for European international services for which national numbers might not be adequate and global numbers might not be available. The designation of a new European country code, 388, allows European international companies, services, and individuals to obtain a single European number to access their services.

Four ETNS services are now available: Public Service Application, Customer Service Application, Corporate Networks, and Personal Numbering. A European service identification (ESI) code is designated for each ETNS service. The one-digit service type code follows the European country code 388 and European service code 3 (3883), as shown in Table 1.1.

TABLE 1.1 ETNS Service and ESI Codes

ETNS Service	ESI Code
Public Service Application	3883 1
Customer Service Application	3883 3
Corporate Networks	3883 5
Personal Numbering	3883 7

There are three parts to an ETNS subscriber number:

▶ The European country code (388) combined with the European service code (3)

▶ The European service code that identifies a particular ETNS service (refer to Table 1.1)

▶ The European subscriber number assigned to a customer

The maximum length of a European subscriber number is 15 digits; for example, 3883 S XXXXXXXXXX, where S is 1, 3, 5, or 7.

EXAM ALERT

Number plans are managed by regional authorities to standardize the format and prevent overlapping numbers.

E.164 Addressing

E.164 is an international numbering plan for public telephone systems in which each assigned number contains a country code, a national destination code, and a subscriber number. An E.164 number can have up to 15 digits. The International Telecommunication Union (ITU) originally developed the E.164 plan.

In the E.164 plan, each address is unique worldwide. With up to 15 digits possible in a number, there are 100 trillion possible E.164 phone numbers. This makes it possible, in theory, to direct-dial from any conventional phone set to any other conventional phone set in the world by inputting no more than 15 single digits.

Most telephone numbers belong to the E.164 numbering plan, although this does not necessarily extend to internal PBX extensions.

The E.164 numbering plan for telephone numbers includes the following plans:

- ▶ Country calling codes
- ▶ Regional numbering plans, such as the following:
  - ▶ ETNS
  - ▶ NANP
- ▶ Various national numbering plans, such as the U.K. National Numbering Scheme

EXAM ALERT

E.164 is an international standard used to create and maintain country codes and authorize regional organizations to manage the regional number plans.

Exam Prep Questions

1. Which of the following items are physical components of the legacy PSTN? (Choose two.)

   ○ **A.** Telephones

   ○ **B.** CO switches

   ○ **C.** SS7

   ○ **D.** PBX

2. What are the primary differences between a PBX and a key system? (Choose two.)

   ○ **A.** Key systems have additional advanced features.

   ○ **B.** Key systems are used in smaller organizations.

   ○ **C.** Key systems are used in organizations that have at least 100 users.

   ○ **D.** Key systems usually provide all CO line appearances on each phone.

   ○ **E.** Key systems are used only in organizations that have 10 or fewer users.

3. How does DTMF create unique detectable dialed digits?

   ○ **A.** Generating a unique frequency for each digit

   ○ **B.** Generating a combination of low and high frequencies for each digit

   ○ **C.** Generating 100ms pulses

   ○ **D.** Changing frequencies to indicate the digit dialed

4. What is the best description of the role SS7 plays in the PSTN?

   ○ **A.** SS7 is used to signal that one PBX wants to set up a call to another PBX.

   ○ **B.** SS7 is a standard developed by leading PBX vendors to allow interoperability.

   ○ **C.** SS7 is used by the carriers to set up calls between CO switches.

   ○ **D.** SS7 is used by ISDN circuits to set up a call.

5. Which of the following statements accurately describe a numbering plan? (Choose two.)

   ○ **A.** A numbering plan is a set of rules used to construct numbers.

   ○ **B.** A numbering plan mandates an international standard.

   ○ **C.** A numbering plan is an internal set of rules configured on a PBX.

   ○ **D.** The NANP regulates all numbering plans.

   ○ **E.** A numbering plan has an authority that regulates number distribution in its territory.

6. A valid E.164 address is made up of which of the following items? (Choose three.)

   ○ **A.** Country code

   ○ **B.** Regional code

   ○ **C.** Office code

   ○ **D.** National destination code

   ○ **E.** National number

   ○ **F.** Subscriber number

   ○ **G.** Circuit number

7. Which of the following accurately defines the standard voltage and current deployed on local loops directly connected to the CO?

   ○ **A.** 48 volts DC and 20ma of current

   ○ **B.** 40 Vrms AC

   ○ **C.** −48 volts DC and 20ma of current

   ○ **D.** −48 volts AC and 20ma of current

8. Which of the following accurately defines the standard voltage used to activate the ringer on an analog phone?

   ○ **A.** 48 volts DC and 20ma of current

   ○ **B.** 40 Vrms AC

   ○ **C.** −48 volts DC and 20ma of current

   ○ **D.** −48 volts AC and 20ma of current

9. Which of the following informational signals provide caller feedback when a call has been placed? (Choose two.)

   ○ **A.** Ringing

   ○ **B.** Ringback

   ○ **C.** Dial tone

   ○ **D.** Busy

10. Which of the following are valid address signaling methods for dialed digits from a phone to the CO? (Choose two.)

   ○ **A.** SS7

   ○ **B.** DTMF

   ○ **C.** E.164

   ○ **D.** Pulse

Answers to Exam Prep Questions

1. **A and B.** Telephones and CO switches are components of the legacy PSTN. Answer C, SS7, is a call setup signaling protocol, and answer D is a private switch connected to the edge of the PSTN, so those options are incorrect.

2. **B and D.** Key systems are typically used for smaller organizations, where each phone has access to all outside lines. Key systems do not have advanced call-routing features such as a PBX and are not limited to either a minimum or maximum number of users, but are typically used for organizations with 50 or less users. Therefore A, C, and E are incorrect.

3. **B.** Each key on the keypad generates a combination of high and low tones or frequencies. Answers A and D are incorrect; two frequencies are required per digit, not one. Answer C is incorrect because it refers to off-on pulses, not tones.

4. **C.** SS7 is used for call routing between COs. SS7 is not used for direct PBX-to-PBX communications, so answers A and B are incorrect. Answer D is incorrect because ISDN places calls to the PSTN using the Q.931 protocol.

5. **A and E.** A numbering plan has a set of addressing rules and an authority that manages the plan within its territory. No international organization mandates numbering plans, so answer B is incorrect. The NANP manages the United States and Canada as its territory, so answer C is incorrect. PBX numbering is controlled within an organization, so D is incorrect.

6. **A, D, and F.** E.164 addresses consist of country code, national destination code, and subscriber number. The terms regional, office, national, and circuit can be associated with regional governing bodies such as NANP administration, so answers B, C, E, and G are incorrect.

7. **C.** Answer A refers to the voltage as positive DC so is incorrect. Answers B and D refer to AC voltage, which is incorrect.

8. **B.** 40 Vrms AC activates the ringer on the phone. Answers A and C refer to the voltage as DC, and ringing takes place when there is no DC circuit established. Answer D is incorrect because it uses a negative AC voltage.

9. **B and D.** Ringback and busy let the original caller identify the currently placed call status. Answer A alerts the called party that there is an incoming call and is incorrect. Answer C is incorrect because it is used to inform the caller that the CO is ready to accept digits.

10. **B and D.** Answer A is incorrect because SS7 is used for call setup between COs, and answer C is a standards-based method for defining numbering plans, and is incorrect.

CHAPTER TWO

Introducing Analog Circuits

Terms you need to understand:

✓ Switch hook

✓ Dual tone multifrequency (DTMF)

✓ Codec

✓ Foreign Exchange Station (FXS)

✓ Foreign Exchange Office (FXO)

✓ Loop start, ground start, and E&M

✓ Answer and Disconnect Supervision

✓ Wink Start, Immediate Start, and Delay Dial Supervision

Techniques you need to master:

✓ Understand the components of the analog telephone

✓ Understand how the telephone components interact for initiating and answering calls

✓ Understand the operation of loop start, ground start, and E&M circuits

✓ Understand Answer and Disconnect Supervision

✓ Understand the E&M signaling, types, and usage

✓ Understand the three types of start types: Wink Start, Immediate Start, and Delay Dial Supervision

Even with the growth of IP telephony in the enterprise network, many analog devices, including phones and facsimile (fax) machines, are still being used today. Therefore, you should understand how analog devices function and connect to the network through routers and gateways, as well as to the central office (CO).

This chapter focuses on the phone. You must understand the components of the phone to know how they interact to initiate and receive calls. Three types of circuits connect phones and trunk lines: loop start, ground start, and E&M. The type of circuit you choose depends on whether you are connecting to a phone, a private branch exchange (PBX), or another type of device. Each of these circuits has its purpose, which you explore in this chapter.

Analog Telephone Components

We begin with the various components of the analog phone, similar to the one you have in your home. The handset is composed of two components: the receiver (within the earpiece) and the transmitter (within the mouthpiece). These two components supply the phone with four wires for the communication path (two wires each from the receiver and transmitter). However, the CO expects only two wires (tip and ring) on most residential circuits. So, how do you convert the four wires from the receiver and transmitter to two wires (tip and ring)? The answer is a 2-wire–to–4-wire hybrid circuit within the phone that provides this conversion.

> **NOTE**
>
> *Tip* and *ring* are common terms in the telephone service industry that refer to the two wires or sides of an ordinary telephone line. Tip is the ground side (positive) and ring is the battery (negative) side of a phone circuit. The terms came about in the early days when all calls went through a manual switchboard with plugs.

Now we're ready to make the call. The switch hook component of the phone enables the phone to signal when a call is ready to begin. The CO detects when the handset is off-hook or on-hook. The phone going off-hook causes a contact closure, joining the ring and tip wires connected to the CO. This action completes the circuit, and –48vDC is available from the CO, causing the current flow through the tip and ring. The CO detects this flow of current and provides the phone with dial tone.

> **EXAM ALERT**
>
> The CO is responsible for detecting when the user has lifted the receiver from the phone, which creates the off-hook or closed-circuit condition using a manual relay in the phone. You should watch this on the exam because it is easy to think that the handset creates the off-hook condition, which is not correct; it is the switch hook (relay) in the phone.

At this point, the user can make a call using the dialer. The dialer produces dual tone multifrequency (DTMF) signaling to the CO for each digit the caller selects. These frequencies are recognized and interpreted as the proper digits at the CO to complete the call to the desired location. The DTMF signals are a combination of two tones (dual tone) produced by each digit at different frequencies (multifrequency), as shown in Table 2.1.

TABLE 2.1 DTMF Signaling

	1209Hz	1336Hz	1477Hz
697Hz	1	2	3
770Hz	4	5	6
852Hz	7	8	9
941Hz	*	0	#

For an incoming call, the CO signals the phone by applying an AC ring voltage, which activates the ringer in the phone. At this point, the called party answers the phone by lifting the handset, which causes the switch hook to create a contact closure between the ring and tip. This off-hook condition signals to the CO to stop the ring voltage. The communication path is now complete, and the conversation can proceed.

Foreign Exchange Trunks

To connect an analog device or telephone line to an IP network, an interface card is needed in a Cisco router. This interface comes in two different types: the Foreign Exchange Station (FXS) and the Foreign Exchange Office (FXO).

Foreign Exchange Station

The FXS interface card is used to connect phones, fax machines, modems, and other types of "station" devices. The FXS interface card is responsible for producing the voltage and dial tone upon switch hook signaling from the attached device, as well as ring voltage for an incoming call. When the user goes off-hook, the FXS interface card supplies proper voltage to the phone so that the caller can use the dialer to complete the call. In essence, the FXS interface simulates what the CO does for residential circuits.

NOTE

The FXS component is defined as the device that connects to the FXS interface card on a Cisco router. This device can be an analog phone, modem, fax, or similar type of device.

When the call setup is complete and you have established a two-way communication path, the FXS interface continues to supply power to the phone for the operation of the receiver and transmitter. The communication from the phone to the FXS interface is entirely analog. However, communication within the router and the IP network is digital. Therefore, you must convert this analog signal to digital for communication through the network. The FXS interface provides a component called a digital signal processor (DSP) that is programmed to operate based on *codec definitions*. The purpose of the DSP/codec combination is to sample the analog signal, convert it to a digital format, and convert from digital to analog communication in the reverse direction. The term *codec* is derived from the words *code* and *decode*.

EXAM ALERT

The DSP/codec combination is responsible for converting analog signals to digital signals for access to the IP network. For the exam, remember that a DSP/codec combination can exist in an FXS interface card and an IP phone, but never in an analog phone.

Foreign Exchange Office

The FXO interface card is used to provide a connection to the network for the CO trunk line. This type of interface terminates the connection from the CO by answering incoming calls and providing access for outgoing calls. Depending on the configuration, the FXO interface card can supply another dial tone (an outside dial tone), or it can make a call directly to a preconfigured number, referred to as a PLAR (private line, automatic ringdown). PLAR circuits are commonly used for security phones or unattended lobby phones, where the phone automatically dials a predefined number when an off-hook condition occurs. This is sometimes referred to as the *hotline* or *Batphone* (remember the old Batman series and Commissioner Gordon's phone?).

The FXO interface can also supply signaling for outbound calls in the form of DTMF tones. The older pulse-dial type can be configured, though these are not as prevalent. In the past, however, the most common types of dialers were pulse dial, which was used by rotary-style phones.

You can install both FXS and FXO interface cards in a Cisco router to provide analog connections to the network. In Figure 2.1, a Cisco router is equipped with both FXS and FXO interface cards. Note how they connect with the two-wire analog circuit.

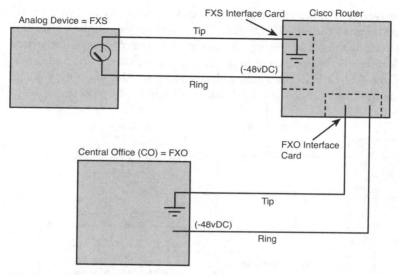

FIGURE 2.1   FXS and FXO connections to a Cisco router

Understanding Circuit Types

There are three analog circuit types that use different physical and logical methods of connecting and transmitting analog voice signals. These three circuit types are loop start, ground start, and E&M.

Loop Start

The loop start circuit is the first signaling type that we examine. This is the two-wire circuit that the telephone company provides to your home and what is used in most residential circuits. The concept is easy to understand if you think about how a circuit works. When the phone is on-hook, the circuit is open between the tip and ring. In this "open" condition, current is prevented from flowing.

When the user picks up the handset, the switch hook creates the off-hook condition, and the circuit is now closed. The CO provides –48vDC on the ring lead, which causes current to flow. This is referred to as *line seizure* because you are literally "seizing" the line. The CO senses this current and provides dial tone to the phone. If the phone is connected to an FXS interface module, the module detects the current and produces the dial tone.

This operation is going to be somewhat different for an incoming call. In this case, you are beginning in the on-hook condition. The CO or FXS interface module signals to the phone that an incoming call is present by applying an AC voltage in addition to the –48vDC signal. The ringer on the phone senses this AC voltage, causing the phone to ring. When the user answers the call, the switch hook again causes the off-hook condition, where current flows. This condition is detected by the CO or FXS interface, where it stops sending the ring voltage. Figure 2.2 defines the on-hook and off-hook conditions of the loop start circuit.

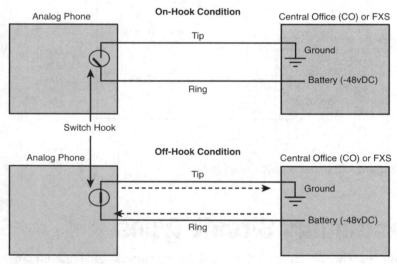

FIGURE 2.2   Loop start circuit

Now that you are familiar with how your home phone works, have you ever noticed a time when you were dialing a friend, and the person picked up the phone and you were connected before hearing it ring? This is a condition called *glare*. It occurs when there is no mechanism to signal the remote "called" location with an off-hook or on-hook condition. Glare occurs when line seizure occurs at both ends of the circuit at the same time. This is one shortcoming of the traditional loop start line, because neither side is able to detect the line seizure from end to end.

EXAM ALERT

Glare is the condition when both parties seize the line at the same time. You should remember this for exam time and understand that both Answer and Disconnect Supervision eliminate this condition. Loop start circuits used in residential areas lack this mechanism.

Glare is not a major issue with residential circuits, but it can be a real problem with business and enterprise, high-volume circuits. The solution to the problem is a different type of circuit called ground start.

Ground Start

Ground start circuits ultimately accomplish the same purpose as the loop start circuit, but without the glare issue. For this reason, ground start circuits are used primarily in businesses to connect to FXO interfaces on routers and gateways and to connect directly to a PBX, where an analog connection is needed. However, they are not used to connect directly to the standard analog phone. Although they are not commonly used in IP networks, ground start circuits overcome the glare issue by signaling line seizure to the remote end. They accomplish this by removing or reversing the current on answer and disconnect. This action provides the signaling to the remote end, eliminating glare, which is called Answer and Disconnect Supervision. For these reasons, ground start circuits require a common ground between the originating and terminating ends of the circuit to function properly.

Figure 2.3 illustrates a ground start call procedure on a line connected from an FXO interface card on a Cisco router to the CO.

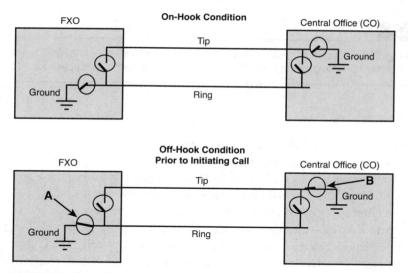

FIGURE 2.3 Ground start circuit

We begin with an FXO interface card that has a two-wire (tip and ring) configured for ground start to the CO. When a call is being made that originates from the IP network (toward the CO), the FXO interface grounds the ring side of the circuit (see A in Figure 2.3). The CO acknowledges this by grounding the tip side of the circuit (see B in Figure 2.3). This action lets the FXO interface know that the CO is ready for the call. Finally, to complete the connection (not shown in Figure 2.3), the FXO interface connects the ring to tip and removes the ground. The line is now seized and the communication path is complete for the conversation to proceed.

EXAM ALERT

You should remember that ground start circuits are more common in business, high-volume analog applications because they don't have issues with glare, as do loop start circuits.

For an incoming call to the gateway, the CO signals the call by grounding the tip side and applying a 90 volt AC (20Hz) signal. This is the ring voltage that the FXO interface uses (along with the tip being grounded) to sense the incoming call. If the line is available, the FXO interface (again) connects the ring to tip and removes the ground. This must occur within 100ms, or a reorder tone will be delivered to the caller. This timeout is another mechanism that helps ground start circuits to prevent glare. When the circuit is complete (ring to tip), the CO senses the incoming current and removes the ring voltage. The line seizure is now complete, and the conversation can proceed. This same action applies to a ground start circuit between a PBX and a CO, or a PBX and an FXS interface.

NOTE

For proper operation, ground start circuits require the current to be reversed or removed to signal on-hook and off-hook conditions, which is called Answer and Disconnect Supervision.

E&M

A third type of circuit, the E&M circuit, uses either two-wire or four-wire connections (one transmit pair and one receive pair of wires) for both the voice connection and either an E-lead or M-lead to provide signaling for on-hook and off-hook conditions. The four-wire is the most common type and is used primarily for connection to an E&M router interface card or a PBX. For each end of the circuit in an E&M circuit, one side is called the *trunk side* (typically a PBX), while the other side is referred to as the *signaling-unit side* (typically, the CO or an E&M interface on a Cisco router). The trunk side uses the E-lead to signal an off-hook condition, whereas the signaling-unit side uses the M-lead.

The *E&M* term comes from the words *Earth* and *Magneto*, where Earth is the ground and Magneto is the electromagnetic portion that generates the voltage. Some might also refer to E&M as "Ear and Mouth" or "rEceive and transMit."

EXAM ALERT

For the exam, you should remember that E&M is accomplished by separate signaling wires called an E-lead and an M-lead and either two wires or four wires for the communication path, even though the typical E&M interface supplies eight wires. Additional wires for Signal Ground (SG) and Signal Battery (SB) are designated for Type II, III, and IV circuits.

The on-hook and off-hook condition can be signaled by an open, ground, or –48vDC state, depending on the type of E&M signaling. Five types of E&M signaling are available. These types are described in Table 2.2.

TABLE 2.2   E&M Signaling Types

		Trunk Side			Signaling Side	
Type	Lead	On-Hook	Off-Hook	Lead	On-Hook	Off-Hook
I	M	Ground	-48v	E	Open	Ground
II	M	Open	-48v	E	Open	Ground
III	M	Ground	-48v	E	Open	Ground
IV	M	Open	Ground	E	Open	Ground
V	M	Open	Ground	E	Open	Ground

Type I is most common in the United States, while Type V is mostly used outside North America. Type IV is not supported on Cisco routers. Types II and V can be used to connect two signaling-unit side devices in a back-to-back configuration.

E&M circuits are most commonly used to connect to IP networks and tie lines. A *tie line*, which is a dedicated direct connect circuit, provides an analog interface between locations and typically terminates on an E&M interface in a Cisco router. For example, Communications Manager Express can use an E&M interface to provide a connection to an external Music on Hold (MoH) service.

For signaling in E&M circuits, you have three possible mechanisms for line seizure and passing address information, which is referred to as Start Dial Supervision, because they determine how dialing is accomplished in E&M circuits:

▶ Wink Start

▶ Delay Start

▶ Immediate Start

Wink Start is the most common and reduces glare by providing Answer Supervision. When the call is being made, the originating side takes the M-lead off-hook (according to the type of E&M being used). The terminating end of the connection provides a "wink," that is, an off-hook pulse, on the E-lead and goes back on-hook, indicating that it is ready to place a call. After 100ms, the originating switch begins the calling process. When the called party answers, the terminating end of the E&M connection indicates an off-hook to the originating end.

Delay Start waits for a configurable time before it begins the call. This solves a problem with some equipment that might start dialing too soon with Wink Start.

Immediate Start is the most basic type of Start Dial Supervision, but it does not include the supervision like Wink Start. The originating end goes off-hook and begins transmitting after 150ms.

Exam Prep Questions

1. Which telephone component is responsible for detecting an off-hook condition?

   ○ **A.** Ringer

   ○ **B.** Switch hook

   ○ **C.** Receiver

   ○ **D.** Transmitter

2. Which of the following is not an analog signaling type?

   ○ **A.** FXO

   ○ **B.** E&M

   ○ **C.** PRI

   ○ **D.** FXS

3. What is the condition that occurs when a user picks up the phone before it rings and is already connected to the caller?

   ○ **A.** Glare

   ○ **B.** Trunk side signaling

   ○ **C.** Answer Supervision

   ○ **D.** Wink Start

4. What type of circuit is most susceptible to glare and used in residential circuits?

   ○ **A.** Ground start

   ○ **B.** Loop start

   ○ **C.** E&M—Type I

   ○ **D.** E&M—Type V

5. What are the names of the wires used in loop start circuits? (Choose two.)

   ○ **A.** Ring

   ○ **B.** E-lead

   ○ **C.** Tip

   ○ **D.** M-lead

6. What is a mechanism used by ground start circuits to overcome issues with glare? (Choose two.)

   ○ **A.** Disconnect Supervision

   ○ **B.** Answer Supervision

   ○ **C.** Wink Start

   ○ **D.** Immediate Start

7. Which of the following is not an E&M signaling type?

   ○ **A.** Type I

   ○ **B.** Type VI

   ○ **C.** Type IV

   ○ **D.** Type II

8. Which of the following E&M signaling types is most common in the United States?

   ○ **A.** Type I

   ○ **B.** Type III

   ○ **C.** Type IV

   ○ **D.** Type V

9. What is used by the trunk side to signal an off-hook condition on an E&M circuit?

   ○ **A.** E-lead

   ○ **B.** M-lead

   ○ **C.** Ring

   ○ **D.** Tip

10. What are three Start Dial Supervision types?

   ○ **A.** Delay Dial

   ○ **B.** Wink Start

   ○ **C.** Loop Start

   ○ **D.** Immediate Start

Answers to Exam Prep Questions

1. **B.** The switch hook detects the off-hook and on-hook condition on the phone when the user lifts the handset. Answers A, C, and D are incorrect, because the ringer is only used to signal an incoming call, and the receiver and transmitter are used only after the call is connected.

2. **C.** PRI is a digital signaling type used in T1 Common Channel Signaling (CCS) circuits. Answers A, B, and D are incorrect. FXO, E&M, and FXS are valid analog signaling types.

3. **A.** Glare is the condition that occurs when both ends of the connection seize the line at the same time, due to the absence of Answer and Disconnect Supervision. Answers B, C, and D are incorrect. Trunk side signaling is used in E&M circuits. Answer Supervision provides remote signaling to eliminate glare. Wink Start is a signaling type used in E&M circuits.

4. **B.** Loop start is most susceptible to glare, because there is no mechanism for Answer and Disconnect Supervision. Answers A, C, and D are incorrect. Ground start and E&M are less susceptible to glare.

5. **A and C.** Ring and tip are leads used in loop start circuits. Answers B and D are incorrect. The E-lead and M-lead are used for signaling in E&M circuits.

6. **A and B.** Answer Supervision and Disconnect Supervision allow remote signaling to the remote end to eliminate glare. Answers C and D are incorrect. Wink Start and Immediate Start are both E&M Start Dial Supervision types.

7. **B.** Type VI does not exist. Answers A, C, and D are incorrect. Type I, Type IV, and Type II are all valid E&M signaling types.

8. **A.** Type I is the most common E&M signaling type in the United States. Answers B, C, and D are incorrect. Type III, Type IV, and Type V are valid signaling types but not as common in the United States. Type V is common outside of North America.

9. **A.** The E-lead is used by the trunk side for signaling. Answers B, C, and D are incorrect. The M-lead is used by the signaling-unit side. Ring and tip are used by loop start and ground start circuits.

10. **A, B, and D.** Wink Start, Immediate Start, and Delay Dial are all valid Start Dial Supervision types. Answer C is incorrect. Loop start is a two-wire circuit type used in residential circuits.

Suggested Reading and Resources

1. Donohue, Denise, David Mallory, and Ken Salhoff. *Cisco Voice Gateways and Gatekeepers*. Indianapolis, IN: Cisco Press, 2007.

2. Goleniewski, Lillian. *Telecommunications Essentials: The Complete Global Source for Communications Fundamentals, Data Networking and the Internet, and Next-Generation Networks*. Boston, MA: Pearson Education, Inc, 2002.

CHAPTER THREE

Introducing Digital Circuits

Terms you need to understand:

✓ Sampling

✓ Quantization

✓ Encoding

✓ Compression

✓ Time-division multiplexing (TDM)

✓ T1

✓ E1

✓ Channel-associated signaling (CAS)

✓ Common channel signaling (CCS)

✓ PRI

✓ BRI

Techniques you need to master:

✓ Understand the various digital circuits

✓ Understand sampling, quantization, encoding, and compression

✓ Understand channel-associated signaling (CAS) and common channel signaling (CCS)

✓ Understand the differences between PRI and BRI

As discussed in the Chapter 2, "Introducing Analog Circuits," analog phone circuits enable users to make a single voice call for each circuit. Unfortunately, this doesn't scale well in today's business environments, where up to hundreds or even thousands of concurrent calls can be required.

Digital circuits provide the needed solution, where a number of calls can be combined over the same physical circuit. You can support and manage one physical connection that provides multiple calls, making the circuits more cost effective. Several types of digital circuits exist: T1 CAS, E1 R2, T1 ISDN PRI, E1 ISDN PRI, and ISDN BRI.

We explore each of these technologies in this chapter.

From Analog to Digital: Coder/Decoder (Codec) Revealed

In the beginning, businesses had few options to provide connectivity to their phone systems. Switched analog circuits carried only one call at a time; therefore, companies had to purchase and install multiple circuits or lines, which became quite expensive and hard to manage. Using multiple analog circuits increases crosstalk and noise on the circuits where they terminate in the phone room of an organization.

The solution to this scalability issue was the digital circuit, which became accepted in the business world during the 1980s. Digital circuits allowed the combination of multiple logical connections over a single physical circuit through a process of multiplexing and demultiplexing.

EXAM ALERT

Multiplexing combines multiple logical circuits and transmits them fairly over a single physical circuit or trunk. One physical connection can carry multiple phone calls.

A translator or converter is required to bridge the gap between analog telephones with an infinite number of frequencies and digital services with limited bandwidth and data represented with two values, 0 and 1. Broadcast TV is switching from analog signals to digital signals, and older analog sets require a converter to translate the digital transmission to analog for existing nondigital televisions. Converting analog signals to digital information follows a four-step pathway: sampling, quantization, encoding, and optional compression. The four-step pathway described in the following sections uses the G.711 pulse code modulation (PCM) codec.

Sampling

The sampling rate for digitizing analog signals is determined using Nyquist's Theorem, which states that the sampling rate should be twice the highest frequency being carried on the circuit. Human voice has a frequency of between 300Hz and 3,300Hz, so with a little rounding up to simplify things, Nyquist set the highest frequency at 4,000Hz and stated that doubling the highest frequency provides the sampling rate for good voice quality, 8,000 samples per second. When digital voice was first proposed, the electronics industry was in its infancy, and the highest-resolution analog-to-digital converter could generate 8-bit sample values between 0 and 255. Based on this information, multiply 4,000Hz by 2 to get an adequate sampling rate of 8,000 samples per second and 8 bits to record each sample defined the number of kilobits per second required to carry a single analog call on a digital circuit, 64Kbps. Figure 3.1 shows an example of how an analog signal is sampled.

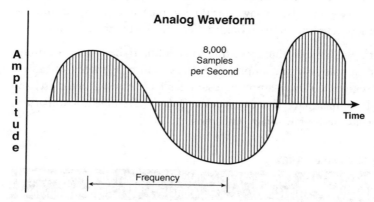

FIGURE 3.1 Sampling the analog signal.

Quantization

After a sample is taken, a logarithmic scale is used to quantize the sample into a binary number. Softer-spoken voice has a lower-amplitude signal, and if a linear scale is used to quantize the sample, softer portions of a conversation would have a low signal-to-noise ratio and become unintelligible. By giving a higher granularity to the softer analog signal, the overall quality is improved.

Each sample is broken down into three fields:

- ▶ Plus or minus (0 or 1)
- ▶ Segment (0–7)
- ▶ Interval (each interval is 125 microseconds)

See Figure 3.2 for an example of quantization using a logarithmic scale.

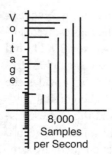

8,000
Samples
per Second

FIGURE 3.2   Quantizing the sample.

Encoding Quantized Values to Binary

The G.711 codec has two variants: mu-law, used primarily in North America, and a-law, used everywhere else. A-law uses the sample values as is, but mu-law inverts both the segment and interval before creating the binary encoding.

Mu-law calculates the binary value by setting the reading to be plus (1) or minus (0) from the last sample, and the amplitude is broken into segments and intervals within the segment. Lower-amplitude samples have more granularity, and higher-amplitude signals have less granularity. Table 3.1 shows a comparison between the mu-law and a-law binary encoding.

TABLE 3.1   Mu-law Versus A-law

	Plus (1) or Minus (0)	Segment (3 bits)	Interval (4 bits)	Binary Number and Decimal Equivalent
Sample	1	001	1100	—
Mu-law	1	110	0011	11100011 = +99
A-law	1	001	1100	10011100 = +28

Compression

The standard for voice communications today is the G.711 codec, which translates analog voice to digital. This is a one-for-one relationship, where 64Kbps is used per call. Service providers wanted better performance from their digital circuits and submitted several additional codecs to the ITU-T to increase the number of calls carried over their digital T1 or E1 circuits.

Adaptive differential pulse code modulation (ADPCM) codecs are waveform codecs that instead of quantizing the speech signal directly like PCM codecs, quantize the difference between the speech signal and a prediction that has been made of the speech signal. If the prediction is accurate, the difference between the real and predicted speech samples will have a lower variance than the real speech samples, and will be accurately quantized with fewer bits than would be needed to quantize the original speech samples. At the decoder, the quantized difference signal is added to the predicted signal to give the reconstructed speech signal. The performance of the codec is aided by using adaptive prediction and quantization so that the predictor and difference quantizer adapt to the changing characteristics of the speech being coded.

In the mid-1980s, the ITU-T standardized a 32Kbps ADPCM, known as G.721, which produced reconstructed speech almost as good as the 64Kbps PCM codecs. Later standards included G.726 and G.727 codecs operating at 40, 32, 24, and 16Kbps.

> **EXAM ALERT**
>
> Key elements of this lesson are the understanding of the sequence and function of the following: sampling, quantization, binary encoding, and compression in the process of converting analog voice to a digital format.

Through the process of sampling, quantization, encoding, and compression, we can transmit an analog signal over a variety of digital transmission facilities. The ability to multiplex a number of conversations over a single circuit provides scalability in today's communications environments.

Introducing TDM

Time-division multiplexing (TDM) is a mechanism that allows multiple logical calls or streams to share the same physical circuit, providing an equal amount of time for each conversation. Without multiplexing, digital circuits would not be scalable, as you learn with analog circuits in Chapter 2. However, using TDM, you can combine a number of conversations over a single circuit to provide the capacity required by today's business environment while maintaining a certain level of scalability.

Multiplexing allows each of the connections to "share" the time on the circuit, allowing each connection to get its turn to transmit. Let's look at this in simple terms. Suppose you own a time-share condominium. In this arrangement, you get one week in August to stay at the condo, and 51 other parties own the other weeks of the year. Every year, you get your one week. This is the same concept as TDM. Each analog incoming circuit owns time on the circuit, but only for that slice of time and assigned to that single channel.

Figure 3.3 demonstrates TDM concepts. Notice that there are five channels, or time slots, that are sending data to the time-division multiplexer. The multiplexer provides equal time to each of the channels by transmitting whatever data is presented over the composite or serial circuit or trunk. In the diagram, notice that the multiplexer cycles through the channels, one by one, providing equal time for each channel. This is designated by the selector switch in the center of the multiplexer. When this cycle reaches the last channel, it begins again at the top of the order. In the last pass, channel 3 had no data to send. Therefore, this time slot is left empty. In TDM, there is no sharing of unused time slots. Now, let's carry this concept to the TDM facility in the digital network.

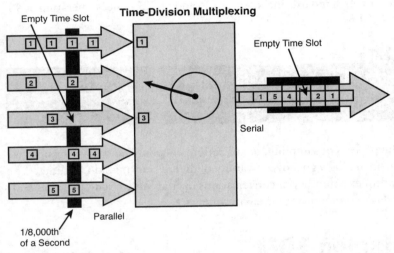

FIGURE 3.3 Time-division multiplexing.

The TDM facilities within the digital network are responsible for combining various analog connections into a single circuit and transmitting them across the network. When this information arrives at the remote end of the circuit, it is retrieved using a process called *demultiplexing*. The multiplexers can perform both multiplexing and demultiplexing functions to perform simultaneous transmission and reception.

Multiplexing and demultiplexing is important in your understanding of all T1, E1, and ISDN digital networking. In the next sections, you look at the various types of digital network circuits available.

EXAM ALERT

There are different types of multiplexing, so for the exam, remember that the type of multiplexing used in today's digital network facilities is time-division multiplexing (TDM).

Understanding Circuit Types

Digital networking covers variations in circuit capacities, signaling characteristics, and feature operations.

T1 Circuits

T1 circuits are digital circuits that provide 24 voice channels multiplexed together into a single digital circuit. Each of these 24 channels provides a single voice conversation of 64Kb each. These 24 voice channels combined with 8Kb for signaling provide a single digital circuit of 1.544Mbps.

The T1 facility provides the same type of TDM shown earlier in Figure 3.3. However, T1 provides this for 24 channels, combining them into a single stream. Each of these channels is referred to as a DS-0, where the resulting stream or trunk is referred to as the DS-1.

Figure 3.4 illustrates the T1 facilities and the various components. Notice that the T1 supports 24 DS-0s of 64Kbps each, resulting in a circuit or trunk being transmitted into the T1 digital facility at a speed of 1.544Mbps. The resulting data stream is actually 1.536Mbps for user traffic. However, framing of the various streams requires 8Kb. Therefore, the resulting T1 stream is transmitting at 1.544Mbps.

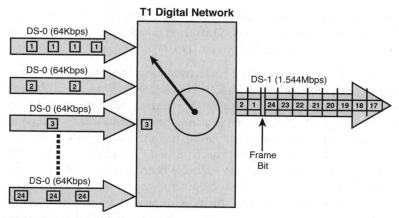

FIGURE 3.4 T1 digital transmission.

EXAM ALERT

T1 is a digital circuit technology that provides twenty-four 64Kbps channels with 8Kbps framing that results in a trunk that carries 1.544Mbps.

Now that we have the data multiplexed on the T1 circuit, we need to know the frame formats that are available. A frame is a combination of individual 1/8,000-second time slices of all 24 channels. There are two main formats available on T1 circuits:

▶ **D4 or Super Frame (SF):** D4 or SF is the original format and designates a frame of 8 bits from each of the 24 DS-0s (192 bits) and adds 1 bit for framing, for a total of 193 bits. Twelve 193-bit time slices or frames combine to create what is called the Super Frame (SF).

▶ **Extended Super Frame (ESF):** ESF is the most commonly used format today. This expands the concept of the Super Frame from 12 to 24 time slices or frames.

The last piece of information that you should know about T1 is something called *line coding*. This defines how the bits are transmitted across the digital facility. The two types of line coding used today are alternate mark inversion (AMI) and binary 8-zero substitution (B8ZS). AMI is mostly used with D4 framing, while B8ZS is the preferred line coding for ESF circuits.

EXAM ALERT

AMI line coding is configured on D4-type circuits. B8ZS line coding is configured on ESF circuits.

T1 circuits can be used to provide voice and/or data to a specific location or between locations. Data and voice can also be mixed together on different channels or DS-0s, occupying the same T1 circuit (DS-1).

When you install a T1 in your company, some equipment is needed to complete the connection. The T1 digital facility (supplied by the telco) is made available on two twisted-pair wires (two wires for receive and two wires for transmit). A device called a channel service unit (CSU) is used to access the T1 digital network at your facility. The CSU is responsible for providing the framing and formatting for the T1 digital signal, as well as providing an interface used for loopback testing. On the customer side, the CSU would then be connected between the T1 connection to the network and the customer-provided equipment, which can be the local-area network or phone system. In many cases, the CSU is provided on a router interface card, where the router then provides gateway services to the IP telephony network. The gateway or router is then programmed with the various gateway protocols (MGCP, H.323, or SIP) for connection to the IP telephony network, to provide access to service providers and network services.

In the next section, you look at the European version of the digital circuit, which is referred to as E1.

E1 Circuits

E1 circuits are found primarily outside North America and are basically the European version of the T1 digital circuit. E1 has many similarities to T1; however, the speed, framing, and line code are quite different. The speed of an E1 circuit is 2.048Mbps, which provides 32 channels of 64Kb each. Two of these channels are reserved for frame synchronization and signaling, leaving 30 channels available for user traffic. Sixteen 1/8,000-second time slices or frames combine to create the multiframe.

> **EXAM ALERT**
>
> E1 is a common circuit type found outside North America.

The type of signaling used in E1 circuit is called *R2 signaling*. This channel-associated signaling (CAS) was developed in the 1960s and is still in use, with some variations.

Figure 3.5 illustrates the E1 R2 frame format, consisting of 32 time slots. Notice that frame 1 is used exclusively for frame synchronization and frame 17 is used for signaling. The multiframe in E1 is made up of 16 of the previously mentioned time slices or frames. Signaling is designated for two channels in each reiteration of frame 17 within the multiframe, as shown in Table 3.2.

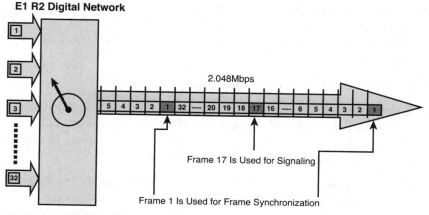

FIGURE 3.5 E1 R2 frame format.

TABLE 3.2   E1 R2 Multiframe (Frame 17)

Frame Number	Signaling Provided for Channel	Signaling Provided for Channel
1	Signals start of multiframe	
2	2	18
3	3	19
4	4	20
5	5	21
.	.	.
.	.	.
.	.	.
16	16	32

EXAM ALERT

E1 circuits provide 32 channels, where channels 1 and 17 are used for framing and signaling, respectively. The resulting stream or trunk is 2.048Mbps.

You can find various types of R2 signaling in different parts of the world, including R2-compelled, R2-noncompelled, and R2-semicompelled.

The concept of address signaling in R2 is slightly different than that used in other CAS systems. In R2 signaling, the exchanges are considered registers, and the signaling between these exchanges is called *interregister signaling*. Interregister signaling uses forward and backward in-band multifrequency signals in each time slot to transfer called and calling party numbers, as well as the calling party category.

There are three types of interregister signaling:

▶ **R2-compelled:** When a tone pair is sent from the switch (forward signal), the tones stay on until the remote end responds (sends an ACK) with a pair of tones that signal the switch to turn off the tones. The tones are compelled to stay on until they are turned off.

▶ **R2-noncompelled:** The tone pairs are sent (forward signal) as pulses, so they stay on for a short duration. Responses (backward signals) to the switch (Group B) are sent as pulses. There are no Group A signals in noncompelled interregister signaling. This is the most common implementation.

▶ **R2-semicompelled:** Forward tone pairs are sent as compelled. Responses (backward signals) to the switch are sent as pulses. It is the same as compelled, except that the backward signals are pulsed instead of continuous.

R2 signaling is defined by the regional telephony administration organization and has different definitions from country to country, and even city to city within a country or geographic area.

EXAM ALERT

E1 CAS circuits use R2 signaling to exchange calling and called party information. The three methods used to exchange the calling and caller party numbers are R2-compelled, R2-noncompelled, and R2-semicompelled.

Understanding Signaling Types

The two types of signaling features used with both T1 and E1 circuits are channel-associated signaling (CAS) and common channel signaling (CCS). The following sections review these signaling features.

Channel-Associated Signaling (CAS)

CAS is a type of signaling transmission used in T1 circuits that transmits the signaling information within the actual voice channel or sets a specific defined relationship between the signaling and the channel information they control.

In a T1 superframe, signaling is performed by a process called *robbed-bit signaling*. This type of signaling robs the low-order bit from every sixth time slice or frame within the voice stream to provide the signaling across the network. The disadvantage is that user bandwidth is being used to provide signaling. This has little effect on the voice quality, because robbed-bit signaling takes only a single low-order bit that is not noticeable to the human ear. CAS T1 circuits are common and available in loop start, ground start, and Earth & Magneto (E&M) signaling.

EXAM ALERT

T1 CAS is a common circuit type found in North America that provides signaling within the channel by using robbed-bit signaling.

In an E1 multiframe, signaling is performed through frame 17. This seems to go against the idea of CAS because all signaling is provided in a separate channel outside user traffic. However, each bit position within frame 17 has a defined meaning and relationship to a specific time slot or channel, so the signaling bits are directly associated with a specific channel. Refer to Table 3.2 for the channel 17 signaling bits' relationship to each traffic channel.

CCS

Common channel signaling (CCS) provides a separate channel for signaling. This signaling type impacts user traffic to provide signaling but sends signaling information using ISDN protocol messages on a separate channel. This signaling information is presented over High-Level Data Link Control (HDLC) at Layer 1, Q.921 at Layer 2, and Q.931 at Layer 3. More information, features, and service information can be communicated end to end, making this type of phone service appealing to the business environment.

The most common type of CCS circuits in the North America are the Primary Rate Interface (PRI) and Basic Rate Interface (BRI) digital circuits. These are referred to as Integrated Services Digital Network (ISDN) type circuits. The following sections describe both of these ISDN circuit types.

PRI

PRI is an ISDN circuit that is provided using a T1 facility. The T1 facility has 24 channels. The first 23 channels (referred to as B-channels) are for user traffic. The 24th channel (referred to as the D-channel) is used for signaling only. The advantage is that user bandwidth is not impacted by signaling. PRI also provides many features to the IP telephony network, such as caller and calling party ID and additional services through the Q.931 signaling protocol used on the D-channel. PRI is sometimes referred to by its signaling format as 23B+D.

PRI is primarily used to provide digital phone service but is also commonly used in data applications.

EXAM ALERT

Primary Rate Interface (PRI) is a common channel signaling (CCS) type of circuit that supplies 23 user channels, or B-channels, and one channel for signaling, referred to as the D-channel.

E1 PRI service, which is available outside North America, supplies an equivalent service to the T1 PRI. The E1 PRI uses the E1 frame format and supplies 30 B-channels and one D-channel. The E1 PRI is a common channel signaling type and is also sometimes referred to as *30B+D*.

BRI

Another type of ISDN circuit is the Basic Rate Interface (BRI). This is a much lower speed digital service that provides a digital circuit of 144Kbps (two 64Kb channels, or B-channels, with 16Kb for signaling, the D-channel). The BRI is also referred to as *2B+D*. This service operates over a standard analog local loop from the CO to the customer premises.

BRI service is used in business for data backup and specific dialup applications for data, where authentication is required. In Europe, BRI circuits are used for residential telephone service, though this is less common in the United States.

> **EXAM ALERT**
>
> Basic Rate Interface (BRI) is a common channel signaling (CCS) type of circuit that supplies two user 64Kbps B-channels and one signaling 16Kbps D-channel and operates over a standard CO local loop.
>
> Primary Rate Interface (PRI) is defined as 23B+D, where Basic Rate Interface (BRI) is defined as 2B+D. E1 PRI, used outside North America, is defined as 30B+D.

Summary

Digital circuits are used in business to provide voice and data services to the enterprise environment. Depending on the specific application, digital circuits have great benefits over the analog variety by providing circuits that are virtually free from noise and crosstalk, easier to manage, and scalable from small to large enterprise networks.

The growth of IP telephony allows us to use the local-area network (LAN) for voice transmission. However, any calls outside our network need to access a gateway. This gateway provides access to either analog or digital circuits to make calls through the various service providers. An understanding of the concepts of digital networks is important in your path to pass the certification exam.

Exam Prep Questions

1. What do digital circuits provide as a benefit over analog circuits? (Choose three.)

   ○ **A.** Scalability

   ○ **B.** Less noise interference

   ○ **C.** Monitoring

   ○ **D.** Manageability

2. Which of the following operate on a digital facility? (Choose two.)

   ○ **A.** T1

   ○ **B.** PRI

   ○ **C.** FXO

   ○ **D.** BRI

3. Which of the following is used in digital circuits to combine multiple streams into a single circuit?

   ○ **A.** Multiplexing

   ○ **B.** Sampling

   ○ **C.** Quantization

   ○ **D.** Encoding

4. What is the sequence used to create a digital representation of an analog signal before transmitting data across a digital circuit?

   ○ **A.** Encoding

   ○ **B.** Sampling

   ○ **C.** Quantization

   ○ **D.** Compression

5. How many channels are available for voice traffic on a CAS T1 digital circuit?

   ○ **A.** 23

   ○ **B.** 24

   ○ **C.** 30

   ○ **D.** 32

6. How many channels are available in PRI digital circuits for voice or data traffic?

- ○ **A.** 23
- ○ **B.** 24
- ○ **C.** 30
- ○ **D.** 32

7. Which type of circuit is used outside North America and can require local signaling settings?

- ○ **A.** T1 CAS
- ○ **B.** T1 PRI
- ○ **C.** E1 PRI
- ○ **D.** E1 R2

8. Which of the following are types of CAS circuits? (Choose two.)

- ○ **A.** T1
- ○ **B.** PRI
- ○ **C.** FXO
- ○ **D.** E1

9. What type of CCS circuit supplies 23B+D channels?

- ○ **A.** T1 CAS
- ○ **B.** T1 PRI
- ○ **C.** FXO
- ○ **D.** E1 PRI

10. Which of the following are valid line-coding types for a T1 digital circuit? (Choose two.)

- ○ **A.** AMI
- ○ **B.** ESF
- ○ **C.** B8ZS
- ○ **D.** R2

Answers to Exam Prep Questions

1. **A, B, and D.** Digital circuits provide better scalability and management and are resilient to crosstalk and interference from noise. Answer C is incorrect; monitoring is not a benefit and not provided on digital circuits.

2. **A and B.** PRI and T1 circuits are implemented on digital facilities. FXO and BRI circuits are implemented over a local loop analog circuit, so answers C and D are incorrect.

3. **A.** Multiplexing is the process of combining multiple streams or calls on a single circuit or trunk. Answers B, C, and D are incorrect because sampling, quantization, and encoding are used to convert the analog stream to the proper digital format.

4. **B, C, A, and then D.** Sampling (B) is the process of taking a sample of the analog signal and creating a digital representation. Quantization (C) is the interpretation and value assignment phase. Encoding (A) is the process of taking the quantized value and encoding the information into a known binary format. Compression (D) is used to reduce the bandwidth requirements for the digital voice stream.

5. **B.** T1 CAS circuits provide 24 channels. Answers A, C, and D are incorrect values.

6. **A.** PRI circuits provide 23 channels for user traffic. The 24th channel is reserved for signaling, which is called the D-channel. Answers B, C, and D are incorrect values.

7. **C and D.** E1 R2 and E1 PRI circuits are found primarily outside North America and can require specific local signaling settings to operate correctly. Answers A and B are incorrect; T1 CAS and T1 PRI are used within North America and typically use standard signaling.

8. **A and D.** T1 and E1 are two CAS circuits. Although both T1 and E1 circuits can also be CCS, they are usually written as T1 or E1 PRI. Answers B and C are incorrect. PRI is a CCS-type circuit (E1 or T1), and FXO is an analog circuit type.

9. **B.** PRI is the digital T1 ISDN circuit that provides 23 B-channels and a single D-channel for signaling. Answers A, C, and D are incorrect. T1 CAS provides 24 channels, E1 provides 32 channels with two of those channels (1 and 17) designated for framing and signaling, and FXO is an analog circuit.

10. **A and C.** Alternate mark inversion (AMI) and binary 8-zero substitution (B8ZS) are line coding used on T1 digital circuits. Answers B and D are incorrect; ESF is the frame format used on T1 circuits, and R2 is the signaling used on E1 CAS circuits.

Suggested Reading and Resources

1. Dodd, Annabel Z. *The Essential Guide to Telecommunications*, Fourth Edition. Upper Saddle River, NJ: Prentice Hall, 2005.

2. Keagy, Scott. *Integrating Voice and Data Networks*. Indianapolis, IN: Cisco Press, 2000.

PART II

VoIP

CHAPTER FOUR

Voice to VoIP

Terms you need to understand:

- ✓ Codec
- ✓ Digital signal processor (DSP)
- ✓ IP
- ✓ Real-Time Transport Protocol (RTP)
- ✓ Real-Time Transport Control Protocol (RTCP)
- ✓ Transmission Control Protocol (TCP)
- ✓ User Datagram Protocol (UDP)

Techniques you need to master:

- ✓ Understand analog and digital VoIP packetization
- ✓ Understand the role of transcoding in VoIP environments
- ✓ Understand the dual tone multifrequency (DTMF) issues in VoIP environments

For analog or digital public switched telephone network (PSTN) voice to be carried across an IP infrastructure, it must be packetized. The process of packetization involves taking the result of digitizing voice signals and packaging it into an IP packet that can then be carried across the IP infrastructure. Special chips called digital signal processors (DSPs) do this packetization. This chapter prepares you to understand the structures and encapsulations that are used for this process.

To accomplish this understanding, we break down the process into the following areas:

- ▸ The function of a DSP

- ▸ How a DSP packetizes voice streams

- ▸ Transmitting voice in RTP packets

- ▸ Codecs used in a Cisco Unified Communications system

- ▸ DSPs that provide additional functionality

This chapter discusses the various compression schemes that are used to transport voice over IP using various coder-decoders (codecs). These compression schemes impact bandwidth utilization and are essential when designing voice traffic quality of service (QoS).

Introducing Digital Signal Processors

DSPs are silicon-based chips that perform specialized voice functions in real time. The DSPs in Cisco Unified Communications systems convert from one voice format to another. Cisco voice gateways that terminate either analog or digital traditional telephony circuits need the voice information converted to IP packets for inbound voice, and need the IP packets converted to the traditional format in the outbound direction. Cisco routers and switches can act as Cisco voice gateways.

DSPs are also found in Cisco Unified IP phones. This DSP converts the voice originating on the receiver of the IP phone to IP packets. Conversely, packets containing voice that are received by the IP phone as data are converted back to an analog format and sent to the transmitter (earpiece), which plays the voice. DSP resources are required for all PSTN terminations on the voice gateways but can perform optional services for conferencing and transcoding between Voice over IP (VoIP) codecs. Figure 4.1 shows the devices that use DSP resources.

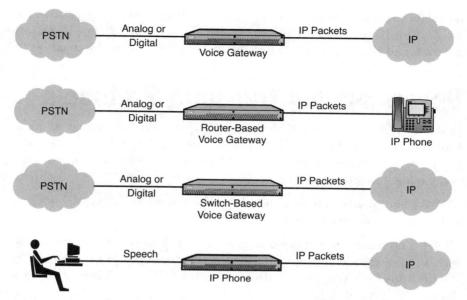

FIGURE 4.1 DSPs are used as translators between different analog and digital voice components and VoIP codecs.

The DSP chip plays a crucial role in the Cisco Unified Communications system. The DSP chip comes in several form factors, including soldered onto the main board of the Cisco Unified IP phone or gateway or to the modular packet voice data module (PVDM2), which can have from 0.5 to 4 C5510 DSPs installed on the module.

The following are the main functions of these DSP chips when they are operating in a voice gateway:

▶ The DSP chip performs the four steps of digitization: sampling, quantization, encoding, and compression in real time.

▶ The DSP chip performs the translation from the traditional PSTN voice format to IP packets and performs the reverse translation.

▶ The DSP chip performs the translation between different VoIP codecs.

The type of DSP chip, number of DSP resources, and type of codec being used all factor in to the calculation of how many simultaneous calls can be handled.

For example, when an inbound call to a channel-associated signaling (CAS) T1 that terminates on a Cisco Unified Communications Manager Express (CME) router or voice gateway is answered, the DSP chip converts the inbound PSTN digital format voice data to IP packets (using the designated codec) that are destined for the receiver on an IP phone. The IP phone outbound voice IP packets get converted by the gateway DSP to the PSTN CAS T1 digital format.

Understanding Transport Protocols

In the TCP/IP protocol stack, the transport layer is used to manage multiple application sessions between two devices. The Transport Control Protocol (TCP) and User Datagram Protocol (UDP) use ports to map incoming and outgoing traffic to applications.

TCP is connection oriented and includes packet retransmission capabilities best suited for call control protocols.

UDP has no retransmission capabilities and is ideally suited for real-time traffic such as voice streams that use both the Real-Time Transport Protocol (RTP) and the Real-Time Transport Control Protocol (RTCP). The following sections describe RTP and RTCP in greater detail.

Real-Time Transport Protocol

RTP provides voice payload transportation in a VoIP environment. RTP for voice offers the following features:

▶ Provides end-to-end delivery services for delay-sensitive, real-time data, such as voice and video

▶ Provides a known UDP port range used by quality of service (QoS) queuing to prioritize RTP voice traffic over other traffic

▶ Randomly picks even ports from UDP port range 16384–32766

▶ Includes the following information for each synchronization source (SSRC) identifier (a single one-way audio stream):

  ▶ **Payload type identification:** This field identifies the format of the RTP payload and determines its interpretation by the application. A profile can specify a default static mapping of payload type codes to payload formats.

  ▶ **Sequence numbering:** The sequence number increments by 1 for each RTP data packet sent and can be used by the receiver to detect packet loss and to restore packet sequence.

▶ **Time stamping:** The time stamp reflects the sampling instant of the first octet in the RTP data packet. The sampling instant must be derived from a clock that increments monotonically and linearly in time to allow synchronization and jitter calculations.

See Figure 4.2 for a graphic layout of the RTP header.

```
0                   1                   2                   3
0 1 2 3 4 5 6 7 8 9 0 1 2 3 4 5 6 7 8 9 0 1 2 3 4 5 6 7 8 9 0 1
+-+-+-+-+-+-+-+-+-+-+-+-+-+-+-+-+-+-+-+-+-+-+-+-+-+-+-+-+-+-+-+-+
|V=2|P|X|  CC   |M|     PT      |         Sequence Number        |
+-+-+-+-+-+-+-+-+-+-+-+-+-+-+-+-+-+-+-+-+-+-+-+-+-+-+-+-+-+-+-+-+
|                         Time Stamp                            |
+-+-+-+-+-+-+-+-+-+-+-+-+-+-+-+-+-+-+-+-+-+-+-+-+-+-+-+-+-+-+-+-+
|              Synchronization Source (SSRC) Identifier          |
+=+=+=+=+=+=+=+=+=+=+=+=+=+=+=+=+=+=+=+=+=+=+=+=+=+=+=+=+=+=+=+=+
```

FIGURE 4.2 RTP header layout.

EXAM ALERT

You should remember the three services provided by RTP: payload type identification, sequence numbering, and time stamping.

RTP runs on top of UDP to use the multiplexing and checksum services of that protocol.

NOTE

RTP is unidirectional, and a typical call will have two RTP streams, one in each direction.

Figure 4.3 shows the layout of a standard RTP packet.

RTP Header			Voice 20 ms Payload	
Payload Type	Sequence Number	Time Stamp	Voice Sample 1	Voice Sample 2

FIGURE 4.3 RTP detailed segment information.

RTP is a critical component of VoIP because it enables the destination device to reorder and retime the voice packets before they are played out to the user. An RTP header contains a time stamp and a sequence number, which allow the receiving device to buffer and remove jitter and latency by synchronizing the packets to play back a continuous stream of sound. RTP uses sequence numbers only to order the packets. RTP does not request retransmission if a packet is lost.

For more information on RTP, refer to the "Suggested Reading and Resources" section at the end of this chapter.

Real-Time Transport Control Protocol

RTCP works with RTP to provide feedback on the quality of an individual one-way voice stream. RTCP provides feedback by

- Monitoring the quality of the voice streams and providing quality feedback information and current network condition.

- Allowing hosts that are involved in an RTP session to exchange information about monitoring and controlling the session. Information exchanged includes the following:

  - Packet count

  - Packet delay

  - Octet count

  - Packet loss

  - Jitter (variation in delay)

- Providing a separate UDP flow from RTP using UDP transport.

> **NOTE**
>
> An RTP stream using port 20000 typically has a corresponding RTCP flow of 20001 (RTCP always uses an odd port number in the range 13385–32767).

RTCP transmits packets as a percentage of session bandwidth but at a specific rate of at least every 5 seconds.

The RTP standard states that the Network Time Protocol (NTP) time stamp is based on synchronized clocks. The corresponding RTP time stamp is randomly generated and based on data-packet sampling. Both NTP and RTP are included in RTCP packets by the sender of the data.

When a voice stream is assigned UDP port numbers, RTP is typically assigned an even-numbered port and RTCP is assigned the next odd-numbered port. Each voice call has four ports assigned: RTP plus RTCP in the transmit direction and RTP plus RTCP in the receive direction.

EXAM ALERT

RTP uses the even port number in an odd-even pair, whereas RTCP uses the odd number. For example, if a device picks UDP port 18222 for RTP, the corresponding RTCP UDP port is 18223.

TIP

Throughout the duration of each RTP call, the RTCP report packets are generated at least every 5 seconds. In the event of poor network conditions, a call can be disconnected because of high packet loss. When using a packet analyzer to view packets, you can check information in the RTCP header that includes packet count, octet count, number of packets lost, and jitter. The RTCP header information helps to determine why calls are disconnected.

Packetizing Voice Streams

This section describes how a DSP packetizes voice streams. Packetization of voice is performed by DSP resources on the voice gateway in the following sequence:

1. The DSP packages voice samples.

2. Packaged voice samples are collected until the packet payload is complete.

3. The voice samples become the RTP payload.

4. The RTP header and payload are encapsulated in a UDP segment.

5. The UDP segment is encapsulated in an IP packet.

6. The IP packet is encapsulated into a Layer 2 frame.

After the voice is digitized, the DSP collects the digitized data for 10 milliseconds and stores the voice sample. If a compressed codec is being used, the data that is passed to the RTP segment is the compressed result instead of the raw samples.

EXAM ALERT

The default payload for RTP is 20ms of voice or two 10ms voice samples. The 20ms per IP packet requires 50 IP packets per second of voice traffic.

The sample time for converting analog and digital voice is 10 milliseconds. Every 10 milliseconds, DSPs accumulate a block of information that represents 10 milliseconds of incoming voice traffic. The amount of memory used to store the final conversion depends on the codec.

After the RTP information is constructed, the IP stack encapsulates the information in a UDP segment and then in an IP packet. The IP packet is finally encapsulated into a Layer 2 frame for transmission between IP routers (see Figure 4.4).

Layer 2 Frame	IP Packet	UDP Segment	RTP Header	Voice Sample 1	Voice Sample 2

FIGURE 4.4 Complete VoIP encapsulation model.

The sections that follow take a deeper look into the G.711 and G.729 codecs used in Cisco Unified Communications.

G.711 Codec

The G.711 codec is the easiest codec to understand. Analog or digital traffic is examined 8,000 times per second, and each time slice is recorded as an 8-bit or 1-octet/byte value. To accumulate 10ms of voice samples, you convert 80 time slices or 80 bytes. To send 20ms of voice traffic in an IP packet, you need two 80-byte voice samples. The RTP information now consists of a 12-byte RTP header plus the 160 bytes of voice samples (see Figure 4.5).

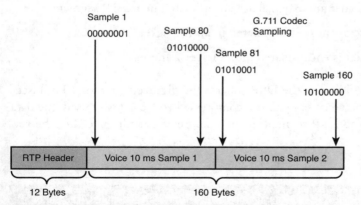

FIGURE 4.5 G.711 codec sampling and packetization.

G.729 Codec

The G.729 codec is an advanced codec that uses a compression algorithm that can create a predictive equation that approximates the original analog traffic and provides an 8-to-1 compression ratio. Analog or digital traffic is examined 8,000 times per second, and each time slice is recorded as an 8-bit or 1-octet/byte value. To accumulate 10ms of voice samples, you convert 80 time slices through the compression algorithm. To send 20ms of voice traffic in an IP packet, you need two 10-byte voice samples. The RTP information now consists of a 12-byte RTP header plus the 20 bytes of voice samples. For traversing wide-area networks, the G.729 codec reduces the bandwidth requirement (see Figure 4.6).

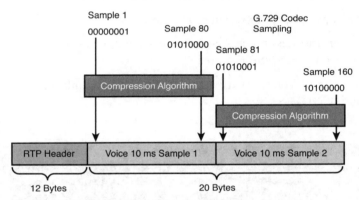

FIGURE 4.6   G.729 RTP sampling and packetization.

Understanding Codecs

ITU-T codecs standardize ways to encode voice for transport across a data network. A coder-decoder (codec) is built using a DSP and a software algorithm that compresses and decompresses speech or audio signals. There are many standardized codecs used in both PSTN and VoIP networks, including pulse code modulation (PCM), adaptive differential PCM (ADPCM), low-delay code-excited linear prediction (LD-CELP), and conjugate-structure algebraic-code-excited linear prediction (CS-ACELP).

The following is a partial list of the codecs that are supported in Cisco Unified Communications environments.

Pulse code modulation (PCM):

▶ **G.711 rate:** 64Kbps = $(2 \times 4\text{kHz}) \times 8$ bits per sample

Adaptive differential pulse code modulation (ADPCM):

- **G.726 rate:** 32Kbps = (2 × 4kHz) × 4 bits per sample
- **G.726 rate:** 24Kbps = (2 × 4kHz) × 3 bits per sample
- **G.726 rate:** 16Kbps = (2 × 4kHz) × 2 bits per sample

Low-delay code-excited linear prediction (LD-CELP):

- **G.728 rate:** 16Kbps

Conjugate-structure algebraic-code-excited linear prediction (CS-ACELP):

- **G.729 rate:** 8Kbps. The codec variants are as follows:

  - **Annex A variant:** Less processor-intensive and allows more voice channels encoded per DSP resource

  - **Annex B variant:** Voice activity detection (VAD) and comfort noise generation (CNG)

EXAM ALERT

G.729 provides 10 milliseconds of voice sampling using 10 bytes of information but uses extensive DSP resources to accomplish this task. G.729a (Annex A) provides the same service but requires 25 percent less "horsepower," measured in millions of instructions per second (MIPS).

Annex B adds VAD and CNG features to either G.729 or G.729a.

G.711 is an ITU-T standard that uses PCM to encode analog signals into a digital representation by regularly sampling the magnitude of the signal at uniform intervals, and then quantizing it into a series of symbols in a digital (usually binary) code. The voice samples created by the PCM process generate 64Kbps of data. This data is carried across a network for a G.711 call.

ADPCM coders, like other waveform coders, encode analog voice signals into digital signals by predicting future encodings based on the immediate past. The adaptive feature of ADCPM reduces the number of bits per second that the PCM method requires to encode voice signals.

ADPCM does this by taking 8,000 samples per second of the analog voice signal and turning them into a linear PCM sample. ADPCM then calculates the predicted value of the next sample, based on the immediate past sample, and encodes the difference. The ADPCM process generates 4-bit words, therefore generating 16 specific bit patterns.

The ADPCM algorithm defined by the ITU-T (formerly the CCITT) transmits all 16 possible bit patterns. The ADPCM algorithm defined by ANSI uses 15 of the 16 possible bit patterns. The ANSI ADPCM algorithm does not generate a "0000" pattern.

Code-excited linear prediction (CELP) is a compression algorithm used in low-bit-rate voice encoding that transforms analog voice signals as follows:

1. Input to the coder is converted from an 8-bit PCM to a 16-bit linear PCM sample.

2. A codebook uses feedback to continuously learn and predict the voice waveform.

3. A white-noise generator excites the coder.

4. The mathematical result (recipe) is sent to the far-end decoder for synthesis and generation of the voice waveform.

Two common variants of CELP are CS-ACELP and LD-CELP.

CS-ACELP is a variation of CELP that performs these functions:

▶ Coding on 80-byte frames that require approximately 10ms to buffer and process.

▶ Adds a look-ahead of 5ms. A look-ahead is a coding mechanism that continuously analyzes, learns, and predicts the next wave shape.

▶ Adds noise reduction and pitch-synthesis filtering to processing requirements.

LD-CELP is similar to CS-ACELP except for the following:

▶ LD-CELP uses a smaller codebook and operates at 16Kbps to minimize look-ahead delay, keeping it to 2 to 5ms.

▶ A 10-bit code word is produced from every five speech samples from the 8kHz input.

▶ Four of these 10-bit code words are called a subframe, which takes approximately 2.5ms to encode.

▶ Two of these subframes are combined into a 5ms block for transmission.

> **NOTE**
>
> Two new supported codecs are being added to the Cisco Unified Communications environment: G.722 and the Internet Low Bit-Rate Codec (iLBC). The G.722 codec samples incoming audio 16,000 times per second for better voice quality and uses a maximum of 64Kbps, matching the same bandwidth requirements of G.711. The iLBC provides higher voice quality closest to G.711, with less bandwidth, 15.2Kbps (75 percent less than G.711), and the same computational requirements of G.729a and is suited for Internet or shared network voice communications.

Comparing G.729 and G.729a Codecs

The G.729 codec has two operational modes, standard and Annex A. The following list details the similarities and differences:

▶ Both codecs are ITU standards.

▶ Both codecs are 8Kbps CS-ACELP.

▶ G.729 is more complex and processor-intensive than G.729a. This is the key issue because more DSP resources are required for standard G.729.

▶ G.729 is slightly higher quality than G.729a.

▶ The compression delay is the same (10 to 20ms).

▶ The Annex B variant can be applied to either G.729 or G.729a.

G.729 is the compression algorithm that Cisco uses for high-quality 8Kbps voice. When you properly implement G.729, it sounds as good as the 32Kbps version of ADPCM. G.729 is a high-complexity, processor-intensive compression algorithm that monopolizes processing resources.

G.729, G.729 Annex A (G.729a), G.729 Annex B (G.729b), and G.729 Annex A with Annex B (G.729ab) are variations of CS-ACELP. There is little difference between the ITU recommendations for G.729 and G.729a. All the platforms that support G.729 also support G.729a.

Although G.729a is also an 8Kbps compression algorithm, it is not as processor-intensive as G.729. G.729a is a medium-complexity variant of G.729 with slightly lower voice quality and is more susceptible to network irregularities such as delay, variation, and tandeming. Tandeming causes distortion that occurs when speech is coded, decoded, then coded and decoded again, much like the distortion that occurs when a videotape is repeatedly copied.

The Annex B variant of CS-ACELP adds voice activity detection (VAD), which is used to detect voice activity in strict compliance with G.729b standards.

When this codec variant is used, VAD is not tunable for music threshold. However, when you configure Cisco VAD, music threshold is tunable.

> **TIP**
>
> On Cisco IOS voice gateways, you must use the variant (G.729 or G.729a) that is related to the codec complexity configuration that is on the voice card. This variant does not show up explicitly in the Cisco IOS command-line interface (CLI) codec choice. For example, the CLI does not display g729r8 (alpha code) as a codec option. However, if the voice card is defined as medium-complexity, the g729r8 option is the G.729a codec.

Table 4.1 summarizes the bandwidth that various codes generate. You should balance the need for voice quality against the cost of bandwidth in the network when choosing codecs. The higher the codec bandwidth, the higher the bandwidth utilization of each call across the network and the better the voice quality.

TABLE 4.1   Bandwidth Implications for Different Codecs

Codec	Bandwidth (Not Including Overhead), Kbps
G.711	64
G.726 r32	32
G.726 r24	24
G.726 r16	16
G.728	16
G.729	8
G.723 r63	6.3
G.723 r53	5.3

The following list details the additional overhead that is added to the Table 4.1 bandwidth values to calculate the total bandwidth per call:

- **RTP/UDP/IP header overhead:**
  - 40 bytes of overhead without compressed RTP (cRTP) enabled

    or
  - 4 bytes of overhead with cRTP enabled
- **Data link overhead (Layer 2):**
  - **Ethernet:** 18 bytes of overhead
  - **MLP:** 6 bytes of overhead
  - **FRF.12:** 6 bytes of overhead
  - **Multilink PPP:** 6 bytes of overhead

You can use cRTP headers on a link-by-link basis to save bandwidth. Using cRTP compresses the IP/UDP/RTP header from 40 bytes to 2 bytes without UDP checksums (Cisco default) and from 40 bytes to 4 bytes with UDP checksums. RTP header compression is especially beneficial when the RTP payload size is small, such as with compressed audio and when you are transmitting over an E1 or slower circuit.

cRTP assumes that most of the fields in the IP/UDP/RTP header do not change or that the change is predictable. Static fields include source and destination IP addresses, source and destination UDP port numbers, and many other fields in all three headers. The cRTP operational stages are shown in Table 4.2 and illustrate the cRTP process for those fields in which the change is predictable.

TABLE 4.2 cRTP Operational Stages

Stage	What Happens
The change is predictable.	The sending side tracks the predicted change.
The predicted change is tracked.	The sending side sends a hash of the header.
The receiving side predicts what the constant change is.	The receiving side substitutes the original stored header and calculates the changed fields.
An unexpected change occurs.	The sending side sends the entire header without compression.

Table 4.3 summarizes the bandwidth utilization for the codecs referenced in this chapter for VoIP to transmit 1 second of audio.

TABLE 4.3 Bandwidth Utilization Summary Table

Codec	Codec Speed, kbps	Sample Size, bytes	Frame Relay, kbps	Frame Relay with cRTP, kbps	Ethernet, kbps
G.711	64,000	240	76,267	66,133	78,933
G.711	64,000	160	82,400	67,200	86,400
G.726r32	32,000	120	44,267	34,133	46,933
G.726r32	32,000	80	50,400	35,200	54,400
G.726r24	24,000	80	37,800	26,400	40,800
G.726r24	24,000	60	42,400	27,200	46,400
G.726r16	16,000	80	25,200	17,600	27,200
G.726r16	16,000	40	34,400	19,200	38,400
G.728	16,000	80	25,200	17,600	27,200
G.728	16,000	40	34,400	19,200	38,400
G.729	8,000	40	17,200	9,600	19,200

TABLE 4.3 Continued

Codec	Codec Speed, kbps	Sample Size, bytes	Frame Relay, kbps	Frame Relay with cRTP, kbps	Ethernet, kbps
G.729	8,000	20	26,400	11,200	30,400
G.723r63	6,300	48	12,338	7,350	13,650
G.723r63	6,300	24	18,375	8,400	21,000
G.723r53	5,300	40	11,395	6,360	12,720
G.723r53	5,300	20	17,490	7,420	20,140

Codec choice, data-link overhead, sample size, and even cRTP all have positive and negative impacts on total bandwidth. To perform the calculations, you must have all the contributing factors as part of the equation.

Consider an example using G.729a. When speech samples are framed every 20ms (default) in a packet voice environment that is using G.729a, a payload of 20 bytes is generated. Without cRTP, the total packet size includes four components:

- ▶ IP header (20 bytes)
- ▶ UDP header (8 bytes)
- ▶ RTP header (12 bytes)
- ▶ Payload (20 bytes)

The header is twice the size of the payload: IP/UDP/RTP (20 + 8 + 12 = 40 bytes) versus the payload (20 bytes). When generating packets every 20ms on a slow link, the header consumes a large portion of bandwidth.

The following points illustrate the Layer 2 overhead for various protocols:

- ▶ **Ethernet:** Carries 18 bytes of overhead—6 bytes for source MAC address, 6 bytes for destination MAC address, 2 bytes for type, and 4 bytes for cyclic redundancy check (CRC).

- ▶ **Multilink PPP (MLP):** Carries 6 bytes of overhead—1 byte for flag, 1 byte for address, 2 bytes for control (or type), and 2 bytes for CRC.

- ▶ **Frame Relay (FRF.3):** Carries 6 bytes of overhead—2 bytes for data-link connection identifier (DLCI) header, 2 bytes for FRF.12, and 2 bytes for CRC.

EXAM ALERT

Make sure you understand the method used to calculate bandwidth requirements based on codec, cRTP, and Layer 2 protocol headers.

Understanding the Effect of VAD

On average, an aggregate of 24 calls or more can contain 35 percent silence. With traditional telephony voice networks, all voice calls use 64Kbps fixed-bandwidth links regardless of how much of the call is conversation and how much is silence. With Cisco VoIP networks, all conversation and silence is packetized. VAD suppresses packets of silence. Instead of sending VoIP packets of silence, VoIP gateways interleave data traffic with VoIP conversations to more effectively use network bandwidth.

VAD provides a maximum of 35 percent bandwidth savings based on an average volume of more than 24 calls. The savings are not realized on every voice call or on any specific point measurement.

NOTE

Bandwidth savings of 35 percent is an average figure and does not take into account loud background sounds, differences in languages, and other factors.

Various features, such as music on hold (MOH) and a fax function, render VAD ineffective. When the network is engineered for the full voice call bandwidth, all savings provided by VAD are available to data applications.

In addition to reducing the silence in VoIP conversations, VAD also provides CNG. Because silence can be mistaken for a disconnected call, CNG provides locally generated white noise so that the call appears normally connected to both parties.

TIP

For the purposes of network design and bandwidth engineering, VAD should *not* be taken into account. Best practice is "no VAD" in VoIP deployments to prevent word and keypad entry clipping.

Additional DSP Functions

DSP resources on the Cisco voice gateway provide hardware support for echo cancellation and additional IP telephony features. These features include hardware-enabled voice conferencing, hardware-based Media Termination Point (MTP) support for supplementary services, and transcoding services.

Echo Cancellation

Echo cancellation is a key function in packet voice. Much of the perceived quality of the connection depends on the performance of the echo canceller. An echo canceller reduces the level of echoes.

Echo cancellation is implemented in DSP firmware on Cisco voice gateways and is independent of other functions implemented in the DSP (the DSP protocol and compression algorithm).

Conferencing

Hardware-enabled conferencing designates the ability to support voice conferences by using DSPs to perform the mixing of voice streams to create multiparty conference sessions. The voice streams connect to conferences through IP packet or time-division multiplexing (TDM) interfaces.

Transcoding and Media Termination Point

Introducing the WAN into an IP telephony implementation forces the issue of voice compression. After a WAN-enabled network is implemented, voice compression between sites, using the G.729a codec, represents the recommended design choice to save WAN bandwidth. This choice presents the question of how WAN users use conferencing services or IP-enabled applications that support only G.711 voice connections. Use hardware-based MTP/transcoding services to convert the compressed voice streams (G.729a) into G.711 voice streams and vice versa. For example, a remote-site VoIP call to the central site arrives as a G.729a stream and is forwarded to voicemail that only operates using the G.711 codec. Without a transcoder, the call would be dropped.

Exam Prep Questions

1. DSP resources perform which of the following tasks in Cisco Unified Communications? (Choose three.)

   ○ **A.** Conversion of G.729 to PAM

   ○ **B.** Conferencing

   ○ **C.** Transcoding

   ○ **D.** Speakerphone

   ○ **E.** Routing of call signaling to the correct phone number

   ○ **F.** Voice media termination

2. Which initial protocol packages 10ms voice samples when going across an IP network?

   ○ **A.** RTP

   ○ **B.** RTCP

   ○ **C.** UDP

   ○ **D.** IP

   ○ **E.** Frame Relay

   ○ **F.** Ethernet

3. RTCP is best described by which of the following statements?

   ○ **A.** Carries voice data, which is then encapsulated into RTP

   ○ **B.** Carries voice data, which is then encapsulated into UDP

   ○ **C.** Provides feedback about an RTP stream

   ○ **D.** Runs on port 2000

   ○ **E.** Is a call-signaling protocol

   ○ **F.** Stands for Real Time Control Point

4. How many bytes of overhead does a VoIP packet have?

   ○ **A.** 4

   ○ **B.** 12

   ○ **C.** 20

   ○ **D.** 40

   ○ **E.** 48

   ○ **F.** 64

5. RTP headers contain which of the following information elements? (Choose three.)

○ **A.** Sequence number

○ **B.** Payload type

○ **C.** Codec type

○ **D.** Time stamp

○ **E.** ACK

○ **F.** Volume

6. The Annex B variant of G.729 or G.729a provides which of the following?

○ **A.** VAD

○ **B.** VAD and CNG

○ **C.** CNG

○ **D.** High-complexity mode

○ **E.** Medium-complexity mode

○ **F.** None of the options is correct.

7. Which codecs are most commonly used in Cisco Unified Communications deployments? (Choose two.)

○ **A.** G.711

○ **B.** G.723

○ **C.** G.726

○ **D.** G.728

○ **E.** G.729

8. When RTP header compression (cRTP) is activated on a point-to-point link, how big is the resulting RTP/UDP/IP header?

○ **A.** 128 bytes

○ **B.** 64 bytes

○ **C.** 40 bytes

○ **D.** 12 bytes

○ **E.** 2 bytes

9. Which of the following are optional DSP functions that are available in a Cisco voice gateway? (Choose two.)

    ○ **A.** VAD

    ○ **B.** Transcoder

    ○ **C.** Music on hold

    ○ **D.** Conferencing

    ○ **E.** CNG

10. In a voice stream traversing an Ethernet segment using the G.711 codec and a sample payload of 160 bytes, which of the following correctly reflects the bandwidth required in bps?

    ○ **A.** 84,600

    ○ **B.** 26,400

    ○ **C.** 86,400

    ○ **D.** 24,600

Answers to Exam Prep Questions

1. **B, C, and F.** Digital signal processors are designed to terminate, convert, and merge voice media streams for PSTN and VoIP call legs. DSPs do not convert G.729 to pulse amplitude modulation (PAM), control a speakerphone, or route calls, so answers A, D, and E are incorrect.

2. **A.** The Real-Time Transport Protocol encapsulates the voice samples produced by a DSP and adds a sequence number, a time stamp, and a media type before handing the information to UDP for further processing. The other answers are Layer 2 through Layer 4 protocols used in the delivery of RTP segments.

3. **C.** The Real-Time Control Protocol takes the receiving device measurements of packet loss, jitter, and delay and sends the information back to the sender. This feedback information is used to identify voice quality of service network issues. RTCP has nothing to do with voice encapsulation, uses odd ports between 16387 and 32767, does not provide call signaling, and stands for Real-Time Control Protocol, so answers A, B, D, E, and F are incorrect.

4. **D.** The TCP/IP packet headers include IP (20 bytes), UDP (8 bytes), and RTP (12 bytes), for a total of 40 bytes. All other answers are incorrect.

5. **A, B, and D.** RTP helps VoIP endpoints identify sequence and missing packet issues by providing a sequence number and a time stamp with every voice sample group. RTP does not provide acknowledgments or control call volume. Answers C, E, and F are incorrect.

6. **B.** The Annex B variant applies to both G.729 and G.729a and is used to implement voice activity detection service with comfort noise generation. VAD and CNG go together and cannot be configured individually. Annex B does not impact the DSP processing power required, nor the codec complexity.

7. **A and E.** G.711 and G.729a are the most commonly used codecs due to their higher voice quality characteristics when compared to the other codecs listed. G.723, G.726, and G.728 provide poorer voice quality than G.711 and G.729 and require more bandwidth than G.729, so answers B, C, and D are incorrect.

8. **E.** Compressed Real-Time Protocol (cRTP) identifies the fields that are unchanged during a voice call, and after the first packet of a voice stream has traversed the link, only the changed header values are forwarded with the payload. cRTP requires only 2 bytes to convey the IP+UDP+RTP header changes for subsequent packets to the destination after the first full 40-byte IP+UDP+RTP header has been transmitted.

9. **B and D.** Answer A, VAD, is used to reduce bandwidth requirements in high-volume environments where low quality is acceptable but is not a DSP function. Answer C, music on hold, is not a DSP function, and answer E, CNG, is not a DSP function.

10. **C.** 86,400 bps is the bandwidth required to transmit a single VoIP stream over an Ethernet segment with a sample size of 160 bytes using a G.711 codec. The other answers are wrong.

Suggested Reading and Resources

1. Schulzrinne, H., S. Casner, R. Frederick, and V. Jacobson. RFC 1889, "RTP: A Transport Protocol for Real-Time Applications." http://www.ietf.org/rfc/rfc1889.txt, January 1996.

2. Schulzrinne, H., S. Casner, R. Frederick, and V. Jacobson. RFC 3550, "RTP: A Transport Protocol for Real-Time Applications." http://www.ietf.org/rfc/rfc3550.txt, July 2003.

3. Schulzrinne, H. and S. Casner. RFC 3551, "RTP Profile for Audio and Video Conferences with Minimal Control." http://www.ietf.org/rfc/rfc3551.txt, July 2003.

4. The ITU website http://www.itu.int.

CHAPTER FIVE

Functions of VoIP Signaling Protocols

Terms you need to understand:

✓ Media Gateway Control Protocol (MGCP)

✓ H.323

✓ Skinny Client Control Protocol (SCCP)

✓ Session Initiation Protocol (SIP)

✓ Peer-to-peer

✓ Client/server

Techniques you need to master:

✓ Understand which signaling protocols are peer-to-peer

✓ Understand which signaling protocols are client/server

✓ Understand which signaling protocols are proprietary and which are based on standards

✓ Understand what type of devices each protocol is typically used with

When a call is placed, more happens than meets the eye (or ear). Most people don't give much thought to this, but anyone tasked with maintaining a voice system needs to have a solid understanding of the mechanisms that set up and maintain a call.

The mechanisms used for call setup, teardown, and maintenance are called *signaling protocols*. Signaling protocols are used in both Voice over IP (VoIP) and traditional voice environments. For example, Signaling System 7 (SS7) is the protocol that is used for the public switched telephone network (PSTN).

Signaling protocols can be categorized in several different ways. The first is based on the path that is used. The path used will either be the same path that the voice travels across or a separate one. When a protocol uses the same path that the voice does, it is referred to as *in-band signaling*. When the signaling is sent across a different path, it is referred to as *out-of-band signaling*. SS7 is out-of-band because it uses a dedicated channel.

Another way that signaling protocols can be categorized is based on their relationship architecture. In a situation in which endpoints and gateways can independently initiate and terminate calls, a peer-to-peer protocol is used. If the endpoints or gateways do not have such capabilities, a client/server protocol is used. In the "SCCP," "H.323," "MGCP," and "SIP" sections of this chapter, we take a closer look at how these two types of protocols work.

The protocols we explore in this chapter are Skinny Client Control Protocol (SCCP), H.323, Media Gateway Control Protocol (MGCP), and Session Initiation Protocol (SIP). Table 5.1 offers a summary of these protocols. Most protocols can be used with both phones and gateways. However, there are some exceptions, as shown in Table 5.1.

TABLE 5.1   VoIP Signaling Protocols Overview

Protocol	Architecture	Cisco IP Phones	Gateways
SCCP	Client/server	Yes	Limited
H.323	Peer-to-peer	No	Yes
SIP	Peer-to-peer	Yes	Yes
MGCP	Client/server	Limited	Yes

We now take a closer look at each of these four protocols.

SCCP

SCCP is a Cisco-proprietary protocol that is used primarily with Cisco IP phones. The signaling information that is sent between an endpoint and the Cisco Unified

Communications Manager can be sent through SCCP, while a separate media stream for the audio is established using Real-Time Transport Protocol (RTP). This is a client/server protocol in which the Cisco Communications Manager acts as the server and the phone acts as the client. A SCCP endpoint is a fairly simple device. The endpoint informs the Communications Manager (CM) when its state changes. When the Cisco Unified Communications Manager receives the information, it tells the phone what it should do. SCCP is sometimes referred to as a stimulus protocol because events trigger messages, which in turn trigger reply messages. The information that is sent between an endpoint and the Cisco Unified Communications Manager is sent through SCCP.

Figure 5.1 shows the types of messages that are sent between a phone and a Cisco Unified Communications Manager that the endpoint registers. The first two messages from the phone let the CM know that the phone is alive and the port number that the phone will use for the audio stream. The next two messages are from the CM, acknowledging the registration and requesting the capabilities of the phone. The phone replies with its capabilities and requests the software version. The CM then sends the version. The phone then requests a phone button template. After receiving the phone button template, the phone requests the date and time.

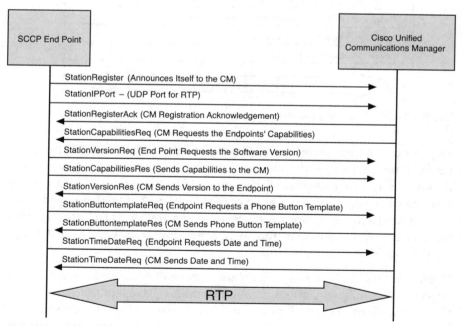

FIGURE 5.1 SCCP messages examples.

To further help you understand this process, Figure 5.2 shows the SCCP messages that are sent when a phone goes off-hook and dials a four-digit extension.

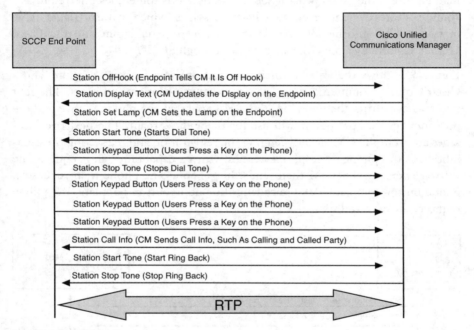

FIGURE 5.2 SCCP call setup messages.

As you can see from these figures, important information is sent between the devices. To ensure that the messages reach their destination, they are sent through TCP. TCP uses acknowledgment packets to ensure a reliable transport. Imagine what would happen if some of the SCCP packets were dropped. If the last message shown in Figure 5.2 (the Station Stop Tone message) were dropped, the phone would continue to ring after it was answered. Because SCCP uses TCP, however, this isn't a concern.

Currently, SCCP is the most widely used protocol when deploying Cisco IP phones in a Cisco Unified Communications Manager, Cisco Unified Communications Manager Express, or Cisco Smart Business Communications System environment. Because SCCP is proprietary, Cisco can implement new features and functionality quickly.

H.323

H.323 is an ITU standard based on ISDN Q.931 and is used widely among many vendors. This protocol is fairly mature; it was first approved in February 1996. H.323 is often referred to as an umbrella under which a number of other protocols sit. This protocol is based on the ISDN Q.931 protocol and allows traditional telephony features to function within an IP network. H.323 is a peer-to-peer protocol, which means that the endpoints need to have a certain level of intelligence. In short, this means that an H.323 endpoint must have its own dial plan. Messages sent between H.323 devices are binary encoded. Typically an H.323 device will have some type of dial plan programmed within it. This dial plan could be simple, such as sending all incoming calls to a single port, or more complex, such as routing calls based on the specific called or calling number.

H.323 is a set of protocols. The following list describes some of these protocols:

- **H.225:** Used for Registration, Admission, and Status (RAS) as well as call signaling

- **H.245:** Used to exchange capabilities and open logical channels

- **RTP:** Used to send the conversation, be it voice, video, or text

This is not all the protocols found within H.323, but it will suffice for the purposes of this discussion.

Note that because H.323 is a peer-to-peer protocol, an H.323 gateway does not register with a Cisco Unified Communications Manager as MGCP gateways do. People sometimes think there is a problem because the H.323 gateway did not register, but this is normal behavior.

NOTE

You should remember that H.323 is not a voice-only protocol. In addition to supporting the G.711, G.729, G.723.1, and G.726 codecs, it also supports video codecs such as H.261, H.263, and H.264.

Figure 5.3 shows the signaling that occurs between two H.323 endpoints. You can see that the setup is initiated by the H.225 messages. After the connect message is sent, capabilities are exchanged through H.245. H.245 then initiates the opening of a logical channel for voice. The voice is transported using RTP.

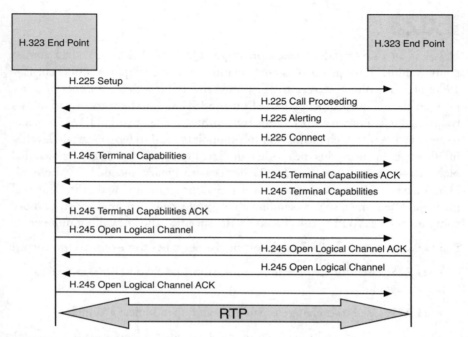

FIGURE 5.3 H.323 call setup messages.

Because H.323 is an industry standard, many vendors support it. Because of this, it is often the protocol of choice when connecting devices from multiple vendors.

EXAM ALERT

H.323 is an open-standard, peer-to-peer protocol that is used for voice, video, and data.

The H.323 protocol supports a number of endpoints. These endpoints are typically broken down into three categories: terminals, multipoint controller units (such as a conference bridge), and gateways and gatekeepers. Within the Cisco IP telephony world, H.323 is most often used with gateways and gatekeepers. While H.323 terminals (endpoints such as phones) are supported, they are not used that widely.

MGCP

The Media Gateway Control Protocol (MGCP) is an Internet Engineering Task Force (IETF)–standard client/server protocol. As with SCCP, MGCP needs a server to instruct what action to perform. The server is often referred to as a *call agent* or *media gateway controller*. While MGCP is similar to SCCP because it is a client/server protocol, devices that use this protocol can perform basic functions without having to be instructed to do so by the call agent, such as play a dial tone. MGCP is often used between a gateway and a Cisco Unified Communications Manager. The Cisco Unified Communications Manager Express and the Cisco Smart Business Communications System do not support MGCP.

EXAM ALERT

MGCP is an open-standard, client/server protocol that is typically used between a gateway and Cisco Unified Communications Manager.

MGCP sends its messages in plain text. These messages are comprised of the following eight commands. In a Cisco IP telephony deployment, these commands are sent over UDP port 2427 between a gateway and a Cisco Unified Communications Manger:

- ▶ **AUEP:** Audit Endpoint
- ▶ **AUCX:** Audit Connection
- ▶ **CRCX:** Create Connection
- ▶ **DLCX:** Delete Connection
- ▶ **MDCX:** Modify Connection
- ▶ **RQNT:** Request for Notification
- ▶ **NTFY:** Notify
- ▶ **RSIP:** Restart In Progress

Unlike H.323, an MGCP gateway does not have a dial plan of its own. It relies on the call agent for all call-routing decisions. When an MGCP gateway has to determine how to route a call, it sends the information about the call to the call agent. Because the call agent has a dial plan, it can instruct the MGCP gateway where the call should be sent. In a Cisco IP telephony deployment, a Cisco Unified Communications Manager is the call agent.

Figure 5.4 shows the MGCP signaling between a Cisco Unified Communications Manager and a gateway. You can see that the setup begins with an off-hook message sent from the MGCP device. After the connection is created, dial tone is played. After the MGCP device sends the message that a digit has been pressed, the dial tone stops. Additional digits are sent, and the call setup proceeds. After the dialed party answers, the setup completes and the voice is sent through RTP.

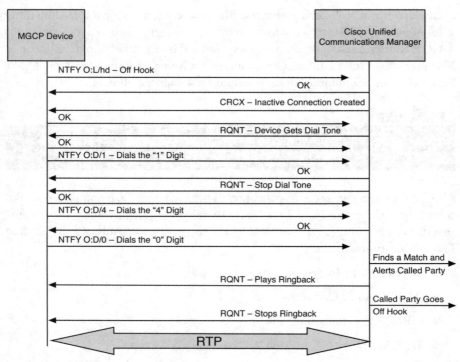

FIGURE 5.4 MGCP call setup messages.

SIP

SIP is an IETF-standard protocol that handles signaling for a number of IP communication formats. This includes voice, video, instant messaging, and presence. SIP is used with a number of devices such as phones, gateways, proxy servers, and soft clients running on a PC. It was developed by the Multiparty Multimedia Session Control (MMUSIC) Working Group of the IETF.

SIP is similar to H.323 in that it is a peer-to-peer protocol. It is similar to HTTP because it uses ASCII-based messages and shares many of the same status indicators. Because the messages are ASCII based, troubleshooting and monitoring are easier.

SIP is based on existing standards. For example, SIP uses other protocols such as Session Description Protocol (SDP) and Session Announcement Protocol (SAP) to send messages about multicast sessions. SIP also uses an addressing scheme that is based on the Simple Mail Transfer Protocol (SMTP) addressing scheme.

SIP typically operates on port 5060 and can be transported using TCP or UDP. It is a signaling-only protocol, which means that while it can be used to set up a voice stream, another protocol must be used to transport the voice. Typically RTP is used for this.

SIP has the following four major components:

> **User Agent (UA):** Typically end-user devices. User Agents are the components that initiate sessions.

> **Registrar Server:** Stores the location of all UAs.

> **Proxy Server:** Accepts session requests and queries the Registrar Server.

> **Redirect Server:** Informs the client of the next-hop information if the destination is in an external domain.

SIP signaling is based on a series of plain-text codes. All codes fall into one of the following six ranges:

> **1xx:** Informational

> **2xx:** Success

> **3xx:** Redirection

> **4xx:** Client Error

> **5xx:** Server Error

> **6xx:** Global Failure

Figure 5.5 shows the SIP signaling between a gateway and phone. You can see in this figure that SIP is a very efficient protocol. An invite is sent to the phone. The gateway is informed that the phone received the invite. The gateway is then told that the phone is ringing. After the phone goes off-hook, the gateway is told that the call is connected, and the setup is complete. When compared to other protocols, you can see SIP requires fewer messages to be sent.

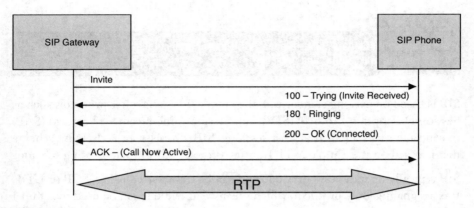

FIGURE 5.5 SIP call setup messages.

Exam Prep Questions

1. Which of the following is a Cisco-proprietary protocol?

   ○ **A.** SIP

   ○ **B.** SCCP

   ○ **C.** H.323

   ○ **D.** MGCP

2. Cisco Unified Communications Manager Express does not support which of the following protocols?

   ○ **A.** H.323

   ○ **B.** SCCP

   ○ **C.** MGCP

   ○ **D.** SIP

3. Which of the following IP communications functions does SIP support? (Choose all that apply.)

   ○ **A.** Instant messaging

   ○ **B.** Voice

   ○ **C.** Email

   ○ **D.** Video

4. Which of the following statements about H.323 is correct?

   ○ **A.** H.323 is an open-standard, client/server protocol that is used for voice, video, and data.

   ○ **B.** H.323 is a proprietary peer-to-peer protocol that is used for voice, video, and data.

   ○ **C.** H.323 is an open-standard, peer-to-peer protocol that is used for voice and video but not data.

   ○ **D.** H.323 is an open-standard, peer-to-peer protocol that is used for voice, video, and data.

5. What is the standard port for SIP?

    ○ **A.** 5066

    ○ **B.** 6050

    ○ **C.** 5060

    ○ **D.** 6055

6. You are going to deploy gateways in a Cisco Unified Communications Manager Express environment, and your customer has requested that you use a peer-to-peer protocol that supports voice and video. Furthermore, the customer would like a protocol that is easier to deal with when troubleshooting. Based on these requirements, which protocol would you choose?

    ○ **A.** IP

    ○ **B.** DMTF

    ○ **C.** H.323

    ○ **D.** SIP

    ○ **E.** MGCP

    ○ **F.** SMDI

7. Which of the following statements about SIP are not true? (Choose all that apply.)

    ○ **A.** SIP can transport voice.

    ○ **B.** SIP messages are sent in ASCII.

    ○ **C.** SIP only uses TCP.

    ○ **D.** SIP is a peer-to-peer protocol.

8. Your customer has a Cisco Unified Communications Manager and is using both Cisco IP phones and third-party phones. Which of the following statements would be true about the customer's environment?

    ○ **A.** The signaling protocol used for all phones is SCCP.

    ○ **B.** The signaling protocol used for all phones is MGCP.

    ○ **C.** The signaling protocol used for Cisco phones is SCCP. The signaling proto-col for the third-party phones is MGCP.

    ○ **D.** The signaling protocol used for Cisco phones is SCCP. The signaling proto-col for the third-party phones is SIP.

9. During routine monitoring, one of your new technicians notices that the H.323 gateway is not registered to your Cisco Unified Communications Manager. What issue might be caused by this?

   ○ **A.** Calls to the PSTN can fail.

   ○ **B.** This does not indicate a problem.

   ○ **C.** Calls from the PSTN can fail.

   ○ **D.** Calls to and from the PSTN can fail.

10. Which of the following is not a SIP component?

    ○ **A.** Registrar Server

    ○ **B.** Proxy Server

    ○ **C.** Peer Server

    ○ **D.** Redirect Server

Answers to Exam Prep Questions

1. **B.** SCCP is a Cisco-proprietary protocol. Answers A, C, and D are incorrect because SIP, H.323, and MGCP are all standards-based protocols.

2. **C.** The Cisco Unified Communications Manager does support MGCP but the Cisco Unified Communications Manager Express system does not. Answers A, B, and D are incorrect because Cisco Unified Communications Manager Express supports these protocols.

3. **A, B, and D.** SIP supports instant messaging, voice, and video. SIP is not an email protocol, so C is incorrect.

4. **D.** H.323 is an open-standard, peer-to-peer protocol that is used for voice, video, and data. Answer A is incorrect because H.323 is not a client/server protocol. Answer B is incorrect because H.323 is not proprietary. Answer C is incorrect because H.323 does support data.

5. **C.** 5060 is the port used for SIP. Answers A, B, and D are incorrect because 5066, 6050, and 6055 are not normally used for SIP.

6. **D.** SIP is a peer-to-peer protocol that uses ASCII messages, which makes troubleshooting easier. Answer A is incorrect because IP is too general of a protocol. Answer B is incorrect because DTMF is not an IP VoIP signaling protocol. Answer C is incorrect because H.323 uses binary messages, which can make troubleshooting more difficult than with SIP. Answer E is not correct because MGCP is not a peer-to-peer protocol. Answer F is incorrect because SMDI is not an IP VoIP signaling protocol.

7. **A and C.** Answer A is correct because SIP cannot transport voice; RTP would be used for voice. Answer C is correct because SIP can use UDP or TCP. Answer B is incorrect because SIP messages are sent in ASCII. Answer D is not correct because SIP is a peer-to-peer protocol.

8. **D.** Cisco phones can use SCCP, and third-party phones can use SIP. Answer A is incorrect because the third-party phones cannot use SCCP. Answer B is incorrect because MGCP is typically used with gateways, not phones. Answer C is incorrect because MGCP is typically used with gateways, not phones.

9. **B.** Because H.323 is a peer-to-peer protocol, an H.323 gateway does not register with a Cisco Unified Communications Manager. For that reason, Answers A, C, and D are incorrect.

10. **C.** Peer server is not a SIP component. The four SIP components are User Agent, Redirect Server, Proxy Server, and Registrar Server.

Suggested Reading and Resources

1. Davidson, Jonathan, James Peters, Manoj Bhatia, Satish Kalidindi, and Sudipto Mukherjee. *Voice over IP Fundamentals*, Second Edition. Indianapolis, IN: Cisco Press, 2006.

2. Wallace, Kevin. *Cisco Voice over IP (CVoice) (Authorized Self-Study Guide)*, Third Edition. Indianapolis, IN: Cisco Press, 2008.

CHAPTER SIX

Connecting Your VoIP System to the Rest of the World

Terms you need to understand:

✓ Analog voice port
✓ Digital voice port
✓ VoIP and POTS dial peer
✓ Preference
✓ Target session
✓ Destination pattern
✓ Port
✓ Default dial peer 0
✓ ITSP

Techniques you need to master:

✓ Understand the steps required to configure a dial peer
✓ Understand the difference between a VoIP dial peer and a POTS dial peer
✓ Understand how inbound dial peer matching works
✓ Understand how outbound dial peer matching works

To make calls to destinations outside of a Cisco Unified Communications Manager Express (CME), you have to have some type of connectivity to outside networks. These foreign destinations can range from a coworker at another site to the pizza parlor down the street to someone on the other side of the world. For the most part, gateways are used to connect a Cisco Unified CME network to another network. This chapter explores the components and configuration of gateways.

The two key components covered in this chapter are call legs and dial peers. This chapter explores these components and describes how they are used within a gateway. Finally this chapter takes a brief look at how Cisco Unified CME can be connected to an Internet service provider (ISP).

Understanding Gateways

The simplest definition of a gateway is a device that connects dissimilar systems. In the case of Cisco Unified CME, a gateway is used to connect to other phone networks. The most commonly connected system is the public switched telephone network (PSTN). The following sections explore the various types and functions of a gateway.

EXAM ALERT

Gateways are used to connect to traditional private branch exchanges (PBXs) as well as the PSTN.

Gateways are often classified by the type of circuit they are connected to. As explained in Chapter 2, "Introducing Analog Circuits," and Chapter 3, "Introducing Digital Circuits," there are two types of telephone circuits: analog and digital. The circuits are plugged into either analog or digital voice ports, depending on the type of circuit. The voice ports are part of the gateways. Gateways that have analog voice ports are referred to as *analog gateways*, and those that have digital voice ports are referred to as *digital gateways*.

NOTE

The hardware that functions as a gateway is most often a router. For that reason, the terms *gateway* and *router* are often used interchangeably. For this chapter, the term *gateway* is used, but on the test, the term *router* or *gateway* might be used.

Analog Gateways and Voice Ports

There are three types of analog voice ports:

- **Foreign Exchange Station (FXS):** FXS ports connect to station equipment, and that station equipment could be an analog phone or fax machine.

- **Foreign Exchange Office (FXO):** FXO ports are ports that are circuits from the telephone central office (CO). You can also use this type of port to connect to a PBX.

- **recEive and transMit (E&M):** E&M ports are typically used to terminate tie lines (a circuit between two sites).

Analog circuits are detailed in Chapter 2, so this section does not cover the details of analog circuits but rather focuses on the details of analog gateways. Analog gateways convert voice to Voice over IP (VoIP) packets for incoming calls and VoIP packets to voice for outbound calls.

Analog gateways are typically divided into two categories: analog station gateways and analog trunk gateways. Analog station gateways have FXS voice ports and are used to connect devices such as phones and fax machine to the VoIP network. An analog trunk gateway has FXO or E&M ports in them and is where circuits from the CO or a tie line are terminated.

> **NOTE**
>
> When connecting to the PSTN, the term *POTS* is sometimes used. POTS stands for plain old telephone system. It is exactly what it says: just the telephone system that we have known and loved for years.

Digital Gateways and Voice Ports

There are a number of different types of digital circuits (described in detail in Chapter 3); therefore, there are a number of types of voice ports that can be used in a digital gateway. These various ports can be categorized into three types:

- Basic Rate Interface (BRI)
- Primary Rate Interface (PRI)
- Channel-associated signaling (CAS)

A BRI circuit would terminate at the BRI port. You might recall from Chapter 3 that a BRI circuit has two 64Kbps channels that can be used for voice or data. These are referred to as B channels, and a separate 16Kbps channel, referred to as the D channel, is for signaling.

A PRI T1 or E1 terminates in a PRI port. PRI T1 circuits have 23 B channels and one D channel, while PRI E1 circuits have 30 B channels and one D channel. Both B and D channels are 64Kbps.

Just as with the PRI ports, a CAS T1 or E1 circuit terminates at a CAS port. The difference is that while the PRI circuits have a separate channel for signaling, the CAS port sends signaling using the same channel as the voice.

NOTE

A T1 port such as the VWIC2-1MFT-T1/E1 can support PRI or CAS. The configuration of the port is what determines whether it is PRI or CAS.

TIP

You should use digital voice ports whenever possible to avoid Answer and Disconnect Supervision issues.

Digital Gateways

Gateways that contain digital ports are referred to as digital gateways. These types of circuits are most often used to connect an IP telephony network to the PSTN, but they can also be used to connect to traditional PBX and voicemail systems. The types of digital circuits that terminate in a digital gateway include BRI, PRI T1/E1, and CAS T1/ E1.

Digital gateways convert the incoming voice to VoIP packets and the outgoing VoIP packets to voice. Digital signal processors (DSPs) are used to accomplish this task.

EXAM ALERT

Digital gateways are often used to connect to a traditional PBX.

Understanding Call Legs

When a call is placed from point A to point B, there are a number of segments to the call. These segments are referred to as *call legs*. A call leg is a logical connection between two devices. Figure 6.1 shows that a call from a phone connected to an

FXS port on a router to a phone connected to another FXS port on a different router has four call legs. At first, this seems odd because it shows two call legs between the two routers. It seems like there should be only one call leg because the call is going from Router A to Router B and there is no device between them. However, you have to look at it from the router's perspective. Router A sees the call as having two call legs: one between itself and phone A (inbound) and one between itself and Router B (outbound). Router B sees the call as having two call legs: one between itself and phone B (outbound) and one between itself and Router A (inbound). Because each router has two call legs, the total number of call legs is four.

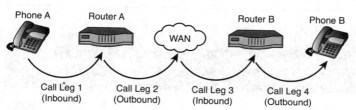

FIGURE 6.1 Call leg.

A good way to think of a call leg is that it is a logical connection between a gateway and any of the following:

- ▶ PBX

- ▶ IP trunk

- ▶ PSTN

- ▶ Another gateway

- ▶ An analog device such as a phone

- ▶ Any Cisco call control product such as a Communications Manager

Understanding Dial Peers

When a call arrives at a gateway, the gateway must route the call to the correct destination. The destination is going to be either a voice port or an IP address. The mechanism used by the types of gateways that the test focuses on to route the call is called a *dial peer*. There are a number of types of dial peers. When the destination is a voice port, it is considered to be a POTS call. When the destination is an IP address, it is considered to be a VoIP call. There are primarily two types of dial peers: POTS dial peers and voice-network dial peers.

Dial Peer Overview

Dial peers are just a set of commands entered on the gateway. A single dial peer can be as simple as just a few lines or as many as eight. The number of commands that a dial peer requires is based on a number of factors. Let's take a look at a simple dial peer.

> **NOTE**
>
> A dial peer is sometimes referred to as an addressable call endpoint.

> **EXAM ALERT**
>
> You should remember that both call legs and dial peers are thought of as logical connections.

To configure a dial peer, you need to be in the configure terminal prompt on the gateway. The prompt looks something like this:

```
GatewayName(config)#.
```

From this prompt, you issue the following commands, which create the dial peer:

```
CME(Config)# dial-peer voice 20 pots
CME(Config)# destination-pattern 2000
CME(Config)# port 0/0/1
```

The first time you enter the first command, the dial peer is created. If, in the future, you want to change the configuration of this dial peer, you would enter the same command. Let's take a closer look at each piece of the first command. The following list defines each part of the `dial-peer voice 20 pots` command:

- ▶ `dial-peer`: Instructs the gateway to create or enter for configuration purposes a dial peer.

- ▶ `voice`: Instructs the gateway that this is going to be a voice dial peer as opposed to a data dial peer.

- ▶ `20`: Denotes what is known as a tag number. The tag number can be anything you like, but each dial peer must have a unique tag number. The tag number is used when referencing this dial peer in other commands.

- ▶ `pots`: Denotes that this dial peer is going to be a POTS dial peer. The valid parameters are `pots`, `voip`, `vofr`, and `voatm`. The next two sections go into more detail on POTS and VoIP dial peers.

The next command determines which numbers will match this dial peer. In this example, `destination-pattern 2000` instructs the gateway that when it receives a call with the destination (dial number) of 2000, it should route it to the destination defined by this dial peer.

The last command determines where the call will be routed. In this example, `port 0/0/1` instructs the gateway to send the call that matches this dial peer to port 0/0/1, which is a physical port on the gateway.

This is a fairly simple example, and we go into more detail on additional settings in the section "Dial Peer Commands," later in this chapter. For now, just understand that dial peers determine how a call is routed and other properties of the call such as quality of service (QoS) markings fax rate, voice activity detection (VAD), and codec.

POTS Dial Peers

The example in the previous section shows how to configure a simple POTS dial peer. POTS dial peers are used when calls that match them are sent to a POTS voice port, such as an FXO or T1. Figure 6.2 shows an example of a configuration that would use a POTS dial peer.

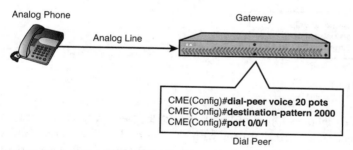

FIGURE 6.2 POTS dial peer.

In this figure, the phone is plugged into an FXS port on the gateway. Dial peer 20 will match if the router receives a call for the digits 2000. It then sends all matched calls to port 0/0/1, which has an analog phone plugged into it.

> **NOTE**
>
> A dial peer is often referred to by its tag number. For example, the dial peer example in Figure 6.2 would be referred to as "dial peer 20."

VoIP Dial Peers

VoIP dial peers are used to route a call to an IP device such as a Cisco Unified CME or another Cisco VoIP gateway. The configuration of a VoIP dial peer is similar to that for a POTS dial peer, but instead of defining a port as the destination of a call, you define an IP address as the destination.

Figure 6.3 shows an example configuration that would use a VoIP dial peer.

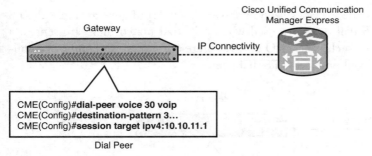

FIGURE 6.3   VoIP dial peer.

This first line in the dial peer found in Figure 6.3, `dial-peer voice 30 voip`, defines this dial peer as a VoIP dial peer with the tag of 30. The second line, `destination-pattern 3...`, instructs the gateway that any call where the dialed number is 3000–3999 matches this dial peer. The reason that `3...` matches any number 3000–3999 is because the period (.) is a wildcard that matches any single digit 0–9. The last line, `session target ipv4:10.10.11.1`, instructs the gateway to route the call that matches this dial peer to the device with the IP address of 10.10.11.1, which in this case is the Cisco Unified CME.

Dial Peer Commands

Now that we have discussed an overview of dial peers and the two types we are dealing with in this book, let's dig deeper into the various commands that can make up a dial peer. The following sections show examples of a number of commands and provide explanations for each of them. The core commands of a dial peer appear in the preceding "Dial Peer Overview" section of this chapter, so let's look at some of the other commands that can be part of a dial peer.

```
dial-peer voice 20 voip
```

For this example, we break down each portion of the command as follows:

- `dial-peer`: Instructs the gateway to create or enter for configuration purposes a dial peer.

- `voice`: Instructs the gateway that this is going to be a voice dial peer as opposed to a data dial peer. Valid parameters are `voice` and `data`.

- `20`: Denotes what is known as a tag number. The tag number can be anything you like, but each dial peer must have a unique tag number.

NOTE

VOFR stands for Voice over Frame Relay, and VoATM stands for Voice over ATM. Neither of these types of dial peers is covered in this book because they are outside the scope of the exam.

`destination-pattern` Command

The `destination-pattern` command determines which dialed digits match this dial peer. For example, in the `destination-pattern 2000` command, the number 2000 means that when the router receives a call for a destination with the dial digits of 2000, the dial peer is a match. The valid parameters that can follow the `destination-pattern` command are a string of numbers and wildcards. A list of valid wildcards follows:

- **Period (.):** Matches a single digit 0 through 9. For example, `500.` matches 5000, 5001, 5002, 5003, 5004, 5005, 5006, 5007, 5008, and 5009.

- **Comma (,):** Inserts a pause. This is useful when a 9 is dialed to signal to the PBX to seize a PSTN trunk. The comma in the string gives the PBX a moment to seize the trunk before the rest of the digits are sent.

- **Plus sign (+):** Indicates that the preceding number occurs one or more times. For example, the pattern `517565.+` matches any number that begins with 517565 and is followed by one or more digits.

- **Percent sign (%):** Indicates that the preceding number occurs zero or more times.

- **Brackets [ ]:** Indicate a range. A range is a sequence of characters enclosed in the brackets. The range can only contain single digits, such as `[0-9]`. For example, `240[2-7]` would match 2402, 2403, 2404, 2405, 2406, and 2047.

- **T:** In short, the T matches any digits and any number of digits. This is useful when a variable-length daily plan is needed, for example, to allow callers to dial local, long-distance, and international calls. Because the T can match a large number of digits (no more than 32), the interdigit timeout value is used to decide when the gateway stops collecting digits and attempts to find a matching dial peer. On certain types of trunks, there can be a pause at the end of dialing equal to the interdigit timeout value, which is normally 10 seconds. The caller can expedite this process by pressing the # button on the phone, which terminates interdigit timeout.

session target **Command**

The `session target` command is used in VoIP dial peers and determines what IP address the call is routed to. For example, in the `session target ipv4:10.10.11.1` command, the call will be routed to the device with the IP address of 10.10.11.1.

> **TIP**
>
> A loopback can be used as a session target. This way, the dial peer is not tied to the state of a physical port. Because of this, the dial peer will always be functional as long as the target device is reachable.

port **Command**

The `port` command is used in POTS dial peers and determines which physical port on the gateway the call will be sent out. For example:

```
port 0/0/1
```

codec **Command**

The codec command determines which codec will be used for this dial peer. The valid codecs that can be selected vary based on the gateway. Typically you can select from the following: g711alaw, g711ulaw, g722-64, g723ar53, g723ar63, g723r53, g723r63, g726r16, g726r24, g726r32, g728, g729r8, and g729br8. The default codec for a VoIP dial peer is g729r8. For example:

```
codec g711ulaw
```

preference **Command**

The preference command is used to determine which dial peer a call should be routed to first when all the dial peer matches are the same, for example, when all matched dial peers have the same destination pattern. This is useful when configuring hunting. Listing 6.1 shows how this might be used.

Listing 6.1   The preference Command
```
dial-peer voice 555 pots
 destination-pattern 5551000
 preference 1
 port 0/0/0

dial-peer voice 55 pots
 destination-pattern 5551000
 preference 2
 port 0/0/1

dial-peer voice 5 pots
 destination-pattern 5551000
 preference 3
 port 0/1/0
```

In Listing 6.1, when a call in which the dialed digits are 5551000 reaches the gateway, three matches are found. Because the preference determines which dial peer should handle the call and the lowest preference is tried first, the call would be routed to port 0/0/0. If the device on port 0/0/0 were busy or unavailable, the call would be sent to port 0/0/1 because the dial peer that points to that port has a preference of 2. Finally, if port 0/0/1 were busy or unavailable, the call would be routed to port 0/1/0 because the dial peer that points to that port has a preference of 3.

NOTE

In Listing 6.1, the dial peer tag numbers have no effect on which dial peer is used. Only the preference number determines the hunting algorithm when there are multiple exact matches.

Often the `preference` command is not seen when you look at a dial peer configuration. That is because the default preference is 0, and most defaults do not show up in a running config.

> **CAUTION**
>
> You should understand that if there are two or more dial peers that a call matches equally—for example, the destination-pattern is the same for all matched dial peers and preference is not assigned—all the dial peers will have a preference of 0 and the gateway will randomly select one of the dial peers. This can result in unexpected call routing.

`vad` Command

The `vad` command determines whether the gateway will use voice activity detection (VAD). The VAD feature allows the gateway to reduce the amount of bandwidth required for a call by only sending data when there is voice. That is to say that when one party is not talking, nothing is sent from that side. Because a conversation can be as much as 60 percent silence, this feature can save a significant amount of bandwidth.

The problem with VAD is that due to the mechanics of how it works, there can often be voice cutoff at the beginning of statements. For that reason, many people issue the `no  vad` command to turn off this feature. While it adds to the required bandwidth, it improves the caller's experience. VAD is enabled by default.

`ip precedence` Command

The `ip precedence` command is used to assign a high priority to the packets coming from the dial peer. The default is 0. The valid options are 0–7, with the higher number having the higher precedence. For example:

```
ip precedence 1
```

`fax rate` Command

The `fax rate` command determines the rate at which a fax is sent to a dial peer. The valid speeds to choose from are 2400, 4800, 7200, 9600, 12000, and 14400. For example:

```
fax rate 9600 voice
```

Matching Dial Peers

So far, we have looked at one way that a call matches a dial peer, that is, by matching the dial digits to the destination pattern of a dial peer. While this is a common method, it is only one of several. The gateway processes two types of calls: inbound and outbound. The way it matches a dial peer is different for these two types of calls. Based on the type of call that is being routed, a dial peer is referred to as an inbound dial peer or an outbound dial peer.

Inbound Dial Peer Matching

For inbound dial peers, the gateway tries to match on four parameters. This is a sequential process. In other words, it tests each of the following in the following order. When it finds a match, it routes the call:

1. The `incoming called number` command is used to define the Dialed Number Identification Service (DNIS) that an inbound call has to match in order to match the dial peer. For example, incoming called number 8105551... would match an incoming call from the DNIS 8105551000–8105551999. This command can be used for both POTS and VoIP dial peers.

2. The `answer address` command is used to match an incoming dial peer based on the E.164 telephone number of an incoming call. This command is only used for VoIP dial peers.

3. The `destination-pattern` command is discussed in the "Dial Peer Commands" section, earlier in this chapter.

4. The `port` command is discussed in the "Dial Peer Commands" section of this chapter. When this command is used, it matches the dial peer based on the port that the call came in on.

5. The default dial peer 0 is a dial peer that you do not have to create and you cannot modify. It is in the system by default and you never see it. It is used to handle calls that do not match any other dial peer.

> **TIP**
>
> You can create what some refer to as a "catch-all" dial peer. This allows you to determine where all calls that do not match any other dial peer are routed to.

The default dial peer configuration for inbound VoIP calls are any codec, VAD enabled, IP precedence 0, fax-rate voice, and no rsvp support. The default dial peer configuration for inbound POTS calls contains the `no ivr application` command.

Outbound Dial Peer Matching

Determining the outbound dial peer is much easier than determining the inbound dial peer. The gateway does a digit-by-digit match on the dial number against the destination pattern and selects the first/best match. The best way to explain this is to look at a couple of examples. Listing 6.2 shows what happens when multiple dial peers with the same-length destination pattern match. The dial peers are configured in a gateway.

Listing 6.2   Dial Peer Matching

```
dial-peer voice 50 VOIP
 destination-pattern 555....
 session target ipv4:10.10.11.1

dial-peer voice 60 VOIP
 destination-pattern 5551...
 session target ipv4:10.10.11.1

dial-peer voice 70 VOIP
 destination-pattern 55512..
 session target ipv4:10.10.11.1

dial-peer voice 80 VOIP
 destination-pattern 5551230
 session target ipv4:10.10.11.1
```

When an outgoing number is 5551230, dial peer 80 is used because even though all the dial peers match, dial peer 80 is the closest. The closet match is determined by how many "matches" each dial peer has, that is, how many different numbers match the destination pattern. Dial peer 50 would match 10,000 numbers (5550000–5559999). Dial peer 60 matches 1,000 numbers (5551000–5551999). Dial peer 70 matches 100 numbers (5551200–5551299). Dial peer 80 only matches one number (5551230).

When an outgoing number is 5552000, dial peer 50 is used because none of the other dial peers match.

Listing 6.3 shows how the first match is chosen when dial peers have different length destination patterns. The dial peers in the gateway are shown.

Listing 6.3   First Match

```
dial-peer voice 50 POTS
 destination-pattern 555
 port 0/0/0

dial-peer voice 60 POTS
 destination-pattern 5551...
 port 0/0/1

dial-peer voice 70 POTS
 destination-pattern 5551230
 port 0/1/0
```

When an outgoing number is 5551230, you would expect dial peer 70 to be used. However, because the matching is done on a digit-by-digit basis, the gateway routes a call as soon as it finds a match. In this case, the first digit the gateway receives is a 5 and is a possible match for all three dial peers, so the gateway waits for another digit. The second digit the gateway receives is a 5. The gateway now has 55, and because that is a possible match for all dial peers, the gateway waits for another digit. The third digit the gateway receives is a 5. Now the gateway has 555, and it is an exact match for dial peer 50, so it routes the call even though there are other digits yet to be sent. In this example, dial peers 60 and 70 would never be used.

Using Internet Telephony Service Providers

This section is a brief overview of how to connect to an Internet telephony service provider (ITSP). ITSPs are relatively new. They basically provide a customer with an IP trunk that the customer uses to route PSTN-bound calls. The ITSP trunks are typically SIP based but can also be H.323. The call is sent to the ITSP through an IP connection, and the ITSP routes the call to the PSTN.

There are many benefits to ITSP trunks. The first and most attractive is the reduced cost.

EXAM ALERT

These trunks are typically less expensive for both the circuit and the long-distance fees. Another benefit is that when the bandwidth is not being used for voice, it can be used to transport data. The number of lines can be incremented one at a time, which is another benefit over a circuit like a T1, which contains 24 channels.

To connect to an ITSP, create a VoIP dial peer using the parameters provided by the ITSP.

Exam Prep Questions

1. Which of the following statements about analog voice is incorrect?

   ○ **A.** A fax machine can be connected to an FXS port.

   ○ **B.** An analog port can be used to connect to a PBX.

   ○ **C.** A circuit from a CO can terminate at an FXO analog voice port.

   ○ **D.** E&M is an analog circuit.

   ○ **E.** None of the options are incorrect.

2. Which of the following is not a digital voice port?

   ○ **A.** PRI T1

   ○ **B.** CAS E1

   ○ **C.** BRI

   ○ **D.** E&M

3. Which of the following statements about call legs is true?

   ○ **A.** A call leg is a logical connection between two devices.

   ○ **B.** A call leg is a required command for dial peers.

   ○ **C.** A call leg determines how a call will be routed.

   ○ **D.** A call leg command must have a unique tag number.

4. Which of the following statements about dial peers is not correct?

   ○ **A.** A VoIP dial peer's session target is the IP address of the destination device.

   ○ **B.** A POTS dial peer contains a `port` command to determine where to route the call.

   ○ **C.** Dial peer tag number must be unique.

   ○ **D.** Outbound dial peers always match based on the most exact match.

5. Which of the following lines would not be part of a VoIP dial peer?

   ○ **A.** `dial-peer voice 10 VOIP`

   ○ **B.** `destination-pattern 1...`

   ○ **C.** `session target 10.10.1.2`

   ○ **D.** `preference 0`

6. Which of the following dial peers would be the first match when the dialed number is 2000?

○ **A.** `dial-peer voice 555 pots`

    `destination-pattern 2000`

    `preference 1`

    `port 0/0/0`

○ **B.** `dial-peer voice 55 pots`

    `destination-pattern 2000`

    `preference 2`

    `port 0/0/1`

○ **C.** `dial-peer voice 550 pots`

    `destination-pattern 2000`

    `preference 3`

    `port 0/1/0`

○ **D.** `dial-peer voice 500 pots`

    `destination-pattern 2000`

    `port 0/1/1`

7. If no match for an inbound dial peer can be found, what happens to the call?

○ **A.** The default dial peer 0 is used.

○ **B.** The call is dropped.

○ **C.** The call is routed to the operator.

○ **D.** The caller is told to please try the call later.

8. Which of the following are not commands that an inbound dial peer is matched on? (Choose all correct answers.)

○ **A.** `codec`

○ **B.** `preference`

○ **C.** `vad`

○ **D.** `ip precedence`

9. When the outgoing number is 5551100, which of the following dial peers will be used?

   ○ **A.** `dial-peer voice 55 pots`

      `destination-pattern 5551100`

      `port 0/0/1`

   ○ **B.** `dial-peer voice 55 pots`

      `destination-pattern 5551100`

      `preference 2`

      `port 0/0/1`

   ○ **C.** `dial-peer voice 55 pots`

      `destination-pattern 5551...`

      `preference 2`

      `port 0/0/1`

   ○ **D.** `dial-peer voice 55 pots`

      `destination-pattern 555...`

      `preference 2`

      `port 0/0/1`

10. What must be created to connect to an ITSP?

    ○ **A.** Create an ITSP dial peer.

    ○ **B.** Create a VoIP dial peer.

    ○ **C.** Create a VoITSP dial peer.

    ○ **D.** Create a SIP dial peer.

Answers to Exam Prep Questions

1. **E.** Answers A, B, C, and D are all correct statements about an analog voice port.

2. **D.** E&M is an analog port. Answers A, B, and C are incorrect because PRI T1, CAS E1, and BRI are all digital voice ports.

3. **A.** A call leg is a logical connection between two devices. Answer B is incorrect because `call leg` is not a command. Answer C is incorrect; a dial peer determines how calls are routed. Answer D is incorrect because `call leg` is not a command and does not have a tag number.

4. **D.** An outbound dial peer matches on the first match, even if it is not the most exact match. Answers A, B, and C are true statements.

5. **C.** While it looks okay, the `session target` command must have the IP version specified. The correct command would have been `session-target ipv4:10.10.1.2`. Answers A, B, and D are all valid commands for a VoIP dial peer.

6. **D.** Remember that the default preference is 0. Also remember that many defaults do not show up in a running config. Because no preference was listed in this dial peer, the preference was 0, and the dial peer with the lowest preference is the one that is selected. Answers A, B, and C are incorrect because each of them has a preference higher than 0.

7. **A.** After searching for an inbound dial peer match based on the `incoming called-number`, the `answer-number`, the `destination-pattern`, and the `port` commands, the default dial peer 0 is used if no other matches are found. Answer B is incorrect because the call does not drop. Answer C is not correct because the call is not routed to the operator. Answer D is not correct because the caller does not hear a message.

8. **A, B, C, and D.** An inbound dial peer matches based on the `incoming called-number`, the `answer-number`, the `destination-pattern`, or the `port` command. If no match is found, it uses the default dial peer 0.

9. **D.** The destination pattern is only five digits long, and the gateway routes based on the fastest match. Because answers A, B, and C all have 7-digit destination patterns, they will never match because the call will have been routed before the gateway receives the seventh digit.

10. **B.** A VoIP dial must be created when connecting to an ITSP. Answers A, C, and D are not valid dial peer types.

Suggested Reading and Resources

1. Cisco. "Understanding Dial Peers and Call Legs on Cisco IOS Platforms." http://tinyurl.com/47g39u.

2. Wallace, Kevin. *Cisco Voice over IP (CVoice) (Authorized Self-Study Guide)*, 2nd Edition. Indianapolis, IN: Cisco Press, 2006.

CHAPTER SEVEN

Configuring the Network to Support VoIP

Terms you need to understand:

✓ Dynamic Host Control Protocol (DHCP)

✓ DHCP relay

✓ Domain Name System (DNS)

✓ Cisco Discovery Protocol (CDP)

✓ Network Time Protocol (NTP)

✓ IEEE 802.1af

✓ Power over Ethernet (PoE)

✓ IEEE 802.1Q

✓ IEEE 802.1p

✓ Virtual LAN (VLAN)

✓ Trivial File Transfer Protocol (TFTP)

✓ Extensible Markup Language (XML)

Techniques you need to master:

✓ Configure and understand VLANs

✓ Understand how CDP is used in Cisco VoIP solutions

✓ Create DHCP scopes on the Cisco IOS router platform

✓ Configure DHCP relay on the Cisco IOS router platform

✓ Understand the importance of NTP

✓ Configure NTP

✓ Understand the Cisco IP phone bootup process

✓ Identify the XML configuration files and understand their use

To deploy Cisco Unified Communications Manager Express, network services need to be established and properly configured on all routers and switches for Cisco IP phones to function. This chapter describes the typical boot process for Cisco IP phones and indicates the best practices related to configuring the network to support Voice over IP (VoIP).

Understanding the Theory of Voice VLANs

A Cisco IP phone can act as a three-port switch. Just like a switch, the phone can support 802.1Q frames between itself and another switch, and more than one VLAN can be supported between the Cisco Unified IP phone and an access switch. Figure 7.1 illustrates how the Cisco IP phone acts as a three-port switch.

> **NOTE**
>
> Not all Cisco IP phones provide a switch port for PC access, and switch port maximum speed is model dependent.

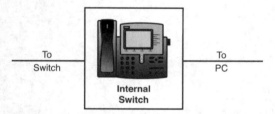

FIGURE 7.1   Cisco IP phones include a three-port switch.

The following are the three ports of the Cisco IP phone:

- ▶ The external port that connects to a 10/100/1000 Ethernet switch
- ▶ The external 10/100/1000 Ethernet port for PC connections
- ▶ An internal 10/100/1000 Ethernet port for VoIP traffic

> **EXAM ALERT**
>
> Cisco IP phone switch ports do not support Inter-Switch Link (ISL) encapsulation, only 802.1Q.

The benefits of this type of configuration include the following:

▶ Cisco IP phones can be deployed on the network without IP address scalability problems. IP subnets usually have more than 50 percent—and often more than 80 percent—of their IP addresses allocated. A separate VLAN and its separate IP subnet to carry the voice traffic allow a large number of new devices, such as IP phones, to be introduced into the network without extensive modifications to the existing IP address scheme.

▶ Voice and data VLANs allow the logical separation of data and voice traffic due to different characteristics. This separation allows you to handle each traffic type individually, applying different quality of service (QoS) policies to each VLAN for monitoring and managing them separately.

The following are IP addressing recommendations when adding Cisco IP phones to an existing data network:

▶ Continue to use existing addressing for data devices (PCs, workstations, and so on).

▶ Add Cisco IP phones and use DHCP to provision IP addresses and operating parameters.

▶ Use new subnets for Cisco IP phones if they are available in the existing address space, or use private addressing such as the 10.0.0.0 network (see RFC 1918 for details) if subnets are not available in the existing address space.

With IP phones residing in a separate VLAN—a voice VLAN—it is easier for you to automate the process of deploying IP phones. The IP phone communicates with the switch, using the Cisco Discovery Protocol (CDP), to request the voice VLAN if present. The switch CDP response provides the phone with the appropriate 802.1Q VLAN ID, known as the voice VLAN ID (VVID). The PC traffic travels across the same connection without the 802.1Q tag inserted.

Configuring Voice VLANs

This and the following sections define how VoIP and data traffic can use the same physical link while operating on separate Layer 2 VLANs. Figure 7.2 shows the PC communicating using untagged frames on VLAN 12 and the IP phone communicating on VLAN 112 with 802.1Q frames. The VLANs are configured on the infrastructure switch, as shown in Figure 7.1.

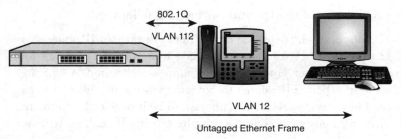

FIGURE 7.2 Voice and data VLANs coexist on a single physical connection.

Listing 7.1 shows a sample switch port configuration.

Listing 7.1   Switch Port Configuration

```
Switch(config)# interface FastEthernet0/1
Switch(config-if)# switchport access vlan 12
Switch(config-if)# switchport mode access
Switch(config-if)# switchport voice vlan 112
Switch(config-if)# spanning-tree portfast
```

The switchport access vlan command statically configures the access VLAN for the PC traffic.

The switchport mode access command statically configures the port in access mode.

The switchport voice vlan *vlan-id* command identifies the VLAN provided by the switch to the Cisco IP phone using CDP so that the Cisco IP phone can insert the voice VLAN ID and the 802.1P class of service (CoS) values for the VoIP control and media frames. By default, the IP phone sets the CoS setting in the 802.1Q header to a priority of 5 for voice streaming traffic and a priority of 3 for the call control traffic.

The spanning-tree portfast command eliminates the normal 30- to 50-second spanning tree delay before traffic is forwarded on a switch port.

You can verify your voice VLAN configuration on the Cisco Catalyst switch using the show interface *mod/port* switchport command, as shown in Listing 7.2.

Listing 7.2   Using the show interface *mod/port* switchport Command

```
Switch# show interface fa0/17 switchport

Name: Fa0/17Switchport: Enabled
Administrative mode: static access
Operational Mode: static access
Administrative Trunking Encapsulation: negotiate
```

Listing 7.2 *Continued*

```
Operational Trunking Encapsulation: native
Negotiation of Trunking: Off
Access Mode VLAN: 12 (VLAN0012)
Trunking Native Mode VLAN: 1 (default)
Voice VLAN: 112 (VLAN0112)
Trunking VLANs Enabled: ALL
Pruning VLANs Enabled: 2-1001
Appliance trust: none
```

EXAM ALERT

There are only two VLANs allowed on a switch port configured for IP phones: the access VLAN with standard untagged Ethernet frames and the voice VLAN with 802.1Q-tagged Ethernet frames.

For IP communications to access the voice and data VLANs, you need to provide a Layer 3 IP interface. There are three methods used to provide this access: an external router connected to a switch, a Layer 3 switch, and a router with built-in switch ports.

VLANs and an External Router

The commands used to connect an external router to access the voice and data VLANs created in the preceding section follow in Listing 7.3.

Listing 7.3 **External Router—Layer 3 VLAN Configuration**

```
CMErouter(config)# interface fa0/0.12
CMErouter(config-if)# encapsulation dot1q 12
CMErouter(config-if)# ip address 10.1.12.1 255.255.255.0
CMErouter(config)# interface fa0/0.112
CMErouter(config-if)# encapsulation dot1q 112
CMErouter(config-if)# ip address 10.1.112.1 255.255.255.0
```

Router with Built-in Switch Ports

Listing 7.4 shows the commands used to connect a Layer 3 switch or a router with internal switch ports to access the voice and data VLANs created previously.

Listing 7.4 **Router with Built-in Switch—Layer 3 VLAN Configuration**

```
CMErouter(config)# interface vlan 12
CMErouter(config-if)# ip address 10.1.12.1 255.255.255.0
CMErouter(config)# interface vlan 112
CMErouter(config-if)# ip address 10.1.112.1 255.255.255.0
```

Power over Ethernet

To simplify deployment and ensure that the Cisco IP phones are powered even in emergencies, power to operate the phones is sourced from the wiring closets by either powered switches or power patch panels running on uninterruptible power supplies (UPSs). Figure 7.3 shows the two methods commonly used to provide power to IP phones.

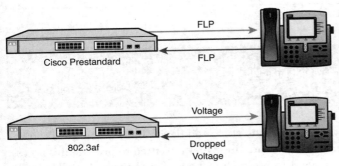

FIGURE 7.3 Power is supplied from the access switch.

Prestandard power uses a relay in the Cisco IP phone that bridges the transmit pair and the receive pair so that the Fast Link Pulse (FLP) can be detected by the Cisco Catalyst switch. After the switch detects the FLP, the switch applies inline power to the Cisco IP phone to activate the relay so that transmit and receive pairs can power the phone and enable communications.

Cisco prestandard power can be supplied on two pairs of a standard four-pair Ethernet cable. Option 1 is pins 1 and 2 and pins 3 and 6, and option 2 is pins 4 and 5 and pins 7 and 8.

Make sure that all the components in your wiring plant are certified to carry the power and voltage levels required to power Cisco IP phones. Components such as cables and patch panels should be Cat 5e or better.

With the IEEE standard 802.3af and the extended 802.3af plus, the method of detecting a powered device connected to Catalyst switches has been modified to measure resistance by sending low power to the powered device, measuring the result, verifying the result by slightly increasing the power, and remeasuring. After the powered device is verified, full power is applied.

EXAM ALERT

You should understand the two methods of delivering power to the Cisco IP phones: Cisco prestandard and IEEE 802.3af.

Essential Network Services: DHCP and NTP

DHCP is a common protocol and is familiar to many network administrators. With DHCP, a scope is defined per subnet and is used to assign IP addresses, along with a subnet mask, from a pool of available addresses. You should assign other values, such as the default gateway and Domain Name System (DNS) server (optional), to the scope by setting option values. Cisco IP phones look for option 150 (multiple servers) or option 66 (single server) from their DHCP server. These options provide the IP address of the TFTP server where the IP phone configuration files are stored. You must configure option 150 with the IP address of the TFTP server for the IP phones to receive their configuration file and successfully boot.

NOTE

The router or server that provides call control typically provides the TFTP function used in a Cisco Unified Communications deployment. Option 150 is the preferred practice.

NTP is used to synchronize the date and time on your network devices and for IP telephony to display the time on the IP phone and record the date and time for voicemail messages.

DHCP Services

You can deploy DHCP on any platform that supports customized scope options. These platforms include Windows, Linux, Novell, UNIX, and other operating systems.

When you set up the DHCP service for IP phones, you can define the address pools in the following ways:

- **Single DHCP IP address pool:** Define a single DHCP IP address pool if the router is a DHCP server and if you can use a single shared address pool for all your DHCP clients.

- **Separate DHCP IP address pool for each Cisco IP phone:** Define a separate pool for each Cisco IP phone if the router is a DHCP server and you need different settings on non–IP phone devices, such as personal computers, on the same subnet.

NOTE

You should avoid separate DHCP scopes for individual devices if possible because of the added configuration complexity.

▸ **DHCP relay server:** Define a DHCP relay server if the router is not a DHCP server and you want to relay DHCP requests from IP phones to a DHCP server on a different subnet.

Listing 7.5 shows router-based DHCP services.

Listing 7.5   Cisco IOS DHCP Configuration

```
CME(config)# ip dhcp excluded-address 10.112.0.1 10.112.0.10
CMERouter(config)# ip dhcp pool mypool
CMERouter(dhcp-config)# network 10.112.0.0 255.255.255.0
CMERouter(dhcp-config)# option 150 ip 10.112.0.1
CMERouter(dhcp-config)# default-router 10.112.0.1
CMERouter(dhcp-config)# dns-server 10.100.0.1 10.100.0.2
CMERouter(dhcp-config)# exit
```

EXAM ALERT

The DHCP pool name is case sensitive.

DHCP Relay Service

Implement DHCP relay when the DHCP server is not on the network where the DHCP clients exist. The Cisco IP phones use a broadcast DHCP request-and-response process, and broadcasts are only valid on the local subnet (VLAN). The solution is to convert and track the DHCP broadcast request to either a unicast or a directed broadcast. The broadcast traverses the network to reach the destination server or subnet and relays the response to the original requesting device. Figure 7.4 shows a router acting as the relay agent, accepting the IP phone broadcasts, obtaining the DHCP information from the server, and forwarding the response to the IP phone.

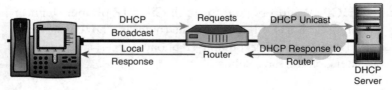

FIGURE 7.4 DHCP relay services.

For the Cisco router to support DHCP relay services, it must have the DHCP service enabled. The Cisco IOS DHCP server is enabled by default. If it has previously been disabled, use the `service dhcp` command in global configuration mode to enable this feature.

The `ip helper-address ip-address` command enables the selective forwarding of certain types of broadcasts, including Bootstrap Protocol (BOOTP) and DHCP. The `ip-address` parameter specifies the DHCP server to which the messages are forwarded. If you have multiple servers, you can configure one helper address for each server. For the IP phone to obtain IP address information, configure the `relay` command on each router interface local to the IP phones pointing to the remote DHCP server.

Listing 7.6 shows the configuration commands to implement DHCP relay services.

Listing 7.6   Implementing DHCP Relay Services

```
CMERouter(config)# service dhcp
CMERouter(config)# interface fastethernet 0/0
CMERouter(config-if)# ip helper-address 10.200.0.1
```

This listing configures an IP helper address of 10.200.0.1 on the Fast Ethernet 0/0 (fa0/0) interface. This interface connects to a network that has IP phones but does not have a DHCP server. This command causes the DHCP broadcasts that enter the router on the Fast Ethernet 0/0 interface to be forwarded to DHCP server 10.200.0.1. Each request is tracked by the router so that DHCP responses are forwarded to the correct local Cisco IP phone.

Network Time Protocol

NTP synchronizes network infrastructure (routers and switches) and computers (PCs and servers) to a single clock on the network, known as the *clock master*. NTP is essential to Cisco Unified Communications deployments.

An NTP network usually gets its time from an authoritative time source. This source can be a radio clock or an atomic clock attached to a time server. NTP then distributes this time across the network. An NTP client initiates a transaction with its server with a polling interval that ranges from 64 to 1,024 seconds. This interval dynamically changes over time, depending on the network conditions between the NTP server and the client. No more than one NTP transaction per minute is needed to synchronize two machines.

One of the strengths of NTP is that it uses Coordinated Universal Time (UTC), which is easily accessed through the GPS satellite system. Because UTC is the same worldwide, networks synchronized to UTC avoid interoperability problems with other networks. This synchronization is particularly important when administrators are troubleshooting IP telephony traffic and need to compare log files from various networks. The time of the internal clock of the Cisco Unified Communications call control platform and the network infrastructure components should be synchronized with an NTP server.

The `clock timezone` *zone hours-offset* command sets the time zone and number of hours that the time zone is offset from the UTC (formerly Greenwich Mean Time [GMT]). This command allows the Cisco router to define the operating time zone. If daylight saving time occurs in the area where the system is located, you must configure it using the `clock summer-time` *zone* `recurring` [*start-date end-date*] command.

Because Cisco Unified Communications call control can run on multiple platforms, the method for enabling NTP varies. To keep the correct time based on the time of a more authoritative source than its own system, perform the following:

- **Cisco IOS router:** The `ntp server` *ip-address* command configures the Cisco router to synchronize with the NTP server specified by the *ip-address* parameter.

- **LINUX-based servers:** Linux-based versions of Cisco Unified Communications Manager have a web-based interface that you can use to set the NTP server to which they can synchronize.

- **Windows-based servers:** Windows-based versions of Cisco Unified Communications Manager can be set from the command line.

Listing 7.7 sets a Cisco router to Pacific Standard Time with daylight saving time configured and synchronizes the router's system time to an NTP server with an IP address of 10.1.2.3.

Listing 7.7   Configuring NTP and Clock Settings

```
Router(config)# clock timezone PST -8
Router(config)# clock summer-time PDT recurring first sunday april 02:00
   last sunday october 02:00
Router(config)# ntp server 10.1.2.3
```

Understanding the Phone Bootup Process

After completing the configuration of the switch and activating DHCP, the Cisco IP phone proceeds through the standard bootup cycle.

After an IP phone receives power, the following happens:

1. Power-on self-test (POST): The phone performs a set of tests to ensure basic functionality.

2. The phone begins the boot process.

3. The phone uses Cisco Discovery Protocol to learn the voice VLAN.

4. The phone initializes a basic IP stack.

5. The IP phone (DHCP client) sends a DHCPDISCOVER request to the 255.255.255.255 broadcast address.

6. A DHCP server returns a DHCPOFFER message and assigns the following for the requested scope: a free IP address, the subnet mask, the default gateway, the DNS server (optional), and the TFTP server (option 150) for the scope. This information is sent to the DHCP client (the IP phone) using the broadcast address 255.255.255.255 (the router uses the IP phone MAC address at Layer 2).

7. The IP phone takes the values received from the DHCP response and applies them to the IP stack of the IP phone.

8. The IP phone uses the value received in option 150 to attempt to retrieve a configuration file from the TFTP server.

The IP phone is prepared and ready to operate on the network, but it needs its unique identity and operating parameters. When the TFTP request for configuration files is issued, there is a sequence of requests issued in an attempt to register with a call agent and operate. The following sections cover the configuration files.

Installing Cisco IP Phone Firmware and XML Configuration Files

Certain files are necessary for the proper operation of a Cisco IP phone or analog device so that it can register successfully with a Cisco Unified Communications call control device. These files are not installed on the Cisco router and must be installed from an external source. The file types are as follows:

- **Firmware:** The firmware is loaded into flash memory on the IP phone and can survive a reboot.

- **SEP*AAAABBBBCCCC*.cnf.xml:** This XML configuration file is specific to one device, and the *AAAABBBBCCCC* part of the name is the MAC address of the device.

- **XMLDefault.cnf.xml:** This XML configuration file specifies the proper firmware and the call agent's address and port, which the new phone needs to register.

The following sections describe each file type in greater detail.

Firmware

Install the firmware required by the Cisco IP phones in the flash memory of the Cisco Unified Communications Manager Express systems. There are two commands required to provide access to these firmware files:

- **tftp-server flash:*firmware-file-name*:** Use this global command to make the file available.

- **load *phone-type firmware-file*:** Use this telephony-service command to associate a type of phone with a firmware file.

All the necessary firmware files for Cisco IP phones are stored internally in the flash memory of the Cisco Unified Communications Manager Express router, so an external database or file server is not required. During registration, Cisco IP phones use TFTP to download firmware files from the router's flash memory. All Cisco Unified Communications Manager Express configuration and language files are located in the memory of the router in the system:/its/ directory.

To make the firmware file(s) available through a TFTP server, use the **tftp-server flash:*firmware-file-name(s)*** command on the Cisco Unified

Communications Manager Express router. The load *phone-type firmware-file* command under telephony service is also required to associate the model of IP phone with the appropriate firmware file(s).

For Cisco Unified Communications Manager, the firmware files are installed on the server(s) in the cluster that run the TFTP service.

Device Configuration XML File

The XML file SEP*AAAABBBBCCCC*.cnf.xml (where *AAAABBBBCCCC* is the MAC address of the IP phone) contains the call agent IP address and port, firmware, locale, directory URL, and many other pieces of information. This file is present when the IP phone has been added to the configuration.

Listing 7.8 shows a configuration file that contains the phone model (7931), IP address (10.6.150.1), and port (2000) for registering; the firmware filename; the language (English United States); and additional information for proper IP phone operation.

Listing 7.8 SEP*AAAABBBBCCCC*.cnf.xml File (*AAAABBBBCCCC* = the MAC Address)

```
<device>
<versionStamp>{7931 Aug 06 2008 14:23:48}</versionStamp>
<devicePool>
<dateTimeSetting>
<dateTemplate>M/D/YA</dateTemplate>
<timeZone>Eastern Standard/Daylight Time</timeZone>
</dateTimeSetting>
<callManagerGroup>
<members>
<member  priority="0">
<callManager>
<ports>
<ethernetPhonePort>2000</ethernetPhonePort>
</ports>
<processNodeName>10.6.150.1</processNodeName>
</callManager>
</member>
</members>
</callManagerGroup>
</devicePool>
<commonProfile>
<callLogBlfEnabled>3</callLogBlfEnabled>
</commonProfile>
<loadInformation>SCCP31.8-3-3S</loadInformation>
<userLocale>
<name>English_United_States</name>
<langCode>en</langCode>
```

Listing 7.8 *Continued*

```
</userLocale>
<networkLocale>United_States</networkLocale>
<networkLocaleInfo>
<name>United_States</name>
</networkLocaleInfo>
<idleTimeout>0</idleTimeout>
<authenticationURL>http://10.6.4.2/voiceview/authentication/authenticate.do
   </authenticationURL>
<directoryURL>http://10.6.150.1:80/localdirectory</directoryURL>
<idleURL></idleURL>
<informationURL></informationURL>
<messagesURL></messagesURL>
<proxyServerURL></proxyServerURL>
<servicesURL>http://10.6.150.1:80/CMEserverForPhone/serviceurl</servicesURL>
<capfAuthMode>0</capfAuthMode>
<capfList>
<capf>
<phonePort>3804</phonePort>
<processNodeName></processNodeName>
</capf>
</capfList>
<deviceSecurityMode>1</deviceSecurityMode>
</device>
```

Default XML File

IP phones and devices that do not find the more specific SEP*AAAABBBBCCCC*. cnf.xml file can use the XMLDefault.cnf.xml file if they have never registered before and an autoregistration method has been enabled. IP phones that download this XML file through TFTP learn the IP address and port to send Skinny Client Control Protocol (SCCP) messages to when attempting to register. The IP phones also learn the version of firmware that is required to function properly with the Cisco Unified Communications call control product to which the phone is registering. Cisco IP phone models 7931 and 7961 are highlighted.

Listing 7.9 shows a default configuration file.

Listing 7.9 XMLDefault.cnf.xml **File**

```
<Default>
<callManagerGroup>
<members>
<member  priority="0">
<callManager>
<ports>
<ethernetPhonePort>2000</ethernetPhonePort>
```

Listing 7.9 *Continued*

```
</ports>
<processNodeName>10.6.150.1</processNodeName>
</callManager>
</member>
</members>
</callManagerGroup>
<loadInformation124  model="Cisco IP Phone 7914 14-Button Line Expansion
   Module"></loadInformation124>
<loadInformation227  model="Cisco IP Phone 7915 12-Button Line Expansion
   Module"></loadInformation227>
<loadInformation228  model="Cisco IP Phone 7915 24-Button Line Expansion
   Module"></loadInformation228>
<loadInformation229  model="Cisco IP Phone 7916 12-Button Line Expansion
   Module"></loadInformation229>
<loadInformation230  model="Cisco IP Phone 7916 24-Button Line Expansion
   Module"></loadInformation230>
<loadInformation30008  model="Cisco IP Phone 7902"></loadInformation30008>
<loadInformation20000  model="Cisco IP Phone 7905"></loadInformation20000>
<loadInformation369  model="Cisco IP Phone 7906"></loadInformation369>
<loadInformation6  model="Cisco IP Phone 7910"></loadInformation6>
<loadInformation307  model="Cisco IP Phone 7911"></loadInformation307>
<loadInformation30007  model="Cisco IP Phone 7912"></loadInformation30007>
<loadInformation30002  model="Cisco IP Phone 7920"></loadInformation30002>
<loadInformation365  model="Cisco IP Phone 7921"></loadInformation365>
<loadInformation348  model="Cisco IP Phone 7931">SCCP31.8-3-3S
   </loadInformation348>
<loadInformation9  model="Cisco IP Conference Station 7935">
   </loadInformation9>
<loadInformation30019  model="Cisco IP Phone 7936"></loadInformation30019>
<loadInformation431  model="Cisco IP Conference Station 7937">
   </loadInformation431>
<loadInformation8  model="Cisco IP Phone 7940"></loadInformation8>
<loadInformation115  model="Cisco IP Phone 7941"></loadInformation115>
<loadInformation309  model="Cisco IP Phone 7941GE"></loadInformation309>
<loadInformation434  model="Cisco IP Phone 7942"></loadInformation434>
<loadInformation435  model="Cisco IP Phone 7945"></loadInformation435>
<loadInformation7  model="Cisco IP Phone 7960"></loadInformation7>
<loadInformation30018  model="Cisco IP Phone 7961">SCCP41.8-3-3S
   </loadInformation30018>
<loadInformation308  model="Cisco IP Phone 7961GE"></loadInformation308>
<loadInformation404  model="Cisco IP Phone 7962"></loadInformation404>
<loadInformation436  model="Cisco IP Phone 7965"></loadInformation436>
<loadInformation30006  model="Cisco IP Phone 7970"></loadInformation30006>
<loadInformation119  model="Cisco IP Phone 7971"></loadInformation119>
<loadInformation437  model="Cisco IP Phone 7975"></loadInformation437>
<loadInformation302  model="Cisco IP Phone 7985"></loadInformation302>
</Default>
```

Exam Prep Questions

1. What are the reasons for using 802.1Q? (Choose two.)

   ○ **A.** Standards based multi-VLAN trunking

   ○ **B.** To allow clients to see the 802.1Q header

   ○ **C.** To provide inter-VLAN communications over a bridge

   ○ **D.** To load-balance traffic between parallel links using STP

   ○ **E.** To provide a voice and data VLAN on a shared connection

2. Which of the following describes the endless flooding or looping of frames in a Layer 2 switched environment?

   ○ **A.** Flood storm

   ○ **B.** Loop overload

   ○ **C.** Broadcast storm

   ○ **D.** Broadcast overload

3. Which command correctly connects an Ethernet subinterface to VLAN 50 using 802.1Q trunking?

   ○ **A.** Router(config) # **encapsulation 50 dot1Q**

   ○ **B.** Router(config) # **encapsulation 802.1Q 50**

   ○ **C.** Router(config-if) # **encapsulation dot1Q 50**

   ○ **D.** Router(config-if) # **encapsulation 50 802.1Q**

4. Which of the following is a Cisco recommendation for IP addressing deployment?

   ○ **A.** Statically apply IP addresses to IP phones to ensure stability.

   ○ **B.** Apply public IP addresses to IP phones so that they can be reached from the PSTN.

   ○ **C.** Add IP phones with DHCP as the mechanism for obtaining IP addresses.

   ○ **D.** Deploy IP phones on the same subnet as data devices.

5. Why would you need to implement a DHCP relay server?

- ○ **A.** If the DHCP server does not have a local interface on the network with the DHCP clients
- ○ **B.** Because the DHCP request and response process is not broadcast
- ○ **C.** To relay the proprietary DHCP request of an IP phone to the standard DHCP request understood by the Cisco IOS Software
- ○ **D.** If an IP phone, a data device, and a DHCP server all reside on the same subnet

6. Which protocol do IP phones use during registration to download firmware files from the flash memory of the router?

- ○ **A.** HTTP
- ○ **B.** DHCP
- ○ **C.** FTP
- ○ **D.** TFTP

7. Which of the following statements accurately describe NTP? (Choose all that apply.)

- ○ **A.** NTP is used to synchronize syslog time stamps.
- ○ **B.** NTP is used to synchronize call detail records.
- ○ **C.** NTP is used to minimize errors during TFTP downloads.
- ○ **D.** The time displayed on the IP phones must come from an NTP server.
- ○ **E.** Cisco Unified Communications Manager Express can synchronize its clock to an NTP server.
- ○ **F.** NTP requires the purchase of an atomic or radio clock.

8. Which of the following filenames could be used by a Cisco IP phone to synchronize its firmware with the call agent? (Choose two.)

- ○ **A.** XMLdefault.cnf.xml
- ○ **B.** ephone-1.cnf.xml
- ○ **C.** SEP001BD5086771.cnf.xml
- ○ **D.** SEP001BB35853C.cnf.xml
- ○ **E.** XMLDefault.cnf.xml

9. Which of the following commands would be used to deliver firmware file SCCP41.8-3-3S.loads at the request of a Cisco IP phone?

   ○ **A.** `ftp-server flash:/SCCP41.8-3-3S.loads`

   ○ **B.** `tftp-server flash:/SCCP41.8-3-3S.loads`

   ○ **C.** `tftp-server flash:/SCCP41.8-3-3S`

   ○ **D.** `tftp-server SCCP41.8-3-3S.loads`

10. DHCP services can be configured on which of the following devices? (Choose two.)

    ○ **A.** Cisco IOS routers

    ○ **B.** Cisco IP phones

    ○ **C.** Cisco IOS Layer 3 switches

    ○ **D.** Cisco IOS Layer 2 switches

Answers to Exam Prep Questions

1. **A and E.** 802.1Q is a standards-based trunking protocol and shares a single physical connection for voice and data traffic. End users typically are not permitted to access the network over multiple VLANs, so answer B is incorrect. Answer C is incorrect; VLANs isolate traffic at Layer 2. Multiple VLANs are not used for load balancing because end stations can only access one VLAN at a time, so answer D is incorrect.

2. **C.** Broadcast storm describes the endless flooding of frames in a Layer 2 switched environment. Answers A, B, and D are incorrect. None of those terms have meaning in the Ethernet switch environment.

3. **C.** The `encapsulation` command followed by the *encapsulation type* and the *VLAN number*. Answers A and B are incorrect; the answers are in global mode, not interface mode. Answer D has the parameters of the encapsulation command backward.

4. **C.** Deploy IP phones using DHCP. Statically applying IP addresses is time consuming and error prone, so answer A is incorrect. Using public IP addresses for phones opens a security threat, so answer B is incorrect. Answer D is incorrect; the goal is to separate voice and data traffic.

5. **A.** No direct connection to the DHCP server. The IP phone DHCP request is a broadcast, so answer B is incorrect. The IP phone uses standard DHCP services, so answer C is incorrect. If the DHCP server is directly attached to the same IP subnet or VLAN, there is no reason to use DHCP relay, so answer D is incorrect.

6. **D.** TFTP is used to provision Cisco IP phones. HTTP, DHCP, and FTP are not used during the automatic provisioning and registration process, so answers B, C, and D are incorrect.

7. **A, B, and E.** NTP is the source for syslog and CDR time stamps, and for Cisco Unified Communications call agent synchronization. NTP is not used during TFTP downloads to minimize errors, so answer C is incorrect. The time displayed on the IP phones comes from the call agent, so answer D is incorrect. There are many free-access NTP servers on the Internet that have atomic clocks and are typically used as NTP sources, so answer F is incorrect.

8. **C and E.** `SEP<12 hex digit MAC address>.cnf.xml` and `XMLDefault.cnf.xml` (case sensitive) are valid files. Answer A is incorrect; file requests are case sensitive and the *d* in default is lowercase. Answer B is an invalid filename and is incorrect. Answer D has only 11 hex digits for the MAC address, not the normal 12, and is incorrect.

9. **B.** The complete filename using the TFTP protocol. FTP service is not supported for firmware upgrades, so answer A is incorrect. The complete filename including extension must be referenced by the `tftp-server` command. The full directory and filename must be defined, not default locations.

10. **A and C.** Layer 3 devices can provide DHCP services. Answer B is incorrect; IP phones cannot provide DHCP services. Answer D is incorrect; Layer 2 devices cannot provide DHCP services.

Suggested Reading and Resources

1. Droms, R. RFC 2131, "Dynamic Host Configuration Protocol." http://www.ietf.org/rfc/rfc2131.txt, March 1997.

2. Mills, David L. RFC 1305, "Network Time Protocol (Version 3) Specification, Implementation and Analysis." http://www.ietf.org/rfc/rfc1305.txt, March 1992.

3. Rekhter, Y., B. Moskowitz, D. Karrenberg, G. J. de Groot, and E. Lear. RFC 1918, "Address Allocation for Private Internets." http://www.ietf.org/rfc/rfc3551.txt, February 1996.

4. IEEE. Information on IEEE 802.1Q and IEEE 802.1af. http://www.ieee.org.

CHAPTER EIGHT

Reviewing QoS and Configuring the Cisco AutoQoS Feature

Terms you need to understand:

✓ Quality of service (QoS)

✓ Propagation

✓ Serialization

✓ Class of service (CoS)

✓ Differentiated Services Code Point (DSCP)

✓ IP Precedence

✓ Real-Time Transport Protocol (RTP)

✓ User Datagram Protocol (UDP)

✓ Transmission Control Protocol (TCP)

✓ Weighted fair queuing (WFQ)

✓ Class-based weighted fair queuing (CBWFQ)

✓ Network-based application recognition (NBAR)

Techniques you need to master:

✓ Understand sources of information to define a QoS policy

✓ Understand the importance of defining a QoS policy

✓ Identify the trust boundary

✓ Know the difference between AutoQoS without and with the trust option

✓ Understand the traffic marking used to implement QoS: CoS, IP Precedence, and DSCP

✓ Understand the techniques used to mitigate issues with bandwidth utilization, end-to-end delay, packet loss, and variable delay or jitter

You need to understand what quality of service (QoS) is and why it is useful in solving problems that arise when different traffic types are converged into a single network infrastructure. This chapter explains the basic concepts and key terminology of QoS. This lesson also includes the three steps involved in implementing a QoS policy, special QoS considerations for LANs, and deploying QoS using Cisco AutoQoS.

The TCP/IP stack has two transport protocols: User Datagram Protocol (UDP) and Transport Control Protocol (TCP). Real-time traffic is carried over UDP and requires the highest priority level for good-quality audio. Call control traffic is carried over TCP and requires a guaranteed minimum amount of bandwidth to provide good call setup times.

Cisco Unified Communications relies on QoS to provide the reliable, predictable network infrastructure to properly transmit quality voice communications.

Defining QoS

QoS is the ability of the network to provide better or *special* service to selected users or applications at the expense of other users or applications. While more bandwidth can appear to solve immediate issues, throwing more bandwidth at voice quality issues is often a temporary fix.

Cisco IOS QoS features enable you to control and predictably service a variety of networked applications and traffic types, thus allowing network managers to take advantage of a new generation of media-rich and mission-critical applications.

The goal of QoS is to provide better and more predictable network service by providing dedicated bandwidth, controlled jitter and latency, and improved packet loss characteristics. QoS achieves these goals by providing tools for managing network congestion, shaping network traffic, using expensive wide-area links more efficiently, and setting traffic policies across the network. QoS offers intelligent network services that when applied correctly, help provide consistent, predictable performance.

Why Converged Networks Need QoS

Before voice, data, and video were converged into a single IP network, each of the three types of traffic had its own dedicated network. In network environments that are not converged, an increase in voice, data, or video traffic impacts only that specific service area. When all three traffic types are converged on a single IP network, the network engineer is challenged to provide proper service levels for each traffic type.

Let's review the transition from separate traffic paths to a single traffic path and identify the characteristics of voice, video, and data traffic.

Networks Before Convergence

Historically, network engineering has been focused on connectivity. Data, voice, and video have different network requirements and traffic characteristics. Few tools existed to handle the needs of the different traffic types, forcing network engineers to build separate networks to handle these traffic requirements. Separate networks meant higher equipment, installation, and operating costs and required segmented support staffs. With the advent of QoS, QoS monitoring tools, and the use of IP to transport traffic, converged networks are a reality. Figure 8.1 illustrates a nonconverged voice, data, and video environment.

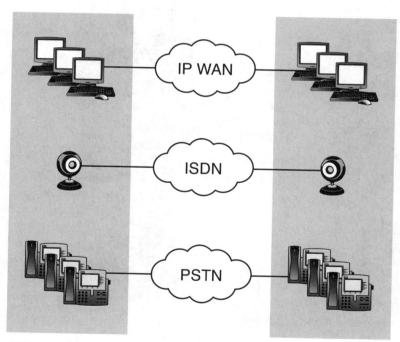

FIGURE 8.1   Networks before convergence.

For traditional data networks that support applications such as file transfer or email, the rates at which data comes onto the network result in bursty data flows. The data arrives in packets and tries to grab as much bandwidth as it can. Traffic is served on a first come, first served basis, and the traffic has to adapt or conform to the existing network conditions.

The protocols that were developed for data networks adapt to the bursty nature of data networks, and brief outages are survivable. Typically, if you are retrieving email, a delay of a few seconds is generally not noticeable. A delay of minutes is annoying, but not serious.

Networks After Convergence

In a converged network, voice, video, and data traffic use the same network facilities. Merging different traffic streams with dramatically differing requirements can lead to a number of service-quality issues. Figure 8.2 illustrates a converged network with one physical link transporting voice, video, and data.

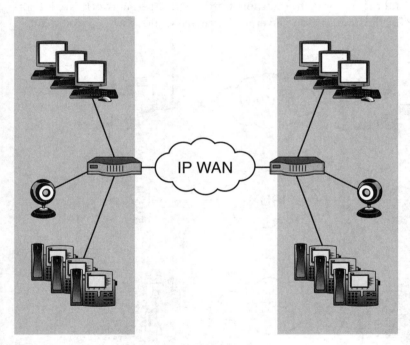

FIGURE 8.2 Single network after convergence.

Packets carrying voice traffic are typically very small, but as real-time data, the packets cannot tolerate delay and delay variation (jitter) as they traverse the network. Delay and jitter affect voice quality; when the audio breaks up, words become difficult to understand.

Packets carrying file-transfer data are typically large and can survive delays and drops. It is possible to retransmit part of a dropped file, but it is not feasible to retransmit a part of an audio conversation or a video stream.

The constant, but small, packet voice flow competes with bursty data flows. Unless some mechanism mediates the overall flow, voice quality suffers terribly at times of network congestion. The critical voice traffic must have priority.

Voice and video traffic are very time sensitive. They cannot be delayed or dropped, or quality suffers.

With inadequate preparation of the network, voice transmission is choppy or unintelligible. Gaps in speech are particularly troublesome, pieces of speech are interspersed with silence, and speech literally disappears. In voicemail systems, this silence is a problem. For example, you dial 68614. When the gaps in speech are actually gaps in the tone, 68614 becomes 6688661144 because the gaps in speech are perceived as pauses in the touch tones.

Poor caller interactivity is the consequence of delay. It causes two problems: echo and talker overlap. Echo is caused by the signal reflections of the voice of the speaker from the far-end telephone equipment into the ear of the speaker. Talker overlap (or the problem of one talker "stepping" on the speech of the other talker) becomes significant if the one-way delay becomes greater than 250 milliseconds. If the problem is severe, calls go to "walkie-talkie" mode, meaning that each caller must conclude his statement by saying "over," which signals the other caller that it is his turn to speak.

Disconnected calls represent the worst cases. If there are long gaps in speech, people hang up, or if there are signaling problems, calls are disconnected. Such events are unacceptable in the voice world yet are quite common in an inadequately prepared data network that is attempting to carry voice.

Multimedia streams, such as those used in IP telephony or videoconferencing, can be extremely sensitive to delivery delays, creating unique QoS demands on the networks that carry them. When packets are delivered using the best-effort delivery model, they might not arrive in order, in a timely manner, or at all. The result is unclear pictures, jerky and slow movement, and sound not synchronized with the image.

Measurable QoS Issues: Bandwidth, Delay, Loss, and Jitter

The following are the four big problems facing converged enterprise networks:

- ▶ Bandwidth capacity
- ▶ End-to-end delay (both fixed and variable)

▶ Packet loss

▶ Variation of delay (also called jitter)

Typical production environments manage all four of these QoS elements, as described in the following sections.

Bandwidth Capacity

You must consider bandwidth on the entire communication path between source and destination. Figure 8.3 illustrates an empty network with four hops between a server and a client. All hops use different media with different bandwidths. The maximum available bandwidth is equal to the bandwidth of the slowest link. So although the workstation has 100Mbps of bandwidth and the server has 100Mbps of bandwidth, packets flowing between these devices must cross the slow-speed WAN link at 256Kbps.

FIGURE 8.3 Maximum available bandwidth is equal to that of the slowest link.

It is rare that only a single communication flow is present on a computer network at a given time. In reality, multiple communication flows are competing for the same bandwidth. The calculation of the available bandwidth is much more complex when multiple flows are traversing the network. The calculation of the available bandwidth in Figure 8.3 is a rough approximation.

End-to-End Delay

End-to-end delay equals the sum of all propagation, processing, serialization, and queuing delays in the path between two end stations, as shown in Figure 8.4. There are two types of delay: fixed and variable.

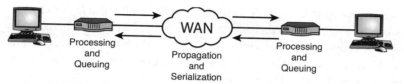

FIGURE 8.4 End-to-end delay components.

Fixed Delay

Propagation and serialization delays are fixed and are based on circuit distances and circuit speeds.

Propagation delays are based on physics and the speed of light. Theoretically, the first bit of a packet traveling from New York City to Sydney, Australia, at 186,000 miles per second takes approximately 65 milliseconds, but practically about 120 milliseconds. Propagation delay is generally ignored, but it can be significant (about 40ms coast to coast across the United States over optical media). Use ping or traceroute to measure the round-trip time of IP packets in a network and divide by 2 for an approximate one-way propagation delay value.

Every time a packet gets processed through an intermediate device, the packet or frame has to be received and retransmitted. Each time a packet is retransmitted, there is serialization delay induced on both input and output sides of the intermediate device. On high-speed circuits, the individual delay is small, but the cumulative effect contributes to the end-to-end delay. Most high-speed service provider connections provide predictable or fixed serialization delay between two end points.

For example, customer routers in New York and San Francisco are connected by a 128Kbps WAN link. The customer sends a 66-byte voice frame across the link. Transmitting the frame (528 bits) requires 4.125ms to clock out (serialization delay), but the last bit does not arrive until 40ms after it clocks out (propagation delay). The total delay is 44.125ms. If you change the circuit to a T1, the 528-bit frame takes 0.344ms to clock out (serialization delay), and the last bit arrives 40ms after transmission (propagation delay), for a total delay of 40.344ms. In this case, the significant factor is propagation delay. In the same situation, but between Seattle and San Francisco, serialization delay remains the same and propagation delay drops to about 6ms, resulting in 528 bits taking 10.125ms on a 128Kbps link and 6.344ms on a 1536Kbps T1 link.

Variable Delay

Processing and queuing variable delays can be created based on traffic levels and types. Processing delays were more significant 10 years ago, but today's router and switch products have been enhanced to the point where processing delays are negligible.

Queuing delays are another story. The higher traffic levels in today's networks are driven by the applications themselves. Retrieving a web-page-based form requires significantly more bandwidth than the text-based interfaces of the recent past. More traffic and faster circuits create a greater potential for queuing bottlenecks in both the LAN and WAN.

Packet Loss

Packet loss occurs when routers or switches run out of buffer space in the output queue for a particular interface. Figure 8.5 illustrates the effects of a full output queue on an interface, which causes newly arriving packets to be tail-dropped. A tail drop occurs when the output buffer can no longer store more packets due to network transmission issues. No room in the queue means that packets are directed to the bit bucket.

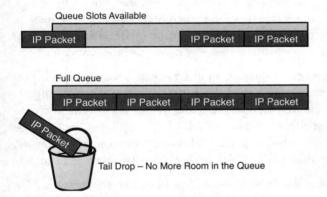

FIGURE 8.5 Where did that packet go?

Variation of Delay: Jitter

Jitter is the voice and video killer when it comes to acceptable quality. With video or audio streaming from the Internet, media players buffer the incoming streams while they measure the incoming data rate. The application then makes sure that there is enough buffer space available to ensure that the streaming media is not interrupted. Based on the download speed and traffic flow, this buffer could be anywhere from a few seconds to minutes. With Voice over IP (VoIP), for example, the Cisco IP phones have a 60-millisecond buffer to smooth out slight variations in the arrival time of the original packets. Without QoS, voice calls sound like Max Headroom (see Wikipedia for definition and video clips). Figure 8.6 illustrates the effects of jitter on voice traffic during the transition, from normal traffic levels to a congested WAN and back to the normal uncongested network.

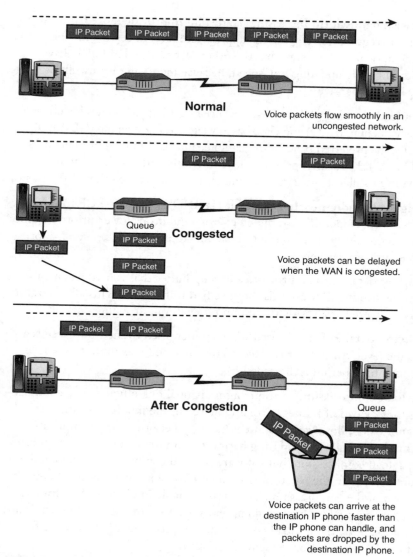

FIGURE 8.6 Jitter effect on VoIP traffic.

Techniques to Solve QoS Issues

Detailed descriptions of mitigation techniques used to solve the four primary QoS issues encountered in converged networks follow:

▶ **Increase bandwidth:** Increasing bandwidth to provide more bandwidth might be required to provide the appropriate level of service for the traffic on the network. Make sure that the other techniques that follow have been explored before updating link speed, because increasing bandwidth is typically more expensive.

▶ **Advanced queuing techniques:** Advanced queuing techniques include low latency queuing (LLQ) and class-based weighted fair queuing (CBWFQ). LLQ is the preferred bandwidth guarantee mechanism for VoIP networks. LLQ establishes a strict priority queue for voice media packets and uses CBWFQ to allocate guaranteed minimum bandwidth for other traffic classes.

▶ **Weighted random early detection (WRED):** Used for TCP traffic flows, WRED identifies traffic by priority and drops lower-priority traffic more aggressively as the output queue fills to provide better service for higher-priority packets.

▶ **Shaping data:** Shaping provides a backup buffer that is used when an identified traffic flow exceeds the specified traffic level. This allows traffic to be delivered at a steady maximum rate without dropping packets.

▶ **Policing data:** Policing is used when an identified traffic flow exceeds a specific level. All traffic that exceeds the allocated maximum traffic level within a time period is discarded.

▶ **Payload compression:** Optimizing individual link efficiency by compressing the payload of frames (virtually) increases the link bandwidth. Compression, however, also increases delay because of the complexity of compression algorithms. Using hardware compression can accelerate packet payload compression, but software payload compression usually induces more delay than the payload without compression. Stacker and Predictor are two of the compression algorithms available in Cisco IOS Software. Voice media packets contain compressed payload that negates much, if not all, of the potential payload compression improvement for voice traffic, but can be effective for reducing data traffic.

▶ **Header compression:** Another link efficiency mechanism is header compression. This mechanism is especially effective in networks where most packets carry small amounts of data (the payload-to-header ratio is small). Typical examples of header compression are TCP header compression, which is effective for Telnet and Secure Shell (SSH), and Real-Time Transport Protocol (RTP) header compression, which is effective for codecs such as G.729a, where the payload is only 33.3 percent of the overall IP packet. This technique is recommended an all point-to-point serial links E1 (2Mbps) or less.

▶ **Link fragmentation and interleaving (LFI):** The physical interface has a first in, first out (FIFO) queue that can create jitter because the hardware buffer can be full or empty when a voice packet arrives at the interface for transmission. LFI takes the nonvoice packets and segments each packet traversing a single physical link into chunks that are approximately the same size as the voice packets. With priority queuing, all the voice packets get to merge into the interface buffer with equal-size nonvoice packets. It is easier to merge onto a parkway that is for cars only than onto a throughway with both cars and trucks. Cisco defines slow-speed links as 768Kbps or slower.

> **TIP**
>
> Implementation experience shows that LFI on an E1 (2048Kbps) WAN circuit or slower can improve voice quality.

Table 8.1 identifies techniques that you can use to mitigate QoS issues in a converged network.

TABLE 8.1 Techniques Used to Mitigate Bandwidth, End-to-End Delay, Packet Loss, and Jitter for Multimedia Traffic

Technique	Applies To				Traffic Types Affected
	Bandwidth Utilization	End-to-End Delay	Packet Loss	Jitter	
Increase bandwidth	Yes	Yes	Yes	Yes	Voice, video, data
Advanced queuing techniques	Yes	Yes	Yes	Yes	Voice, video, data
Weighted random early detection	Yes	—	—	Yes	Data
Shaping data	Yes	—	—	Yes	Data
Policing data	Yes	Yes	Yes	Yes	Data
Payload compression	Yes	No	No	No	Data
RTP header compression	Yes	—	—	Yes	Voice
Link fragmentation and interleaving	Yes	—	—	Yes	Voice, video, data

QoS Traffic Tagging for IP and LAN Traffic

Two types of traffic tagging are used to identify traffic by traffic class: the type of service (TOS) field for IP and the class of service (CoS) field for LAN traffic.

Establish a trust boundary as close to the endpoints in the IP network as possible. Classify and mark incoming traffic with no more than six classes of service to simplify long-term monitoring and management of the network.

The IP Header TOS Field

The TOS field is 1 byte or 8 bits long and is used to identify traffic for QoS processing. Figure 8.7 illustrates the TOS field in the IP header.

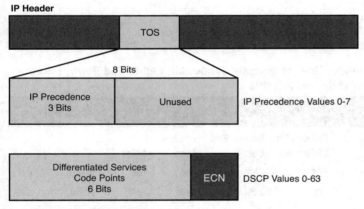

FIGURE 8.7   The TOS field in the IP header.

The first 3 bits define eight levels of priority, 0–7. Priority 6 and 7 are reserved for network infrastructure operations, and priority levels 0 through 5 are used for normal network traffic. This priority field has been defined and in use since 1981 and is referred to as IP Precedence.

The TOS field was updated in 1998 to implement Differentiated Services Code Points (DSCPs); the field is 6 bits long. The DSCP definition uses the first 3 bits for priority to be backward compatible with IP Precedence. The next 3 bits create a potential granularity down to 64 different IP packet classes of service. Currently only the first 2 bits are used to provide drop preference for priority classes 1 through 4. The explicit congestion notification (ECN) bits are used to inform endpoint applications of congestion in the network, similar to the signs on a highway telling drivers there is an accident ahead.

The CoS Field for Layer 2 Frames

The Layer 2 CoS field is 3 bits long, part of the 802.1Q trunk tag or Inter-Switch Link (ISL) header, and is used to identify Layer 2 Ethernet frames. This CoS field is used by the hardware queuing mechanism built into Cisco switch ports to prioritize traffic entering and leaving switch ports. Figure 8.8 illustrates the CoS field.

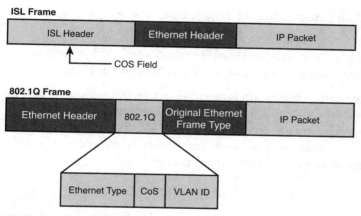

FIGURE 8.8 The CoS field in the frame header.

Understanding QoS Traffic Requirements

The following sections profile traffic requirements in a converged network.

Voice

QoS traffic requirements for voice include the following:

- ► End-to-end delay < 150ms, one way
- ► Jitter < 30ms, one way
- ► Packet loss < 1 percent, one way
- ► 17–106Kbps guaranteed priority bandwidth per call

Voice traffic has extremely stringent QoS requirements for jitter. Voice traffic generates a smooth and steady demand on bandwidth on a per-call basis. When QoS has been properly applied, voice traffic has a minimal impact on other traffic.

Video

QoS traffic requirements for video include the following:

- End-to-end delay < 150ms, one way
- Jitter < 30ms, one way
- Packet loss < 1 percent, one way
- Guaranteed minimum bandwidth required per session

Videoconferencing has similar QoS requirements to voice. Videoconferencing traffic is often bursty in nature and, as a result, can affect other traffic.

The minimum guaranteed bandwidth for a videoconferencing session should be the actual bandwidth of the stream plus 20 percent overhead. For example, a 384Kbps video stream actually requires a total of 460Kbps of priority bandwidth. Video traffic is not considered as critical as voice traffic and is provided a minimum guaranteed bandwidth rather than strict priority.

Data

QoS traffic requirements vary for data, as described in the following list:

- Different applications have different traffic characteristics, for example, text-based applications such as Telnet versus web-based applications.
- Different versions of the same application can have different traffic characteristics, for example, HTML-based web applications migrated to Java-based web applications.
- Data should be classified into a relative-priority model with no more than four or five data traffic classifications.

The QoS requirements for data traffic vary greatly, and it can be difficult to determine potential traffic flows prior to installation. Always test new or updated applications prior to production to determine traffic characteristics.

While data traffic can demonstrate either smooth or bursty characteristics, depending on the application, data traffic differs from voice and video in terms of delay and drop sensitivity. Most data applications can tolerate some delay and generally can tolerate higher drop rates when using TCP as a transport mechanism with TCP's retransmission capability. Voice and video streams use UDP, and when a UDP packet is gone, it is gone forever.

By identifying and tagging data applications as they enter the network, you can start the QoS process up front. Do not classify data traffic into more than four or five traffic classes. While it might seem like a good idea at the time, managing very granular QoS policies is a difficult task; simple is better.

Building a QoS Policy for Converged Networks

A QoS policy is a network-wide definition of the specific levels of service assigned to different classes of network traffic. Having a QoS policy is just as important in a converged network as having a security policy. A written QoS policy allows management to align the network QoS to business priorities.

Let's take a look at ABC Corporation's network traffic and define a QoS policy to align network resources with business priorities. Defining a QoS policy requires the following steps:

1. Identify the traffic on the network.

2. Divide the traffic into service classes.

3. Define policies for each service class.

Identifying the Network Traffic

The first step in implementing a QoS policy is to identify the traffic on the network. ABC Corporation has three primary network applications that require special consideration:

▶ **Enterprise resource planning (ERP):** ERP applications have a high QoS priority and must be available at all times to support replication between systems. Peak traffic is 220Kbps during the normal business day.

▶ **Video applications:** Video applications are guaranteed 100Kbps of bandwidth per session, with a maximum of three sessions operating at any time.

▶ **Voice traffic:** Voice traffic requires a guaranteed delay of less than 150ms in each direction and top priority for the voice traffic and guaranteed bandwidth for call control. Peak calling traffic on the network between sites is seven simultaneous calls.

Divide the Traffic into Service Classes

The next step is to divide the traffic into service classes:

▶ ERP requires higher priority than the balance of the data traffic and requires a guaranteed minimum bandwidth of 220Kbps.

▶ Video traffic requires a guaranteed minimum bandwidth of 300Kbps.

▶ Voice media is using the G.729a codec, which requires 26Kbps per call. With a peak of seven calls crossing the network, the voice traffic requires 182Kbps of priority bandwidth.

▶ Call control, for both voice and video calls, is the key to the voice and video call experience. Bandwidth requirements are approximately 150bps per call. Define a service class with a guaranteed minimum bandwidth of at least 1.5Kbps for call setup quality.

▶ All other data traffic is considered best effort, with Internet web traffic limited to 300Kbps.

Define Policies for Each Service Class

The next step in the process is to define the policies for each class of service. The components we can use for each class are as follows:

▶ Set a minimum bandwidth guarantee or a maximum priority bandwidth.

▶ Set maximum bandwidth limits for traffic such as best-effort web browsing using policing.

▶ Manage congestion with weighted random early detection and shaping.

For ABC Corporation, we can define the following classes and class policies:

▶ **Mission-critical:** Minimum guaranteed bandwidth is 220Kbps. Use QoS marking to mark ERP data packets as priority 2 when they enter the network. Use LLQ-CBWFQ to provide the guaranteed bandwidth.

▶ **Video:** Use QoS marking to mark video streaming packets as priority 4. Use LLQ-CBWFQ to ensure that video traffic flows are guaranteed 300Kbps.

▶ **Voice:** Priority bandwidth is 182Kbps. Use QoS marking to mark these data packets as priority 5. Use LLQ-CBWFQ to prioritize the voice media packets.

- **Call control:** Minimum guaranteed bandwidth of 8Kbps. Use QoS marking to mark these control packets as priority 3.

- **Best-effort:** The balance of the traffic falls into this category. Best-effort traffic is guaranteed a minimum of 25 percent of each circuit bandwidth on the WAN. Internet web traffic is limited to 300Kbps.

Table 8.2 illustrates the QoS policy.

TABLE 8.2 Sample QoS Policy

Traffic	Priority	Queuing Method	Bandwidth
Voice	5	Priority	182Kbps
Video	4	Guaranteed minimum	300Kbps
Call control	3	Guaranteed minimum	8Kbps
Mission-critical	2	Guaranteed minimum	220Kbps
Best-effort	0	Guaranteed minimum	At least 25 percent of circuit bandwidth

An AutoQoS Primer

Cisco AutoQoS enables customer networks to deploy QoS features for converged IP telephony and data networks much faster and more efficiently. It simplifies and automates the Modular QoS CLI (MQC) definition of traffic classes and the creation and configuration of traffic policies. Cisco AutoQoS generates traffic classes and policy maps using command-line interface (CLI) templates. Therefore, when Cisco AutoQoS is configured on the interface or a permanent virtual circuit (PVC), the traffic automatically receives the required QoS treatment.

In-depth knowledge of the underlying technologies, service policies, link efficiency mechanisms, and Cisco QoS best-practice recommendations for voice requirements are not required to configure Cisco AutoQoS.

Cisco AutoQoS can be beneficial for the following reasons:

- Reduces cost of deployment

- Ensures consistency of configurations

- Simplifies network administration

- Contains Cisco best practices for deploying QoS for voice deployments

- Builds configuration and adds to the router or switch configuration

- Lends itself to tuning of all generated parameters and configurations

Cisco AutoQoS simplifies and shortens the QoS deployment cycle. Cisco AutoQoS helps in all five major aspects of successful QoS deployments:

- **Application classification:** Cisco AutoQoS leverages intelligent classification on routers, utilizing Cisco Network Based Application Recognition (NBAR) to provide deep and stateful packet inspection. Cisco AutoQoS uses Cisco Discovery Protocol for voice packets to ensure that the device attached to the LAN is really an IP phone. NBAR examines all IP packet headers, and optionally the content of the packets, to provide a very granular identification of network traffic. For example, instead of identifying HTTP traffic, NBAR provides the mechanism to identify traffic flows based on the web page URL.

- **Policy generation:** Cisco AutoQoS evaluates the network environment and generates an initial policy. It automatically determines WAN settings for fragmentation, compression, encapsulation, and Frame Relay-ATM interworking, which eliminates the need to understand QoS theory and design practices in various scenarios. Customers can meet additional and special requirements by modifying the initial policy as they normally would.

  AutoQoS provides the necessary Cisco AutoQoS VoIP feature to automate QoS settings for deployments. This feature automatically generates interface configurations, policy maps, class maps, and access control lists (ACLs). Cisco AutoQoS VoIP uses a canned network policy to classify voice traffic and mark it with the appropriate QoS marking. Cisco AutoQoS-VoIP can be instructed to rely on, or trust, the DSCP markings previously applied to the packets.

- **Configuration:** With one command, `auto qos voip`, Cisco AutoQoS configures the port to prioritize voice traffic without affecting other network traffic while still offering the flexibility to adjust QoS settings for unique network requirements. Not only does Cisco AutoQoS automatically detect Cisco IP phones and enable QoS settings, but it also disables the QoS settings when a Cisco IP phone is relocated or moved to prevent malicious activity. Cisco AutoQoS–generated router and switch configurations are customizable using the standard Cisco IOS CLI.

- **Monitoring and reporting:** Cisco AutoQoS provides visibility into the classes of service deployed using system logging and Simple Network Management Protocol (SNMP) traps, with notification of abnormal events, such as VoIP packet drops.

- **Consistency:** Cisco AutoQoS enables automatic and seamless interoperability between all the QoS features and parameters across the network topology, including LAN, metropolitan-area network (MAN), and WAN.

Trust Boundaries

The Cisco QoS model assumes that the CoS carried in a frame might or might not be trusted by the network device. Switches are the primary entry point in the network, and trust boundaries are typically set in the switch.

For scalability, classification should be done as close to the edge of the network or source device as possible. End hosts cannot be trusted to tag a packet priority correctly. The outermost trusted devices represent the trust boundary. If the end device can perform traffic classification, the trust boundary for the network is at the access layer in the wiring closet. If the device cannot perform traffic classification, or if the wiring closet switch does not trust the classification done by the end device, the trust boundary should shift to the first device with QoS capabilities.

The concept of trust is an important and integral part of deploying QoS. After the end devices have set priority values, the switch has the option of trusting them or not. If the switch trusts the priority values, it does not need to do any reclassification; if it does not trust the values, it must reclassify the traffic for appropriate QoS.

To configure the Cisco AutoQoS VoIP feature on an interface, use the auto qos voip command in interface configuration mode or Frame Relay data-link connection identifier (DLCI) configuration mode. To remove the Cisco AutoQoS VoIP feature from an interface, use the no form of the command. The auto qos voip trust command uses DSCP values to create the policies instead of using access lists to identify the traffic by protocol type and port ranges.

The bandwidth of the serial interface is used to determine the speed of the link. The speed of the link is one element that is used to determine the configuration that is generated by the Cisco AutoQoS VoIP feature. The Cisco AutoQoS VoIP feature uses the bandwidth at the time the feature is configured and does not respond to changes made to bandwidth after the feature is configured.

For example, if the auto qos voip command is used to configure the Cisco AutoQoS VoIP feature on an interface with 1000Kbps, the Cisco AutoQoS VoIP feature generates configurations for high-speed interfaces. However, if the bandwidth is later changed to 500Kbps, the Cisco AutoQoS VoIP feature does not use the lower bandwidth. It retains the higher bandwidth and continues to use the generated configurations for high-speed interfaces.

To force the Cisco AutoQoS VoIP feature to use the lower bandwidth (and thus generate configurations for the low-speed interfaces), use the no auto qos voip command to remove the Cisco AutoQoS VoIP feature and then reconfigure the feature.

Cisco Devices That Support AutoQoS

Several models of Cisco routers and switches support AutoQoS. The following sections describe the features of those routers and switches and indicate how to configure AutoQoS on each.

Routers

The Cisco AutoQoS VoIP feature is supported on the Cisco 1760 Modular Access Router; Cisco 1800, 2800, and 3800 Series Integrated Services Routers; Cisco 3700 Series Multiservice Access Routers; and Cisco 7200 Series Routers but only on the following interfaces and PVCs:

► Serial interfaces with Point-to-Point Protocol (PPP) or High-Level Data Link Control (HDLC)

► Frame Relay DLCIs for point-to-point subinterfaces only

► ATM PVCs

EXAM ALERT

Cisco AutoQoS does not support Frame Relay multipoint interfaces.

NOTE

Cisco AutoQoS VoIP is supported on low-speed ATM PVCs on point-to-point subinterfaces only (link bandwidth less than 768Kbps). Cisco AutoQoS VoIP is fully supported on high-speed ATM PVCs (link bandwidth greater than 768Kbps).

The following are examples of WAN router configurations.

Listing 8.1 shows the configuration of Cisco AutoQoS on a high-speed serial interface.

Listing 8.1   Configuring the Cisco AutoQoS VoIP Feature on a High-Speed Serial Interface

```
Router(config)# interface s1/2
Router(config-if)# bandwidth 1544
Router(config-if)# ip address 10.10.100.1 255.255.255.0
Router(config-if)# auto qos voip trust
```

EXAM ALERT

For WAN AutoQoS implementations, the trust option uses DSCP matching, and without the option, AutoQoS generates access lists that identify traffic.

Listing 8.2 provides a standard QoS policy to support VoIP and modifies the link connection from HDLC to PPP to implement link fragmentation and interleaving.

Listing 8.2 Configuring the Cisco AutoQoS VoIP Feature on a Low-Speed Serial Interface

```
Router(config)# interface 4/1:23
Router(config-if)# bandwidth 512
Router(config-if)# ip address 10.10.100.1 255.255.255.0
Router(config-if# auto qos voip trust
```

Listing 8.3 provides a standard QoS policy to support VoIP and modifies the link connection from HDLC to PPP to implement link fragmentation and interleaving.

Listing 8.3 Generated Configuration for the Cisco AutoQoS VoIP Feature on a Low-Speed Serial Interface

```
interface multilink 8934257    (Auto QoS Genterated)
ip address 10.10.100.1 255.255.255.0
service-policy output AUTOQOS_NAME    (Auto QoS Genterated)
ppp multilink fragment delay 20
ppp multilink interleave
ppp multilink group 8934257
!
interface serial 4/1:23
bandwidth 512
no fair-queue
ppp multilink
ppp multilink group 8934257
```

EXAM ALERT

AutoQoS for WAN connections triggers additional commands to implement PPP and link fragmentation and interleaving (LFI) when the WAN circuit is less than or equal to 768Kbps.

Switches

The Cisco Catalyst 2950, 2960, 2970, 3550, 3560, 3750, 4500, and 6500 series switches support Cisco AutoQoS.

NOTE

The Cisco Catalyst 2950 series switches requires the Enhanced Image software.

To configure the QoS settings and the trusted boundary feature on the Cisco IP phone, you must enable Cisco Discovery Protocol version 2 or later on the port. If you enable the trusted boundary feature, a syslog message warns you if Cisco Discovery Protocol is not enabled or if the device is running Cisco Discovery Protocol version 1.

You only need to enable Cisco Discovery Protocol when you are using the `ciscoipphone` automatic QoS configuration option; Cisco Discovery Protocol does not affect the other components of the automatic QoS features. When you use the `ciscoipphone` keyword with the port-specific automatic QoS feature, a warning displays if the port does not have Cisco Discovery Protocol enabled.

When executing the port-specific automatic QoS command with the `ciscoipphone` keyword without the trust option, the trust-device feature is enabled. The trust-device feature depends on Cisco Discovery Protocol. If Cisco Discovery Protocol is not enabled or not running version 2, a warning message appears.

Cisco AutoQoS enables you to configure the QoS capabilities of Cisco switches without extensive knowledge of trust boundaries, Layer 2 and Layer 3 priority markings, or queuing parameters.

Listing 8.4 shows the configuration of AutoQoS on switch ports.

Listing 8.4   Configuring AutoQoS on Switch Ports

```
Switch(conf)# interface fa0/1
Switch(conf-if)# auto qos voip trust
Switch(conf)# interface fa0/2
Switch(conf-if)# auto qos voip cisco-phone
```

When you enable the Cisco AutoQoS feature on fa0/1, the first interface, QoS is globally enabled. When you enter the `auto qos voip trust` interface configuration command, the ingress classification on the interface is set to trust the class of service (CoS) QoS label received in the frame, and the egress queues on the interface are reconfigured. QoS labels in the ingress frames are trusted.

When you enter the `auto qos voip cisco-phone` interface configuration command on fa0/2, the trusted boundary feature is enabled. It uses the Cisco Discovery Protocol to detect the presence or absence of a Cisco IP phone. When a Cisco IP phone is detected, the ingress classification on the interface is set to trust the QoS label received in the frame. When a Cisco IP phone is not detected, the ingress classification is set to *not* trust the QoS label in the frame. The egress queues on the interface are also reconfigured.

EXAM ALERT

Understanding the difference between `auto qos` switch interface options is important; `trust` is a static assignment and `cisco-phone` is a dynamic assignment.

Exam Prep Questions

1. How much one-way delay can a voice packet tolerate?

   ○ **A.** 15ms

   ○ **B.** 150ms

   ○ **C.** 200ms

   ○ **D.** 300ms

2. Voice media traffic uses which of the following transport layer protocols?

   ○ **A.** UDP

   ○ **B.** TCP

   ○ **C.** XNS

   ○ **D.** HTTP

3. Voice call control traffic uses which of the following transport layer protocols?

   ○ **A.** UDP

   ○ **B.** TCP

   ○ **C.** XNS

   ○ **D.** HTTP

4. QoS policy definition could contain which of the following components? (Choose three.)

   ○ **A.** User-validated

   ○ **B.** Network-wide

   ○ **C.** Specific levels of QoS

   ○ **D.** Different classes of network traffic

   ○ **E.** 802.1Q

   ○ **F.** DSCP

   ○ **G.** Network-validated

5. How many bits are in the DSCP field in the IP header?

   ○ **A.** 8

   ○ **B.** 3

   ○ **C.** 6

   ○ **D.** 2

6. Which of the following commands provides static QoS operation for Cisco IP phones plugged into a switch port?

   ○ **A.** `Switch(conf)# auto qos voip trust`

   ○ **B.** `Switch(conf)# auto qos voip cisco-phone`

   ○ **C.** `Switch(conf-if)# auto qos voip trust`

   ○ **D.** `Switch(conf-if)# auto qos voip cisco-phone`

7. Which of the following bandwidth values defines the difference between high-speed and low-speed WAN interfaces for AutoQoS?

   ○ **A.** 256Kbps

   ○ **B.** 512Kbps

   ○ **C.** 768Kbps

   ○ **D.** 1024Kbps

8. What is the number of recommended QoS classes of service?

   ○ **A.** 2 to 3

   ○ **B.** 4 to 5

   ○ **C.** 14

   ○ **D.** 64

9. Which of the following statements is true when determining the QoS trust boundary?

   ○ **A.** Identify all traffic as it is transmitted out each interface.

   ○ **B.** Identify and mark all traffic as it is received at the Layer 3 core.

   ○ **C.** Identify and mark all traffic as close to the source as possible at either Layer 2 or Layer 3.

   ○ **D.** Always have the end stations mark the traffic before entering the network.

10. Which encapsulation protocol is used when AutoQoS is applied to a low-speed point-to-point serial link?

   ○ **A.** HDLC

   ○ **B.** PPP

   ○ **C.** Frame Relay

   ○ **D.** MPLS

Answers to Exam Prep Questions

1. **B.** The ITU-T defines one-way delay of 150ms as acceptable. Lower values such as 15ms work fine but are not a requirement, so answer A is incorrect. Higher values impact the quality of the call experience to the users, so answers C and D are incorrect.

2. **A.** Voice media traffic uses UDP. TCP uses retransmission of dropped packets and the voice media traffic would sound like Max Headroom, so answer B is incorrect. XNS is the Xerox Network Protocol, and HTTP is used for web browsing, so answers C and D are incorrect.

3. **B.** Voice call control traffic uses TCP. UDP does not retransmit dropped packets and the call setup would fail, so answer A is incorrect. XNS is the Xerox Network Protocol and HTTP is used for web browsing, so answers C and D are incorrect.

4. **B, C, and D.** The information for QoS policies should include network-wide information, define the specific levels of QoS required, and define the different classes of service required. User-defined information does not provide information specific to the QoS policy, so answer A is incorrect. 802.1Q and DSCP are QoS tagging fields, and network-validated traffic levels might not be valid for developing QoS policies, so answers E, F, and G are incorrect.

5. **C.** The DSCP field length is 6 bits long. The TOS field is 8 bits long, the IP Precedence field is 3 bits long, and the ECN field is 2 bits long, so answers A, B, and D are incorrect.

6. **C.** QoS is enabled on this interface even if the phone is not connected. Incorrect answers A and B are in the wrong configuration mode. Incorrect answer D provides dynamic QoS and is active only when a Cisco IP phone is connected to the port.

7. **C.** 768Kbps. AutoQoS generates additional commands to implement PPP and LFI on circuits that are 768Kbps or slower, and not on higher-speed circuits. Answers A, B, and D are incorrect.

8. **B.** Best practice is to use 4 to 5 traffic classes. Answer A could be used but only to add a single service such as voice and is incorrect. Answer C defines the standard 14 RFC-based classes of service and is incorrect. Answer D is the maximum number of DSCP values available in the 6-bit DSP field and is incorrect.

9. **C.** Identify and mark all traffic as close to the source as possible. Answer A is incorrect because it generates enormous amounts of router and switch configurations for each interface. Answer B is incorrect because all traffic should be marked prior to entering the network core. Answer D is incorrect because all network endpoints cannot mark traffic before entering the network.

10. **B.** All point-to-point serial links 768Kbps or slower are converted to PPP encapsulation. Answer A, HDLC, is the default serial link encapsulation and is not recommended for voice traffic on slow-speed links and is incorrect. Answers C and D, Frame Relay and MPLS, are service provider encapsulation methods and are typically multipoint implementations and are incorrect.

PART III

Cisco Unified CME and Unity Express in Business

CHAPTER NINE

Introducing Cisco Unified CME

Terms you need to understand:

✓ Trunks

✓ Endpoints

✓ Cisco Unified Communications Manager Express (CME)

Techniques you need to master:

✓ Know the benefits of Cisco Unified CME

✓ Understand platform requirements

✓ Understand software requirements

✓ Understand licensing requirements

Cisco offers a number of IP telephony call control products and applications. Cisco Unified Communications Manager Express (CME) is the call control system that the test focuses on. This chapter offers an introduction to the features, hardware, and software that Cisco Unified CME supports.

Understanding the Benefits of Cisco Unified CME

The Cisco Unified CME is attractive to customers for a number of reasons. The Cisco Unified CME system offers cost benefits as well as advanced features that are beneficial for small- to medium-sized companies.

Cisco Unified CME is considered an entry-level solution in part because its top-end capacity is 240 phones. The term *entry-level* should not lead you to believe that it is limited in features. It is normally a perfect fit for small companies and branch offices. It is a complete standalone telephony system that offers each site the ability to manage its own needs.

EXAM ALERT

The Cisco Unified CME uses a multiservice or integrated services router as its hardware platform. As the name implies, this device can also be used for other services such as routing, firewall, quality of service (QoS), video, and XML.

Also, because it runs on a Cisco router, you can leverage existing IOS knowledge to manage it using the command-line interface (CLI). The system can also be configured using a graphical user interface (GUI), but those who are used to the CLI might find it a more efficient way to perform many administrative tasks.

Another benefit of Cisco Unified CME running on a router is the total cost of ownership (TCO) of using a single device to handle many network services.

Understanding Cisco Unified CME Features

Cisco Unified CME offers most of the features that the typical small- and medium-sized business users are familiar with. However, it also offers more advanced features that these companies might not have been able to take advantage of previously. The following sections look at the features offered in four different areas: phone, system, trunk, and voicemail.

Phone Features

The phone features available to the user can vary based on the model of phone. The following are the features that you should be familiar with. Each of the following features is available on many of the phone models:

- Enhanced 911 services.

- Media encryption using Secure Real-Time Transport Protocol (SRTP).

- Ability to log in to a phone (Extension Mobility).

- XML services on certain Cisco IP phones.

- Up to 240 phones per system.

- On-hook dialing.

- Local directory lookup.

- Configurable ringers.

- Message Waiting Indicator (MWI) (light and or icon).

- Customization of softkeys.

- Do Not Disturb (DND) feature to divert calls directly to voicemail.

- DND state display.

- Enable and disable call-waiting notification for each line.

- Monitor-line button speed dial. A monitor line monitors the status of another phone and can also be used as a speed dial. When used as a speed dial, it is also referred to as a direct station select.

- Speed dial and last-number redial.

- Analog phones and fax machines are supported using the Cisco Analog Telephone Adaptor 186 (ATA 186) and ATA 188.

In addition, some phone models offer additional features, as follows:

- 7911 and 7931G support Audible Message Line Indicator.

- 7960G and 7961G can support six line appearances.

- 7970G and 7971G-GE can support eight line appearances.

- Add a number of lines to an attendant's phone by adding a 7914 (14-button sidecar) to any of the following phones: 7940G, 7941G, 7960G, or 7961G.

- Display custom URL on the screen of the phone when idle, also known as Idle URL. The 7940G, 7941G, 7960G, 7961G, 7970G, and 7971G models include this feature.

System Features

The following is a list of system features. Most are self-explanatory; for those that are not, a brief description is offered.

User-facing features:

- Consultation call transfer: Lets the party you are transferring to know who is calling.

- Blind call transfer: Transfer the call without speaking to the transferred party.

- Call hold and call retrieve.

- Call pickup of on-hold calls.

- Call waiting.

- Paging.

- Intercom.

- Extension assigner: Allows the addition of an extension by someone who does not have administrative rights.

- Music on hold (MOH) and music on transfer for external calls: Internal callers hear a tone when placed on hold or transfer.

- Different rings for internal and external calls.

- System speed dial.

- Directory services.

System-side features:

- MOH: The audio source is a file on the router.

- MOH live feed: The source is a live feed such as a CD.

- Interoperability with Cisco Unified Contact Center Express.

- Signaling encryption.

- Conferencing capabilities: Hardware and software.

- International language support: German, French, Italian, and Spanish.

- GUI administrative access for moves, adds, and changes through a web browser.

- Interactive voice response (IVR) Auto Attendant.

▶ Class of restriction (COR) to restrict calling capabilities.

▶ Inline power for IP phones.

▶ Call transfer and call forwarding (standards-based: H450.2 and H450.3).

▶ Computer telephony integration (CTI) support with Telephony Application Programming Interface (TAPI) Lite: Allows things such as dial from Outlook.

▶ Call detail record (CDR) generation through RADIUS.

▶ Cisco and NetCentrex gatekeepers support.

▶ Hookflash pass-through to a central office (CO) for analog phones.

▶ Date and time synchronization with Network Time Protocol (NTP).

▶ Longest-idle hunt group.

▶ Hunt group dynamic login and logout.

▶ Hunt group statistics.

▶ Caller ID display for hunt group.

▶ Called name directory lookup for Dialed Number Identification Service (DNIS).

▶ Called name display for overlay dialed number (DN).

▶ Conference initiator drop-off: Can configure whether a conference call stays active after the initiator hangs up.

▶ Consultative transfer when transferring using direct station select.

▶ The night service notification can repeat every 12 seconds.

▶ Translation-profile support for ephone-dn.

Trunk Features

The trunk features have grown as the Cisco Unified CME product has matured. The following is a list of trunk features:

▶ Direct Inward Dialing (DID) and Direct Outward Dialing (DOD).

▶ BRI and PRI support for all switch types that Cisco IOS supports.

▶ Caller identification display and blocking, calling name display, and automatic number identification support.

- ▶ DID for Foreign Exchange Office (FXO) trunks.

- ▶ T1 and E1 trunk support.

- ▶ Frame Relay, ATM, Multilink PPP (MLP), and DSL support for WAN links.

- ▶ H.323 network calls.

- ▶ Map a phone button directly to a dedicated trunk.

- ▶ H.323 to Session Initiation Protocol (SIP) call routing to Cisco Unity Express.

- ▶ SIP trunks support RFC 2833.

- ▶ Transcoding.

> **NOTE**
>
> The features included in this list were current at the time of this writing. Visit the Cisco Unified CME website for information about any feature changes: http://www.cisco.com/en/US/products/sw/voicesw/ps4625/products_data_sheets_list.html.

Voicemail Features

You can integrate Cisco Unified CME with a number of voicemail systems. The CCNA Voice Exam focuses on the integration with Cisco Unity Express, which is discussed in Chapter 11, "Configuring Cisco Unity Express." In addition to integrating with Unity Express, Cisco Unified CME can also integrate with Unity Express using Skinny Client Control Protocol (SCCP) integration. It can also integrate with a number of third-party voicemail systems through H.323 or dual tone multifrequency (DTMF) signaling.

Knowing the Hardware and Software Requirements

As stated earlier in the section "Understanding the Benefits of Cisco Unified CME," Cisco Unified CME runs on a Cisco router. The following sections take a closer look at exactly which routers it runs on as well as other requirements such as memory, software, and licensing.

Required Platform

The supported router platforms for Cisco Unified CME 4.2 are the Cisco 2800 and 3800 series integrated services routers and the Cisco 3700 series multiservice router. These routers are available in a number of configurations, and the exact configuration you order depends on what additional functions you want the router to perform. For example, you might want an integrated switch module or a T1 port.

> **TIP**
>
> When determining which router you are going to use, make sure to use the Cisco online configuration tool. This tool can help verify that all the required components will work in the selected router.

In addition to the interface modules that you need, you must also ensure that there is enough RAM and flash memory in the router to support Cisco Unified CME and any other functions you want the router to perform.

> **EXAM ALERT**
>
> Cisco Unified CME requires a minimum of 64MB flash and 256MB RAM when installed on a Cisco 2800, 3800, or 3700 series router.

The minimum memory requirements are for Cisco Unified CME only, and more memory must be added for additional functions.

When selecting the platform, make sure that it can support the number of endpoints and directory numbers you are going to have in your environment. Each platform has its own limitations, as shown in Table 9.1.

TABLE 9.1 Phone and Directory Support per Platform

Cisco Router Platform	Maximum Number of Phones	Maximum Directory Numbers
2801	24	120
2811	36	144
2821	48	144
2851	96	288
3725, 3745	144	500
3825	168	500
3845	240	720

Software and Licensing

After you have determined the hardware platform, you need to make sure that you have the proper Cisco IOS Software. To support Cisco Unified CME 4.2, Cisco IOS Release 12.4-11XW6 with the IP voice feature set is required. After you have the proper IOS loaded, you need to load the Cisco Unified CME software. You can obtain the Cisco Unified CME software from Cisco.com. You need to install the base Cisco Unified CME files at a minimum. You might also want to install additional software such as the GUI files, which allow you to administer the system from a web browser, and phone firmware files.

A license is also required. While the platform you choose determines the maximum number of phones and directory numbers that can be supported, the license determines how many you can actually have installed and working. Table 9.2 lists the licenses that are available and the number of phones that each supports.

TABLE 9.2 Available Licenses

License	Maximum Number of Phones
FL-CCME-SMALL	24
FL-CCME-36	36
FL-CCME-MEDIUM	48
FL-CCME-96	96
FL-CCME-144	144
FL-CCME-168	168
FL-CCME-240	240

When you order a license, you can order based on your current needs. You can upgrade these licenses because they are cumulative. For example, if you have an FL-CCME-36 license and add an FL-CCME-SMALL license, you are licensed for a total of 60 phones.

Exploring Supported Endpoints

Cisco Unified CME 4.2 supports several types of endpoints. The following is a list of the phones that are supported broken down into three categories: entry-level, mid-level and high-end:

- **Entry-level phones:**
    - 3911
    - 7902G

- ► 7905G

- ► 7906G

- ► 7910G+SW

- ► 7911G

- ► 7912G

- ► **Mid-level phones:**

  - ► 7931G

  - ► 7940G

  - ► 7941G

  - ► 7941G-GE

  - ► 7942G

  - ► 7945G

  - ► 7960G

  - ► 7961G

  - ► 7961G-GE

  - ► 7962G

- ► **High-end phones:**

  - ► 7965G

  - ► 7970G

  - ► 7971G

  - ► 7975G

In addition to these phones, a number of devices that are also supported by Cisco Unified MCE 4.2 fall into a miscellaneous category. They are as follows:

- ► **7985G:** Videophone

- ► **7920 and 7921G:** Wireless phones

- ► **7914:** 14-button sidecar that can be attached to a 7960 series phone

- ► **7936 and 7937G:** Conference phone (Polycom)

Exam Prep Questions

1. Which of the following is *not* a benefit of deploying a UCME solution?

   ○ **A.** Reduces TCO

   ○ **B.** Leverages existing knowledge

   ○ **C.** Supports up to 240 phones

   ○ **D.** Runs on low-end routers

2. Cisco Unified CME supports which of the following phone features? (Choose all that apply.)

   ○ **A.** DND

   ○ **B.** Call waiting

   ○ **C.** On-hook dialing

   ○ **D.** XML services

   ○ **E.** Flash tone

3. A customer needs the following system features: music on hold, Auto Attendant, standards-based call transfer, and recording of call details. How would you respond?

   ○ **A.** While Cisco Unified CME supports call transfers, it uses proprietary signaling to do so. All other requested features are supported.

   ○ **B.** No problem. Cisco Unified CME can do it all.

   ○ **C.** To have an Auto Attendant, you need to purchase Unity Express.

   ○ **D.** A third-party package is needed for call detail records.

4. A customer needs the following trunk features: analog DID support, SIP trunk, T1/E1 support, and automatic number diversion. How would you respond?

   ○ **A.** No problem. Cisco Unified CME can do them all.

   ○ **B.** Ask the customer to clarify some of his requests because you are not familiar with automatic number diversion.

   ○ **C.** Currently Cisco Unified CME does not support T1s.

   ○ **D.** Currently DID is only available on T1/E1s.

   ○ **E.** SIP trunks will not be supported until 4.31.

5. Which of the following Cisco router platforms support Cisco Unified CME 4.2? (Choose all that apply.)

   ○ **A.** 2811

   ○ **B.** 2822

   ○ **C.** 2821

   ○ **D.** 2855

   ○ **E.** 2851

6. A customer purchased a license for 24 phones. She is using a 2801 as the UCME platform. She decides she is going to need to add 10 more phones. Which of the following must she do? (Choose all that apply.)

   ○ **A.** Buy an FL-CCME-MED license

   ○ **B.** Buy an FL-CCME-SMALL license

   ○ **C.** Buy an FL-CCME-24 license

   ○ **D.** Buy an FL-CCME-10 license

   ○ **E.** Buy a 2811

7. A customer needs a system that is going to support 100 phones. Which of the following would work?

   ○ **A.** Cisco 2851 router with 64MB of flash, 256MB of RAM, and the FL-CCME-144 license

   ○ **B.** Cisco 3725 router with 64MB of flash, 128MB of RAM, and the FL-CCME-144 license

   ○ **C.** Cisco 3825 router with 64MB of flash, 512MB of RAM, and the FL-CCME-144 license

   ○ **D.** Cisco 2851 router with 64MB of flash, 512MB of RAM, and the FL-CCME-144 license

8. Which of the following is supported when deploying UCME 4.2 on a Cisco 3640?

   ○ **A.** DND

   ○ **B.** Call waiting

   ○ **C.** On-hook dialing

   ○ **D.** XML services

   ○ **E.** None of the above

9. Which of the following best describes a monitor line?

  ○ **A.** When a button is configured as a monitor-line button, the voice stream of an active call can be monitored.

  ○ **B.** When a button is configured as a monitor-line button, the status of the line can be monitored.

  ○ **C.** When a button is configured as a monitor-line button, the video stream of an active call can be monitored.

  ○ **D.** When a button is configured as a monitor-line button, an alternate voice-mail box can be monitored.

10. What is the maximum number of phones that a 3845 can support?

  ○ **A.** 96

  ○ **B.** 144

  ○ **C.** 168

  ○ **D.** 240

Answers to Exam Prep Questions

1. **D.** Cisco Unified CME does not run on lower-end routers such as the Cisco 2600. Answer A is incorrect because Cisco Unified CME can help reduce TCO. Answer B is incorrect because you can leverage your existing IOS knowledge. Answer C is incorrect because UCME does support up to 240 phones.

2. **A, B, C, and D.** Cisco Unified CME does support DND, call waiting, on-hook dialing, and XML services. Answer E is incorrect because flash tone is not a feature.

3. **B.** Cisco Unified CME does support music on hold, Auto Attendant, standards-base call transfer, and recording of call details. Answer A is incorrect because Cisco Unified CME uses H.450 standards for call transfer. Answer C is incorrect because Cisco Unified CME has an Auto Attendant feature. Answer D is incorrect because Cisco Unified CME supports CDR through RADIUS but does not require a third-party package.

4. **B.** Automatic number diversion is not a trunk feature. Answer A is incorrect because automatic number diversion is not a trunk feature. Answer C is incorrect because DID is supported on FXOs. Answer D is incorrect because SIP trunks are currently supported.

5. **A, C, and E.** The Cisco 2811, 2821, and 2851 routers are supported platforms for Cisco Unified CME. Answers B and D are incorrect because 2822 and 2855 are not valid router model numbers.

6. **B and E.** The FL-CCME-SMALL license is a license for 24 phones, and the 2811 is required because the 2801 only supports 24 phones. Answer A is incorrect because FL-CCME-MED is not a valid license. Answer C is incorrect because FL-CCME-24 is not a valid license. Answer D is incorrect because an FL-CCME-10 is not a valid license.

7. **C.** A Cisco 3825 router with 64MB flash and 512MB RAM can support 144 phones, and the FL-CCME-144 is a 144-phone license. Answer A is incorrect because a Cisco 2851 router only supports 96 phones. Answer B is incorrect because you need a minimum of 256MB RAM to support Cisco Unified CME. Answer D is incorrect because a Cisco 2851 router only supports 96 phones.

8. **E.** UCME 4.2 is not supported on the 3640. Answers A, B, C, and D are incorrect because UCME 4.2 is not supported on the 3640.

9. **B.** A monitor-line button can monitor the status of the line. Answer A is incorrect because the monitor-line button cannot monitor a voice stream. Answer C is incorrect because the monitor-line button cannot monitor a video stream. Answer D is incorrect because the monitor-line button has nothing to do with voicemail.

10. **C.** The 3825 can support 168 phones. Answer A is incorrect; the 2851 supports 96 phones. Answer B is incorrect; the 3725 and 3745 support 144 phones. Answer D is incorrect; the 3845 supports 240 phones.

Suggested Reading and Resources

1. Cisco. Cisco Unified CallManager Express 4.0 Data Sheet. Cisco.com.

2. Cisco. Cisco Unified CallManager Express Solution Reference Design Guide. Cisco.com.

CHAPTER TEN

Configuring Cisco Unified CME to Support Endpoints

Terms you need to understand:

- ✓ Ephone
- ✓ Ephone-dn
- ✓ Max-ephones
- ✓ Max-dns
- ✓ Button
- ✓ IP Source-address
- ✓ Dialplan-pattern
- ✓ User-locale
- ✓ Network-locale
- ✓ TFTP server
- ✓ Load
- ✓ Auto-reg-ephone
- ✓ Auto-assign

Techniques you need to master:

- ✓ Configure phones
- ✓ Configure various type of ephone-dns
- ✓ Configure auto registration
- ✓ Verify phone configuration and registration

In this chapter, you learn about the configuration needed to allow phones to register to a Cisco Unified CME. For each physical phone that can register to a Cisco Unified CME, you must configure an ephone in the Cisco Unified CME. In addition, for each phone number assigned to a phone, you must configure an ephone-dn. So, before we look at global telephony configurations, let's take a look at these two concepts.

Ephones and Ephone-dns

An ephone is just a set of Cisco Unified CME entries that define how a phone will be configured. The ephone configuration defines the number of directory numbers (DNs), speed dials, and MAC address. While the ephone configuration defines which DNs are assigned to the phone, the DNs themselves must be configured separately. This is done by creating ephone-dns. A good way to think of this is that an ephone is the software configuration of the hardware device.

Configuring Ephones

Before you can create ephones, you need to define how many ephones will be allowed to register to the Cisco Unified CME. While the hardware platform determines the maximum number of phones that the hardware can support, you might not want that many phones to register to the Cisco Unified CME. The router reserves memory based on the number of phones it is configured to support. By default, the maximum is set to 0. The command used to set the maximum number of ephones is

`max-ephones` *number*

For example, if you want to configure the Cisco Unified CME to allow 15 phones to register, you would enter `max-ephones` `15`. This command must be issued from telephony-service configuration. You can enter telephony-service configuration by entering `telephony-service` from the global configuration prompt.

NOTE

The number you set for max-ephones must be within the limitation of the router and the license.

After you define the maximum number of ephones, you can create ephones. Creation of an ephone is done from the global configuration mode on the Cisco Unified CME router. The command to create an ephone is as follows:

`ephone` *phone-tag*

The *phone-tag* parameter is a number that is used to identify this ephone. A phone-tag can be any number you choose, but each ephone must have a unique phone-tag. To create an ephone using 10 as the phone tag, you would enter **ephone 10**.

Using the ephone *phone-tag* command creates an ephone. However, that alone does not allow a phone to register. After you create the ephone, you must configure it. After an ephone is created, the prompt changes to show that you are in ephone configuration. The prompt looks something like the following:

```
router (config-ephone)#
```

From this prompt, you can define various parameters of the ephone. You first must define the MAC address of the phone and the DN(s) that will be assigned to the phone. To define the MAC address, enter the mac-address command followed by the MAC address. The MAC address must be in the proper format. As you know, a MAC address is 12 hexadecimal characters long. The format used to assign one to an ephone is four sets of four hexadecimal characters. The following is an example for defining the MAC address of 00CC0001A1231ABF to ephone:

```
mac-address 00CC.0001.A123.1ABF
```

To assign a DN to the phone, you must first create an ephone-dn. The next section covers how to create and assign ephone-dns.

Configuring Ephone-dns

An ephone-dn represents a line that can be assigned to an ephone to allow a voice channel. An ephone-dn can have one or more numbers assigned to it. Just think of an ephone-dn as being equal to a line on a phone.

The configuration of an ephone-dn is fairly simple, but before you create one, you should define the maximum number of DNs that you want the Cisco Unified CME to allow to register. By default, this is set to 0. This is similar to how you had to define the maximum number of ephones that could register. The command is max-dn *number*, where *number* is the number of DNs the router is to support. To configure the router to support 24 DNs, you would issue the following command at telephony-service configuration:

```
max-dn 24
```

EXAM ALERT

Before adding phones, you must set the max-ephone and max-dn parameters.

To create an ephone-dn, two commands must be entered. First, use the following command to create the ephone-dn:

```
ephone-dn dn-tag
```

The *dn-tag* parameter is a number that is used to identify this ephone-dn. It is not a directory number. It is only used to identify the ephone-dn. A dn-tag can be any number you choose, but each ephone-dn must have a unique dn-tag. To create an ephone-dn using 101 as the dn-tag, you would enter **ephone-dn 101**.

Next you need to define the directory number that will be associated with this ephone-dn. This is done using the `number` command. After you create an ephone-dn, you will be in ephone-dn configuration mode.

The following commands show how to create an ephone-dn with a dn-tag of 101 and a directory number of 2001:

```
ephone-dn 101
number 2001
```

Now that you know how to create a basic ephone-dn, let's take a look at how it is assigned to an ephone. To enter the configuration mode for an ephone, you issue the same command you did when you first created the ephone, which is `ephone phone-tag`. If the ephone exists, you will enter the configuration mode for it; if it doesn't, the ephone will be created and you will enter the configuration mode for it. After you are in ephone configuration mode, you assign an ephone-dn to a button on the phone by using the `button` command. The syntax for the button command is `button button-number{separator}dn-tag`. For example, to assign the ephone-dn 101 to the second button on the phone, you would enter **button 2:101**. This command does not assign the extension number 101 to the second button. It assigns the extension number that is associated with ephone-dn 101. Let's take a look at a complete example of creating a phone with the following characteristics:

- Ephone tag of 10
- MAC address of 00CC0001A1231ABF
- Two extension numbers, 2000 and 2001

Listing 10.1 includes the router prompts so that you can see what config mode the commands are entered in.

Listing 10.1   Ephone and Ephone-dn Configuration

```
Router# config t
Router(config)# ephone-dn 101
Router(config-ephone-dn)# number 2000
```

Listing 10.1   *Continued*

```
Router(config-ephone-dn)# ephone-dn 102
Router(config-ephone-dn)# number 2001
Router(config-ephone-dn)# exit
Router(config)# ephone 10
Router(config-ephone)# mac-address 00CC.0001.A123.1ABF
Router(config-ephone)# button 1:101
Router(config-ephone)# button 2:102
```

To better understand each of these commands, take a look at Table 10.1, which lists each command and offers a brief explanation.

TABLE 10.1   Example Configuration of an Ephone

Command	Explanation
`Router# config t`	Enter global config mode
`Router(config)# ephone-dn 101`	Create an ephone-dn with a tag of 101
`Router(config-ephone-dn)# number 2000`	Assign 2000 as the extension number for ephone-dn 101
`Router(config-ephone-dn)# ephone-dn 102`	Create an ephone with a tag of 102
`Router(config-ephone-dn)# number 2001`	Assign 2001 as the extension number for ephone-dn 102
`Router(config-ephone-dn)# exit`	Exit ephone-dn config
`Router(config)# ephone 10`	Create an ephone with a tag of 10
`Router(config-ephone)# mac-address 00CC.0001.A123.1ABF`	Associate the MAC address of 00CC0001A1231ABF to ephone 10
`Router(config-ephone)# button 1:101`	Assign extension 2000 to the first button on ephone 10
`Router(config-ephone)# button 2:102`	Assign extension 2001 to the second button on ephone 10

As you know, the `button` command defines what ephone-dn is assigned to a button on the phone. But it does more than that: It also defines how the ephone-dn is assigned. How an ephone is assigned to a button impacts how it will function. In the command `button 1:101` the colon (:) is referred to as a *separator*. The separator is used to define how the button will function. There are nine different separators. So far, we have only looked at the colon, which configures the line to act normally, that is, to ring normally and function in much the way you would expect a phone line to function. The following is a list of the other operators that can be used and a brief explanation for each one:

▶ b (Beep): Does not ring incoming calls, but beeps are heard when you are on the phone and another call is coming in. The lights and other visible indicators function normally.

▶ o (Overlay): Assigns multiple ephone-dns to a single button, a maximum of 25 on a button.

▶ c (Call waiting): Allows call waiting for an overlaid ephone-dn.

▶ x (Overlay rollover): Allows a call to an occupied overlay button to ring on this button.

▶ f (Feature ring): Causes the phone to play a ringer three times quickly to differentiate calls coming in on this line.

▶ m (Monitor): Allows you to monitor the status of the DN. Cannot be used to place or receive calls.

▶ s (Silent): Does not play ringing and call waiting beep for incoming calls. The flashing icon is the only indication that a call is coming in on the line.

▶ w (Watch): Shows the status of all lines on a phone that have the primary number assigned in this command.

Let's take a look at a couple of examples. If you were to configure a button as follows, the ephone-dn 101 would be assigned to the first button on the phone, and when a call came in on that line, it would not ring. But, if a person were already on a call when a new call arrived, the person would hear the call waiting beep:

```
button 1b101
```

If a button were configured as follows, ephone-dn 101 would be assigned to the fourth button and would be used to monitor the status on the extension assigned to ephone-dn 101. This line could not be used to place or receive calls:

```
button 4m101
```

You should now understand how to create basic ephones and ephone-dns and associate ephone-dns to buttons. Up to now, we have been discussing basic single-line ephone-dns. Ephone-dns can be configured to function in a number of different manners. The following sections explore six types of ephone-dns:

▶ Single-line   ▶ Shared

▶ Dual-line   ▶ Multiple ephone-dns

▶ Dual-number   ▶ Overlay

Single-Line

This section describes the single-line ephone-dn. A single virtual voice port is created when a single-line ephone-dn is configured. A virtual voice port allows a single call. If you need a line that can support more than a single call, a single-line ephone-dn will not work. Features such as call waiting, call transfer, and conferencing do not work on single-line phones. If you want these features with single-line ephone-dns, you must configure more than one single-line ephone-dn on the phone.

Single-line ephone-dns have a single number assigned to them, but a secondary number might also be assigned. Typical uses for single-line ephone-dns are intercoms, paging, Music on Hold (MoH) sources, loopbacks, and Message Waiting Indicators (MWIs). They are also useful when phones are configured to have a one-to-one relationship to public switched telephone network (PSTN) lines.

EXAM ALERT

Typical uses for single-line ephone-dns are intercoms, paging, MoH sources, loopbacks, and MWIs.

The following commands are required to create a single-line ephone-dn and assign 2001 as its extension number:

```
ephone-dn 101
number 2000
```

Dual-Line

A dual-line ephone-dn allows two active calls on a single line (single button). There is still a single virtual voice port, but the voice port has two channels, thereby allowing two calls. It can have a primary and secondary number associated with it and supports features such as call waiting, call transfer, and conferencing.

EXAM ALERT

Dual-line ephone-dns should not be used for intercoms, paging, MoH sources, loopbacks, MWIs, or call park slots.

The following commands are required to create a dual-line ephone-dn and assign 2001 as its extension number:

```
ephone-dn 101 dual-line
number 2000
```

Dual-Number (Primary and Secondary)

A dual-number ephone-dn is just an ephone-dn with two numbers, a primary and secondary, assigned to it. You can configure single-line ephone-dns and dual-line ephone-dns as dual-number ephone-dns. The type of ephone-dn allows you to assign two numbers to a single button. This is often used to assign the internal and fully qualified number to an ephone-dn.

The following commands are required to create a dual-number ephone-dn and assign both 2001 and 5155552001 as extension numbers:

```
ephone-dn 101 dual-line
number 2000 secondary 5155552001
```

These commands create the ephone-dn as a dual-line, but it could also have been a single-line ephone-dn.

> **NOTE**
>
> When creating a single-line ephone-dn with dual numbers (primary and secondary), the line can still only handle a single call.

Shared

A shared ephone-dn is an ephone-dn that is assigned to multiple phones. This allows a call coming to that DN to be answered from any phone that has the ephone-dn assigned to it. After the call is answered, the shared-line appearance on the other phones is not available for use. If the call is placed on hold, it can be picked up from any phone that has that an ephone-dn assigned to it. Listing 10.2 shows how a shared ephone-dn is configured.

Listing 10.2   Configuring a Shared Ephone-dn

```
Router(config)# ephone-dn 101 dual-line
Router(config-ephone-dn)# number 2000
Router(config)# ephone 10
Router(config-ephone)# mac-address 00CC.0001.A123.1ABF
Router(config-ephone)# button 1:101
Router(config)# ephone 12
Router(config-ephone)# mac-address 00C0.0011.A145.1DDA
Router(config-ephone)# button 1:101
```

Listing 10.2 shows how extension number 2000 is assigned to the first button of ephone 10 and ephone 12.

Multiple Ephone-dns

You can create multiple ephone-dns that have the same extension number. You might want to do so for a number of reasons. For example, it is common in some older systems to have multiple line appearances with the same number, or you might want a phone to be able to accept more than two calls on the same extension number.

> **EXAM ALERT**
>
> You must understand that creating more than one ephone-dn with the same extension number and placing each of them on different phones is not the same as having a shared line. Each ephone-dn is a separate extension, even if the same number is assigned.

The concept of multiple ephone-dns can sound confusing, but it is no different than two people that have the same name. Even though both of them can have the name Toby, they are not the same person. So the question is, when a call comes in to 1001 and there are two ephone-dns that have 1001 assigned, how does Cisco Unified CME know which ephone-dn to send the call to? The decision is made based on the preference that is assigned to the ephone-dn. Chapter 6, "Connecting Your VoIP System to the Rest of the World," covers preference in the dial-peers discussion. Preference works the same way with ephone-dns as it does with dial-peers. The ephone-dn with the lower preference is selected if available.

Let's look at the configuration. We look at scenarios for two common uses of multiple ephone-dns. In the first scenario, you need to have two phones with the same extension, but you do not want a shared line. For example, you might have a main receptionist that answers incoming calls, but if the receptionist is unable to take the call, it can be routed to another phone. Listing 10.3 shows the configuration for two phones to accomplish this. The commands that are grayed are associated with the phone that has the MAC address of 0C00011A1451DDA. The other commands are associated to the other phone.

Listing 10.3 Multiple Ephone-dns with the Same Number on Separate Phones

```
Router(config)# ephone-dn 101 dual-line
Router(config-ephone-dn)# number 2000
Router(config-ephone-dn)# Preference 1
Router(config)# ephone-dn 201 dual-line
Router(config-ephone-dn)# number 2000
Router(config)# ephone 10
Router(config-ephone)# mac-address 0CC.0001.A123.1ABF
Router(config-ephone)# button 1:101
Router(config)# ephone 12
Router(config-ephone)# mac-address 0C0.0011.A145.1DDA
Router(config-ephone)# button 1:201
```

The commands that are associated for each phone are highlighted. You see that phone A has been defined as ephone 10. Ephone 10 has ephone-dn 101 assigned to it, and the extension 2000 is associated with ephone-dn 101. Phone B has been defined as ephone 12. Ephone 12 has ephone-dn 201 assigned to it, and the extension 2000 is associated with ephone-dn 201. The result is that both phones have the extension 2000 assigned to their first button, but because different ephone-dns were used, this is not considered a shared line. Therefore, when a call arrives for extension 2000, Cisco Unified CME needs to decide which of these two devices the call will be sent to. Looking at Listing 10.3 again, you see that ephone-dn 101 has a preference of 1. Ephone-dn 201 has no preference assigned. Remember, if no preference is assigned, the default preference used is 0. Because ephone-dn 201 has a lower preference, the call will be routed to phone B. If phone B is busy, the call can be routed to phone A, if so configured.

The huntstop command is used to determine whether a call will be routed to phone A when phone B is busy. Huntstop determines whether hunting will occur. *Hunting* is when a call goes from one ephone-dn to another until it finds an available voice channel. In other words, a call will "hunt" for an available line. A dual-line ephone-dn has two virtual voice channels; therefore, if the ephone-dn is a dual-line, huntstop for the channel is also configured. The huntstop command with no keywords configures huntstop for the ephone-dn. The huntstop command with the channel keyword configures hunting for the channels; that is, the huntstop channel configuration determines whether the call will hunt to the second channel of a dual-line ephone-dn. Huntstop is enabled on an ephone-dn by default. This means that, by default, a call will not hunt to another ephone-dn if the ephone-dn with the lowest preference is busy or not answered. However, no huntstop channel is the default for channel huntstop. This means that if the first channel of an ephone-dn is busy, the call will hunt to the second channel.

Let's expand on the previous listing. Listing 10.4 shows the same example that was seen in Listing 10.3 with the addition of huntstop commands.

Listing 10.4   Multiple Ephone-dns with the Same Number on Separate Phones and Huntstop Configured

```
Router(config)# ephone-dn 101 dual-line
Router(config-ephone-dn)# number 2000
Router(config-ephone-dn)# huntstop channel
Router(config-ephone-dn)# Preference 1
Router(config)# ephone-dn 201 dual-line
Router(config-ephone-dn)# number 2000
Router(config-ephone-dn)# huntstop channel
Router(config-ephone-dn)# no huntstop
Router(config)# ephone 10
Router(config-ephone)# mac-address 00CC.0001.A123.1ABF
Router(config-ephone)# button 1:101
Router(config)# ephone 12
Router(config-ephone)# mac-address 00C0.0011.A145.1DDA
Router(config-ephone)# button 1:201
```

You see that ephone-dn 201 has `no huntstop` configured. This means that if ephone-dn 201 is busy or unanswered, the call will continue to hunt, but because `huntstop channel` is also configured, it will not hunt to the second channel of the ephone-dn. Instead, it will hunt to an other ephone-dn that has 2000 as its extension; therefore, it will hunt to ephone-dn 101. Ephone-dn 101 has `huntstop channel` configured but no other `huntstop` command, which means the default will be used. The default for huntstop is enabled; therefore, the hunting will stop if the first channel of ephone-dn 101 is busy or unanswered.

> **NOTE**
>
> The `no huntstop channel` command disables call waiting on that line.

Now that you understand how to configure multiple ephone-dns with the same number of separate phones, let's look at how you configure multiple ephone-dns on a single phone. By doing this, you can allow a phone to accept more than two calls placed to the same extension. The best way to understand this is by looking at an example. Listing 10.5 shows the configuration of a phone that has two ephone-dns with the same number assigned to it. The dark gray commands define the ephone. The light gray commands define an extension of 2000 that is assigned to the second button. The other commands define an extension of 2000 that is assigned to the first button.

Listing 10.5   Multiple Ephone-dns with the Same Number on a Single Phone with Huntstop Configured

```
Router(config)# ephone-dn 101 dual-line
Router(config-ephone-dn)# number 2000
Router(config-ephone-dn)# no huntstop
Router(config)# ephone-dn 201 dual-line
Router(config-ephone-dn)# number 2000
Router(config-ephone-dn)# Preference 1
Router(config)# ephone 10
Router(config-ephone)# mac-address 00CC.0001.A123.1ABF
Router(config-ephone)# button 1:101
Router(config-ephone)# button 2:201
```

In Listing 10.5, ephone-dns 101 and 201 have the same extension. Ephone-dn 101 is assigned to the first button on the phone, and 201 is assigned to the second button. This results in two lines with the same extension. When the Cisco Unified CME receives a call for 2000, it uses the `preference` command to determine which line to send the call to. Because ephone-dn 101 has no preference set, it uses the default of 0. Because ephone-dn 201 has a higher preference (1), the call is routed to ephone-dn 101. If the first voice channel on ephone-dn 101 is busy, the call will roll over to the second channel on 101. This happens because the huntstop channel is set by default. If both channels on ephone-dn 101 are busy, the call will hunt to ephone-dn 201. This happens because ephone-dn 101 has no huntstop configured. If the first channel of ephone-dn 201 is busy, the call will roll over to the second channel and, if that channel is busy, hunting will stop because huntstop is the default of an ephone-dn.

Overlay

The last type of ephone-dn that is discussed is the overlay. An overlay ephone-dn allows you to assign as many as 25 numbers to a single button. So an overlay ephone-dn is really a set or group of ordinary ephone-dns. All the ephone-dns that are part of an overlay group must all be either single- or dual-line ephone-dns. That is, you cannot mix single- and dual-line ephone-dns in the same overlay group. The number assigned to the ephone-dns can have unique numbers or the same numbers as other ephone-dns within the overlay group. The same overlay group can be assigned to multiple phones.

An overlay ephone-dn is created when you assign an ephone-dn to a button. You already know that you assign an ephone-dn to a phone using the button command. You might also remember that when you use the letter o as a separator instead of the colon (:), it defines the button as an overlay. Listing 10.6 shows the commands required to configure a button on a phone as an overlay.

Listing 10.6   Configuring an Overlay

```
Router(config)# ephone-dn 101 dual-line
Router(config-ephone-dn)# number 1000
Router(config)# ephone-dn 201 dual-line
Router(config-ephone-dn)# number 2000
Router(config)# ephone-dn 301 dual-line
Router(config-ephone-dn)# number 3000
Router(config)# ephone 12
Router(config-ephone)# mac-address 00C0.0011.A145.1DDA
Router(config-ephone)# button 1o101,201,301
```

This listing would assign the extensions 1000, 2000, and 3000 to the first button of ephone 12. The first ephone-dn assigned appears on the display, which in this case is 1000. Cisco Unified CME will route calls placed to extensions 1000, 2000, or 3000 on this line. An overlay ephone-dn can be assigned as a shared line on multiple phones. As you recall, normally when a shared line is in use, the other phones that share that line cannot use it. This is not the case when an overlay is assigned as a shared line. Listing 10.7 expands the previous example by assigning the overlay to three phones.

Listing 10.7	Assigning Overlay to Three Phones

```
Router(config)# ephone-dn 101 dual-line
Router(config-ephone-dn)# number 1000
Router(config)# ephone-dn 201 dual-line
Router(config-ephone-dn)# number 2000
Router(config)# ephone-dn 301 dual-line
Router(config-ephone-dn)# number 3000
Router(config)# ephone 12
Router(config-ephone)# mac-address 00C0.0011.A145.1DDA
Router(config-ephone)# button 1o101,201,301
Router(config)# ephone 14
Router(config-ephone)# mac-address 00C0.0011.A145.B0BC
Router(config-ephone)# button 1o101,201,301
Router(config)# ephone 16
Router(config-ephone)# mac-address 00C0.0011.A145.65EF
Router(config-ephone)# button 1o101,201,301
```

In Listing 10.7, ephones 12, 14, and 16 are assigned extensions 1000, 2000, and 3000. If ephone 12 takes a call placed to extension 1000, ephones 14 and 16 can still use line 1 to place outbound calls because extensions 2000 and 3000 are available. Also, if a call comes in on extension 2000 or 3000 while ephone 12 is on a call using extension 1000, ephones 14 and 16 will ring.

EXAM ALERT

When using the o as a separator to create an overlay, call waiting is disabled. To have call waiting available on an overlay ephone-dn, use the c separator.

Configuring Telephony Service

In the previous sections, you learned about two commands that you can enter to configure telephony services. The max-ephones and max-dns commands are used to determine how many phones and directory numbers can register to the Cisco Unified CME. You still need to configure telephony service parameters before the phones can register to Cisco Unified CME and make phone calls.

Telephony Service Commands

The following sections describe the commands to configure telephony service parameters.

IP Source Address

The Cisco Unified CME communicates with endpoints through a number of protocols; one of the most commonly used protocols is Skinny Client Control Protocol (SCCP). You must configure Cisco Unified CME so that it knows which interface and TCP port to use when communicating with SCCP endpoints. The default TCP port is 2000 and is typically not changed. The command used to configure this is ip source-address followed by the IP address of the interface on the Cisco Unified CME that will service SCCP requests. To configure the interface with the IP address of 10.1.1.10 to receive and respond to the SCCP requested, use the following command:

```
ip source-address 10.1.1.10
```

To include a port number other than 2000, add the keyword port and then the port number. For example, to issue the same command but change the TCP port to 2020, use the following command:

```
ip source-address 10.1.1.10 port 2020
```

Keepalive

Another setting that you configure in telephony-service configuration mode is keepalives. This command determines how often keepalive packets are sent between the Cisco Unified CME and Cisco IP phones. The default is 30. To change this value, use the keepalive command followed by the number of seconds you want to set it to. The range is 10–65535 seconds. For example, to change the keepalive value to 45 seconds, issue the following command:

```
keepalive 45
```

Dialplan-pattern

Extensions for ephone-dns are often the last four or five digits of the E.164 number that is to be associated with the phone. When placing an outbound call, you typically want the full E.164 number to be sent out. The dialplan-pattern command is used to accomplish this.

You also can use the dialplan-pattern command to transform full E.164 incoming numbers to their extension numbers. This is useful in an environment in which there are multiple Cisco Unified CMEs. When a call leaves one Cisco Unified CME, it matches the dialplan-pattern and is expanded into the full E.164. When the call reaches the other Cisco Unified CME, it again matches the dialplan-pattern and is reduced to its extension number so that the called party sees the calling party's extension number instead of the full E.164. This also causes the incoming call to have a ring that is different than a normal external call, hence alerting the called party that it is an internal call.

The following is an example of a `dialplan-pattern` command:

`dialplan-pattern 1 2485479... extension-length 4 extension-pattern 90..`

Let's take a closer look at each section of this command:

▶ `dialplan-pattern 1` defines that a dialplan-pattern is being configured. The 1 in the command is simply a tag. The tag defines this dialplan-pattern as dialplan-pattern number 1.

▶ `2485479...` determines what numbers will match this dialplan-pattern and what outbound numbers it will be expanded to.

▶ `extension-length 4` determines how many digits inbound numbers that match this pattern will be stripped to. For example, if the dial number was 4085551001 and the extension length was set to 4, the number would be stripped to 1001.

▶ `extension-pattern 90..` determines how the number will further be transformed before appearing as internal caller ID.

So, with the preceding example, an outbound caller ID would be changed for the 4-digit extension of, say, 9091 to 2485479091. The caller ID of an inbound call for 2485479023 would match this dialplan-pattern and be transformed to 9023.

Date and Time

You also need to configure the date and time format. Two commands are used to do this. The first is the `date-format` command. The syntax for this command is `date-format` followed by one of the four following format options: `mm-dd-yy`, `dd-mm-yy`, `yy-dd-mm`, or `yy-mm-dd`. The other command is the time format, and it determines whether a 12- or 24-hour clock is used. The command is `time-format` followed by either `12` or `24`.

Locale

The last configuration commands are those used to configure locale information. There are two locale commands. One determines the language that is displayed on the phone and the other determines the progress tones. Use the `user-locale` command followed by the two-letter language code for the language you desire. The valid language codes are

- ▶ DE: German
- ▶ DK: Danish
- ▶ ES: Spanish
- ▶ FR: French
- ▶ IT: Italian
- ▶ JP: Japanese
- ▶ NL: Dutch
- ▶ NO: Norwegian
- ▶ PT: Portuguese
- ▶ RU: Russian
- ▶ SE: Swedish
- ▶ US: United States

You use the `network-locale` command to set the progress tones. Just as with the `user-locale` command, the `network-locale` command is followed by the language code for the desired progress tones. The valid language codes for progress tones are

- ▶ AT: Austria
- ▶ CA: Canada
- ▶ CH: Switzerland
- ▶ DE: Germany
- ▶ DK: Denmark
- ▶ ES: Spain
- ▶ FR: France
- ▶ GB: United Kingdom
- ▶ IT: Italy
- ▶ JP: Japan
- ▶ NL: Netherlands
- ▶ NO: Norway
- ▶ PT: Portugal
- ▶ RU: Russian Federation
- ▶ SE: Sweden
- ▶ US: United States (default)

Firmware Provisioning

Phones require the correct firmware to register to and work with Cisco Unified CME. There are specific firmware files for each model of Cisco IP phone. The phone retrieves these files through TFTP. TFTP must be configured on the Cisco Unified CME to allow the serving of the required firmware files. The tftp-server command is done in global config mode. The tftp-server command is used to determine which files are going to be available. The command syntax follows:

```
tftp-server flash:filename
```

The flash keyword specifies that the file is in flash. The filename parameter is the name of the file that needs to be served. Because some Cisco IP phone models need multiple files, the tftp-server command needs to be issued a number of times.

Consider the Cisco Unified IP Phone 7961G running SCCP, for example. Listing 10.8 shows the commands that need to be entered to make all the required firmware files available. Keep in mind that the names of the firmware files change based on the version of Cisco Unified CME.

Listing 10.8   TFTP Configuration for Firmware Files

```
tftp-server flash:SCCP41.8-3-3S.loads
tftp-server flash:term61.default.loads
tftp-server flash:apps41.8-3-2-27.sbn
tftp-server flash:cvm41sccp.8-3-2-27.sbn
tftp-server flash:cnu41.8-3-2-27.sbn
tftp-server flash:dsp41.8-3-2-27.sbn
tftp-server flash:jar41sccp.8-3-2-27.sbn
```

NOTE

Not all phone models require multiple firmware files; some require only one.

The total number of files that need to be made available depends on the number of different phone models you are using. Also, if phones are using Session Initiation Protocol (SIP) instead of SCCP, different firmware files are required, which could increase the total number of files being served.

Making the firmware files available through TFTP is only half the job of configuring Cisco Unified CME to serve the files for the phones. The other step that is required is to define what firmware file each phone model should request. This needs to be done because, as upgrades are made, new firmware files are released, and there needs to be a way to tell the phone which file it should be using. The load command is used for this.

The syntax for the load command is load followed by the model of the phone and the name of the firmware file. For example, the load command for a 7941 phone would look something like the following:

```
load 7941 SCCP41.8-3-3S.loads
```

You execute this command from telephony-service configuration mode. Only one firmware file is associated with each phone model. When a phone needs more than one firmware file, such as in the case of the Cisco 7961G, the firmware file that has a .loads extension is used. If more than one firmware file ends with .loads, use the one that begins with SCCP (or SIP if running SIP). For example, the command to associate the correct firmware file to a Cisco 7961G is load 7961 SCCP41.8-3-3S. Notice that you do not include the .loads extension in the command. When specifying the model phone in the load command, make sure that you use the correct syntax. The following is a list of valid model names for the load command:

- 12SP: 12SP+ and 30VIP phones

- 7902: Cisco Unified IP Phone 7902G

- 7905: Cisco Unified IP Phone 7905G

- 7910: Cisco Unified IP Phones 7910 and 7910G

- 7911: Cisco Unified IP Phone 7911G

- 7912: Cisco Unified IP Phone 7912G

- 7914: Cisco Unified IP Phone 7914 Expansion Module

- 7915-12: Cisco Unified IP Phone 7915 12-Button Expansion Module

- 7915-24: Cisco Unified IP Phone 7915 24-Button Expansion Module

- 7916-12: Cisco Unified IP Phone 7916 12-Button Expansion Module

- 7916-24: Cisco Unified IP Phone 7916 24-Button Expansion Module

- 7920: Cisco Unified Wireless IP Phone 7920

- 7921: Cisco Unified Wireless IP Phone 7921

- 7931: Cisco Unified IP Phone 7931G

- 7935: Cisco Unified IP Conference Station 7935

- 7936: Cisco Unified IP Conference Station 7936

- 7937: Cisco Unified IP Conference Station 7937

- 7941: Cisco Unified IP Phone 7941G

- 7941GE: Cisco Unified IP Phone 7941G-GE

- ▶ 7942: Cisco Unified IP Phone 7942

- ▶ 7945: Cisco Unified IP Phone 7945

- ▶ 7960-7940: Cisco Unified IP Phones 7960 and 7960G and Cisco Unified IP Phones 7940 and 7940G

- ▶ 7961: Cisco Unified IP Phone 7961G

- ▶ 7961GE: Cisco Unified IP Phone 7961G-GE

- ▶ 7962: Cisco Unified IP Phone 7962

- ▶ 7965: Cisco Unified IP Phone 7965

- ▶ 7970: Cisco Unified IP Phone 7970G

- ▶ 7971: Cisco Unified IP Phone 7971G-GE

- ▶ 7975: Cisco Unified IP Phone 7975

- ▶ 7985: Cisco Unified IP Phone 7985

- ▶ ata: Cisco ATA-186 and Cisco ATA-188

Before registering phones, you need to run the create cnf-files command. When a phone registers, it requests a configuration file. The create cnf-files command creates these files for SCCP phones. It creates these files based on the current configuration. It creates a configuration file for each phone that is configured in the system.

> **EXAM ALERT**
>
> The create cnf-files command also creates a default file called XMLDefault.cnf.xml. Phones that are not configured in the system use this default file.

Registration Configuration

Using everything you have learned so far, you can configure Cisco Unified CME so that phones can register and make calls. This, however, would require you to add every phone individually, and while adding a phone is not difficult, having to add 100 could be quite time consuming. One way to speed up the process is to allow phones to autoregister. This is done by using the auto-reg-ephone command. This command is entered in telephony-service configuration mode. After the command is entered, phones are allowed to register, even if an ephone has not been configured for them. To disable autoregistration, issue the no auto-reg-ephone command. When autoregistration is disabled, Cisco Unified CME records any MAC address that attempts to register. You can view these MAC addresses by using the show ephone attempted-registration command.

To assign an ephone-dn to a phone that autoregisters, you must use the `auto assign` command. This command defines which ephone-dns will be assigned to phones as they register. You define a range of ephone-dns, and they are assigned on a first come, first served basis. You can also define which types (models) of phones are assigned an ephone-dn from a given range. For example, you could have Cisco 7960 Phones assigned ephone-dns 101–150 and Cisco 7971 Phones assigned ephone-dns 54–100. The `auto assign` command also allows you to define what number a call will be routed to if the ephone-dn is busy or not answered. The following command assigns ephone-dns 101–145 to 7961 phones and forwards busy calls or calls that go unanswered for 10 seconds to extension 2001:

```
auto assign 101 to 145 type 7961 cfw 2001 timeout 10
```

In this example, the values that are highlighted are the variables that you define. You see that 101 to 145 are the ephone-dns that will be assigned to the 7961 type of phone. The call forward (cfw) is set to 2001, and the timeout for ringing is set to 10 seconds.

> **NOTE**
>
> You do not need to use the `type` keyword. If it is not used, any type of phone can be assigned an ephone-dn from this range. If there is a type defined in some ranges and not in others, the ephone-dn will be assigned from the range that has its type defined. When that range is used up, it will assign the ephone-dn from the range that has no type assigned.

There are a few caveats that you should be aware of when using the `auto assign` command:

▶ You cannot use the command to configure the 7914 sidecars. You must configure these manually.

▶ The ephones in a range must all be the same type, that is, either single-line or dual-line.

▶ The ephone-dns cannot be assigned as paging, intercom, MWI, or MoH ephone-dns.

Endpoint Verification

After all required configuration is complete, you should be able to plug phones in and they should register. Of course, the operative word here is *should*. From time to time, something can occur that causes phones to fail to register. This section covers common issues and describes how you can verify that the endpoint registered. All the commands discussed in this section are issued from global configuration mode.

First, you should verify that the VLAN and IP configuration in the phone are correct. The VLAN and IP configuration can be viewed on the phone's screen by pressing the Settings button and selecting Network Configuration. If the IP address settings are not correct, check the DHCP configuration.

If the DHCP configuration is correct and the phone is not registering, check to see whether the firmware files are in the flash on the Cisco Unified CME and whether the load commands are in the configuration and correct.

Next, check to see what files the phone is requesting. This is done by using the `debug tftp events` command. This command displays the files that the TFTP server is sending; this includes the firmware, XML configuration, and locale files.

You can then use the `debug ephone register` command to see the registration process. After issuing this command, reset the phone and watch the registration process. You should look for the `Load=` parameter. On this line, you should see what firmware file and version it is loading.

You can use the `show ephone` command to see which phones have successfully registered. This command also shows some configuration information, such as the ephone-dn assigned to the buttons. You can also see the current status, such as whether the phone is ringing or off-hook.

To verify that locale files are being used, issue the `show telephony-service tftp-bindings` command. This command displays all configuration files that are available to phones through TFTP, which includes the user-locale and network-locale.

And, of course, we can't forget the arguably most used command, `show running-config`. This command shows the configuration of the router. Many configuration errors are often found by simply spending a little time looking at the running-config.

Endpoint Reboot

From time to time, you might need to reboot a phone. This is required after updating certain configuration information or while troubleshooting. There are two commands used to reboot a phone: `reset` and `restart`. The `reset` command is the more drastic of the two. Reset is similar to powering the phone off and on. This is the type of reboot that would be used when the firmware, user-locale, network-locale, and URL parameters change.

The `restart` command is like soft reboot. This is useful for changes to phone button, phone line, and speed dial number. The `restart` command does not cause the phone to go through the DHCP and TFTP process, so it is faster than `reset`.

Exam Prep Questions

1. Which of the following do you have to configure before you can configure Cisco Unified CME to allow phones to register?

   ○ **A.** max-ephone-dns

   ○ **B.** max-ephones

   ○ **C.** max-auto-assign

   ○ **D.** auto-reg-assign

2. Which of the following is correct when creating an ephone?

   ○ **A.** Router(config-telephony)# **ephone 10**

      Router(config-ephone)# **mac-address 00CC.0001.A123.1ABF**

      Router(config-ephone)# **button 1:101**

      Router(config-ephone)# **button 2:102**

   ○ **B.** Router(config)# **ephone 10**

      Router(config-ephone)# **mac-address 00CC.0001.A123.1ABF**

      Router(config-ephone)# **button 1:101**

      Router(config-ephone)# **button 2:102**

   ○ **C.** Router(config)# **ephone tag 10**

      Router(config-ephone)# **mac-address 00CC.0001.A123.1ABF**

      Router(config-ephone)# **button 1:101**

      Router(config-ephone)# **button 2:102**

   ○ **D.** Router(config)# **ephone 10**

      Router(config-ephone)# **mac-address 00CH.0001.A123.1ABF**

      Router(config-ephone)# **button 1:101**

      Router(config-ephone)# **button 2:102**

   ○ **E.** Router(config)# **ephone**

      Router(config-ephone)# **mac-address 00CC.0001.A123.1ABF**

      Router(config-ephone)# **button 1:101**

      Router(config-ephone)# **button 2:102**

3. Which of the following commands is not valid when configuring ephones or ephone-dns?

   ○ **A.** `ephone-dn 101`

   ○ **B.** `ephone 10`

   ○ **C.** `mac address 00CC.0001.A123.1ABF`

   ○ **D.** `button 1:101`

   ○ **E.** `number 2000`

4. Which of the following definitions for these button separators is not correct?

   ○ **A.** o: Multiple ephone-dns assigned to a single button, maximum of 25 on a button.

   ○ **B.** b: Does not ring incoming calls, but beeps are heard when you are on the phone and another call is coming in. The lights and other visible indicators function normally.

   ○ **C.** m: Allows you to monitor the status of the DN. Cannot be used to place or receive calls.

   ○ **D.** c: Allows call waiting for an overlaid ephone-dn.

   ○ **E.** f: Causes the phone to flash only on incoming calls.

5. Which of the following statements about ephone-dns is true?

   ○ **A.** Single-line ephone-dns can have more than one number assigned.

   ○ **B.** Dual-line ephone-dns can have only one number assigned.

   ○ **C.** Dual-line ephone-dns should not be used for paging.

   ○ **D.** Single-line ephone-dns should not be used for MWI.

   ○ **E.** Up to 15 numbers can be assigned to an overlay.

6. A customer is complaining that phones sometimes reset for what seems like no reason. You run some debug commands and notice within a few minutes that keepalives are not being sent to the phones. What could cause this?

   ○ **A.** The `keepalive.prc` process has failed.

   ○ **B.** This means nothing because keepalives are only sent every 5 minutes.

   ○ **C.** The keepalive value might have been changed.

   ○ **D.** The system has reached critical memory use, and more memory must be added.

7. The following `dialplan-pattern` command is configured on your system:

   ```
   dialplan-pattern 1 2485477... extension-length 4
   extension-pattern 90..
   ```

   What effect will it have? (Choose all that apply.)

   ○ **A.** An outbound call from extension 9001 will be sent out with the caller ID of 2485477001.

   ○ **B.** The caller ID that appears on an internal phone on an inbound call from 2485477010 will by transformed to 9010.

   ○ **C.** An inbound call from 2485477012 will cause the phone to ring differently than when a call comes for 2485479100.

   ○ **D.** An outbound call from extension 9011 will be sent out with the caller ID of 12485477011.

8. When configuring a Cisco Unified CME so that phones can retrieve the correct firmware, which of the following are necessary? (Choose all that apply.)

   ○ **A.** Copy the required files from the flash.

   ○ **B.** Issue the appropriate `tftp-server` commands.

   ○ **C.** Use the `load` command to assign the firmware that should be used for each type of phone.

   ○ **D.** Run the `create-cnf.xml` command.

9. You have decided to use the `auto assign` command to allow ephone-dns to be assigned to phones when they register. You created three ranges and assigned the 7960 phone type to one range and the 7961 phone type to another range. You did not assign a phone type on the last range so that all non-7960 and non-7961 phones could register using that range. Based on this, which of the following is true?

   ○ **A.** When the range assigned to the 7960s runs out of ephone-dns, no other 7960s will be able to register.

   ○ **B.** When the range assigned to the 7961s runs out of ephone-dns, the range assigned to the 7960s will be used.

   ○ **C.** When the range assigned to the 7960s runs out of ephone-dns, the range with no type assigned will be used.

   ○ **D.** When the range assigned to the 7960s runs out of ephone-dns, a random ephone-dn will be assigned.

10. Which of the following commands is not helpful when trying to determine why a phone will not register?

   ○ **A.** `debug ephone register`

   ○ **B.** `debug tftp events`

   ○ **C.** `show running-config`

   ○ **D.** `show telephony-net-cfg`

Answers to Exam Prep Questions

1. **B.** You have to configure max-ephones before you can configure Cisco Unified CME to allow phones to register. Answers A, C, and D are incorrect because none of them are valid commands.

2. **B.** Answer A is incorrect because you do not issue the `ephone` command from telephony-service config mode. Answer C is incorrect because the `ephone` command should not have the word `tag` after it. Answer D is incorrect because the MAC address is invalid. Answer E is incorrect because ephones must have a tag number.

3. **C.** The command is missing the hyphen between `mac` and `address`. Answers A, B, D, and E are incorrect because they are all valid commands.

4. **E.** The f separator is for feature ring, not flash only. Answers A, B, C, and D are incorrect because the definitions are correct.

5. **C.** Dual-line ephone-dns should not be used for intercoms, paging, Music on Hold sources, loopbacks, MWIs, and call park slots. Answer A is incorrect because single-line ephone-dns can have a primary and a secondary number. Answer B is incorrect because a dual-line ephone-dn can have more than one number. Answer D is incorrect because single-line ephone-dns should be used for intercoms, paging, Music on Hold sources, loopbacks, and MWIs. Answer E is incorrect because up to 25 numbers can be assigned to an ephone-dn.

6. **C.** The keepalive default value is 30 seconds, but it can be from 10 to 65535. Answer A is not correct because there is no such thing as the `keepalive.prc` process. Answer B is incorrect because the default is 30 seconds, not 5 minutes. Answer D is wrong because keepalives not going out do not point to a memory issue.

7. **A, B, and C.** Answer D is not correct because the 1 in the `dialplan-pattern` command is the tag number, not part of the pattern.

8. **A, B, and C.** Answer D is not correct because `create-cnf.xml` is not a valid command. The command should be `create cnf-files`.

9. **C.** When a range with a specific type of phone defined runs out of ephone-dns, ephone-dns from a range that does not have a type defined will be used. Answer A is not correct because the range with no type defined will be used. Answer B is not correct because ephone-dns will only be assigned to phones of the type that is defined in the range. Answer D is not correct because autoassign only assigns number is the specified range.

10. **D.** This is not a valid command. Answers A, B, and C are incorrect because they are helpful commands when trying to determine why a phone will not register.

Suggested Reading and Resources

1. Search Cisco.com for "Cisco Unified Communications Manager Express Reference."

CHAPTER ELEVEN

Configuring Cisco Unity Express

Terms you need to understand:

- ✓ Session Initiation Protocol (SIP)
- ✓ File Transfer Protocol (FTP)
- ✓ Trivial File Transfer Protocol (TFTP)
- ✓ Advanced Integration Module (AIM)
- ✓ Network Module (NM)
- ✓ Voice Profile for Internet Messaging (VPIM)
- ✓ Command-line interface (CLI)
- ✓ Graphical user interface (GUI)
- ✓ Message Waiting Indicator (MWI)

Techniques you need to master:

- ✓ Create a common FTP and TFTP server directory and activate FTP and TFTP services
- ✓ Know the Cisco Unity Express platform differences
- ✓ Configure HTTP access to Cisco Unified Communications Manager Express (CME) during the Cisco Unity Express Initialization Wizard process
- ✓ Activate and deactivate host router CLI debug commands

Cisco Unity Express is a small-platform voicemail system that integrates into a Cisco Integrated Services Router. Cisco Unity Express has additional services, such as Internet Message Access Protocol (IMAP) access to voice messages from Microsoft Outlook or Outlook Express, Automated Attendant programming, and greeting management using the phone.

Setting Up Cisco Unity Express Voicemail

Cisco Unity Express provides voicemail services for small- to medium-size organizations up to 250 users. Command-line and graphical user interfaces are available for configuration, long-term management, and configuration and message store backup and restore. The command-line interface is used for initial installation and upgrades.

Cisco Unity Express Platforms and Capacities

Cisco Unity Express operates on a Linux platform with command-line installation and upgrade procedures. Administration is performed with either the command-line interface (CLI) or a graphical user interface (GUI). There are three primary hardware components used to implement Cisco Unity Express: the Advanced Integration Module CUE (AIM-CUE), the Network Module CUE (NM-CUE), and the Network Module Extended Capacity CUE (NM-CUE-EC).

> **NOTE**
>
> The preceding three hardware components are covered on the exam, but current Cisco products include the AIM-CUE and the Extended Network Module CUE (NME-CUE). The NME-CUE has the same operating characteristics as the NM-CUE-EC.

AIM-CUE

The AIM-CUE platform is a daughter card installed in the Cisco Unified Communications Express router and uses flash memory for the Linux file system and message store. Table 11.1 shows the capacities and capabilities of the AIM-CUE.

TABLE 11.1   AIM-CUE Capacities and Capabilities

Maximum Mailboxes	Voice Sessions	Internal Slot	Storage Media	Mailbox Storage Hours
50	6	Yes	Flash	14

NM-CUE

The NM-CUE platform requires a Network Module slot in the Cisco Unified CME router and uses a hard drive for the Linux file system and message store. Table 11.2 covers the capacities and capabilities of the NM-CUE.

TABLE 11.2   NM-CUE Capacities and Capabilities

Maximum Mailboxes	Voice Sessions	Network Module	Storage Media	Mailbox Storage Hours
100	8	Yes	Hard disk	100

NM-CUE-EC

The NM-CUE-EC platform requires a Network Module slot in the Cisco Unified Communications Manager Express router and uses a hard drive for the Linux file system and message store. Table 11.3 covers the capacities and capabilities of the NM-CUE-EC.

TABLE 11.3   NM-CUE-EC Capacities and Capabilities

Maximum Mailboxes	Voice Sessions	Network Module	Storage Media	Mailbox Storage Hours
250	16	Yes	Hard Disk	300

EXAM ALERT

Platforms (AIM versus NM), voice sessions (ports), message storage components, and mailbox storage hours are key elements.

Cisco Unity Express Features and Functionality

The following is a quick look at the features and capabilities of Cisco Unity Express:

▶ Voicemail storage configurable per mailbox

▶ End-user tutorial, enabling self-service mailbox setup

- End-user mailboxes and General Delivery Mailboxes (GDMs)
- Standard and alternate greetings
- Subscriber features including notifications and distribution lists
- Caller features such as dial by extension or dial by name
- Voice Profile for Internet Messaging (VPIM) networking between Cisco Unity Express and other voicemail systems
- Integrated messaging using IMAP
- VoiceView Express for visually reviewing voicemail messages from a display phone

EXAM ALERT

Integrated messaging and VoiceView Express are not supported on the AIM-CUE *for the test only*. The AIM-CUE with software version 3.0 and higher does support these two features.

Preintegration CLI Configuration

There is a minimum CLI configuration required on the host router before any installation and configuration commands can be issued on the Cisco Unity Express module.

Use the `show run` command to identify the service engine slot and module for the Cisco Unity Express module. Create a loopback interface and configure the service engine interface to reference the loopback interface with the `ip unnumbered loopback` command. This IP addressing option reduces the number of subnets that are used but requires a static route used to direct Cisco Unity Express traffic through the service engine interface. Listing 11.1 shows the configuration of the service module interface.

Listing 11.1 Service Module Interface Configuration

```
interface Loopback 0
 ip address 10.10.10.1 255.255.255.0
interface Service-Engine1/0
 ip unnumbered Loopback 0
 service-module ip address 10.10.10.2 255.255.255.0
 service-module ip default-gateway 10.10.10.1
ip route 10.10.10.2 255.255.255.255 service-engine 1/0
```

With this configuration in place, you can issue a series of commands to control and connect to the Cisco Unity Express module from the host router command line. The command format follows:

```
service-module engine-type module/0 (options on next line)
        [reload ¦ reset ¦session ¦ shutdown ¦ status]
```

The following is a brief description of the options for the preceding `service-module` command:

- ▶ *engine-type*: Service-engine for Cisco Unity Express; integration-engine for a Unified Messaging Gateway.

- ▶ *module*: Physical AIM slot or Network Module slot.

- ▶ `reload`: Normal shutdown and restart.

- ▶ `reset`: Forced power off shutdown and restart (not recommended).

- ▶ `session`: Used to create a Telnet session to the Cisco Unity Express module.

- ▶ `shutdown`: Used to shut down the Cisco Unity Express module used prior to powering down the host router. The Linux file system can be corrupted by just powering off the host router.

- ▶ `status`: Used to determine the current operating status of the Cisco Unity Express module.

> **NOTE**
>
> For remote access, use Telnet to connect to the host router, and then use the `session` command to reach the Cisco Unity Express module.

There are additional commands required to complete the Cisco Unity Express integration, as shown in Listing 11.2:

- ▶ `ip http` commands: Used to activate the GUI interface.

- ▶ `dial-peer voice 1900 voip` section: Used to define the communications protocol and operating parameters to connect the host router and the Cisco Unity Express module. The `codec g711ulaw` and `no vad` commands are requirements.

- ▶ `ephone-dn` commands: Two sections are used to activate the Message Waiting Indicator (MWI) on the phone (ephone-dn 18 and ephone-dn 19). The destination pattern of 1999 . . . . represents the MWI activation number followed by a period (.) for each digit of the extension length. Four dots are used for a 4-digit extension length.

Listing 11.2   Router Host Commands to Integrate Cisco Unity Express

```
interface Loopback 0
 ip address 10.10.10.1 255.255.255.0
. . .
!
interface Service-Engine1/0
 ip unnumbered Loopback0/0
 service-module ip address 10.10.10.2 255.255.255.0
 service-module ip default-gateway 10.10.10.1
!
ip http server
ip http path flash:
!
ip route 10.10.10.2 255.255.255.255 Service-Engine1/0
!
dial-peer voice 1900 voip
 destination-pattern 19 . .
 session protocol sipv2
 session target ipv4:10.10.10.2
 dtmf-relay sip-notify
 codec g711ulaw
 no vad
. . .
ephone-dn 18
 number 1999 . . . .
 mwi on
!
ephone-dn 19
 number 1998 . . . .
 mwi off
```

EXAM ALERT

Understanding the CLI integration commands on the host router are important, especially the SIP dial peer.

There are several telephony-service commands that complete the integration
between the Cisco Unified CME host router and the Cisco Unity Express module, as shown in Listing 11.3:

▶ voicemail 1900: Activates the Messages button on the Cisco IP phone.

▶ call-forward .T and call-transfer .T: Permit forward to and transfer to voicemail because the default operation only permits forwarding
  and transferring to local extensions.

> **CAUTION**
>
> Use of the .T pattern can introduce toll fraud in a production environment.

▶ `web admin system name` *username* `password` *userpassword*: Permits the use of the GUI directly by an administrator and for integration with the Cisco Unity Express module GUI.

▶ `dn-webedit`: Allows system administrators to manage directory numbers.

Listing 11.3   Additional Commands to Complete the Voicemail Integration

```
telephony-service
 voicemail 1900
 call-forward pattern .T
 call-transfer pattern .T
 web admin system name admin password admin
 dn-webedit
```

With these commands in place, you can proceed with the Cisco Unity Express installation, upgrade, or integration process.

Installation and Upgrade Procedure

Cisco Unity Express modules are distributed with the latest version of software. If there is a newer version that you want to upgrade to, you can connect to the Cisco Unity Express module and perform the installation or upgrade as needed.

Let's walk through the upgrade process step by step:

Step 1   Download files for installation, language updates, and version upgrades from Cisco.com.

Step 2   Install software files to upgrade the software.

Step 3   Install license files to expand the number of licensed users and ports.

Step 4   Reset Cisco Unity Express to factory defaults.

Step 5   Complete the standard setup process.

Step 1: Download Files

Download the appropriate files from Cisco.com or copy the files from a distribution CD. The following is a list of sample files for a full installation. These files should be in a common directory on a server with both TFTP and FTP services configured to use the software directory where the files are stored.

System software:

- ► `cue-vm.3.1.1.pkg`

- ► `cue-vm-full-k9.nm-aim.3.1.1.prt1`

Installation utilities:

- ► `cue-installer.nm-aim.3.1.1`

- ► `cue-vm-installer-k9.nm-aim.3.1.1.prt1`

Cisco Unified Communications Manager Express licenses (only one is used: _cme_ for Cisco Unified Communications Manager Express or _ccm_ for Cisco Unified Communications Manager):

- ► `cue-vm-license_12mbx_cme_3.1.1.pkg`

- ► `cue-vm-license_25mbx_cme_3.1.1.pkg`

- ► `cue-vm-license_50mbx_cme_3.1.1.pkg`

- ► `cue-vm-license_100mbx_cme_3.1.1.pkg`

- ► `cue-vm-license_150mbx_cme_3.1.1.pkg`

- ► `cue-vm-license_200mbx_cme_3.1.1.pkg`

- ► `cue-vm-license_250mbx_cme_3.1.1.pkg`

Language files:

- ► `cue-vm-lang-pack.nm-aim.3.1.1.pkg`

- ► `cue-vm-en_US-lang-pack.nm-aim.3.1.1.prt1` (example)

- ► Other language packs (`.prt1` files) that might be required

Step 2: Install Software Files

Connect to the Cisco Unity Express module using the session option from the host router CLI to get to the Cisco Unity Express CLI. Using the following command, install the appropriate software from the files listed in step 1:

```
CUE# software install clean url
➥ftp://10.10.10.227/cue-vm-k9.nm-aim.3.1.1.pkg
```

Step 3: Install License File

Install the appropriate license file from the files listed in step 1:

```
CUE# software install clean
↪url ftp://10.200.1.2/cue-vm-license_50mbx_cme_3.1.1.pkg
```

Step 4: Reset to Factory Defaults

During an initial installation, make sure that the integration with Cisco Unified Communications Manager Express will be clean by resetting the Cisco Unity Express module to the factory defaults using the following CLI sequence. Go offline using the Cisco Unity Express CLI `offline` command to reset Cisco Unity Express to the factory default settings. After the factory default reset, the process gives you one more chance to use the latest existing configuration stored on the Cisco Unity Express module. For a clean start, enter **n** for no, as shown in Listing 11.4.

Listing 11.4   Resetting Factory Defaults

```
CUE# offline
!!!WARNING!!!: Putting the system offline will terminate all active calls.
Do you wish to continue[n]?: y
CUE(offline)# restore factory default
!!!WARNING!!!: This operation will cause all configuration and data
on the system to be erased. This operation is not reversible.
Do you wish to continue[n]?: y
Would you like to restore the saved configuration? (y,n) n
```

Step 5: Complete the Standard Setup Process

After the factory default has been completed, you are walked through the standard setup process. The following information is required:

► Host name

► Domain Name System (DNS) server address if DNS is activated (recommended practice is to use IP addresses)

► NTP server address (reference should be to the host router)

► Time zone (region of world and country)

► Administrator credentials, username, and password

EXAM ALERT

You should understand the basic setup entries in the preceding list.

After the basic CLI configuration process is completed, the Cisco Unity Express module is ready for Cisco Unified CME integration.

GUI Initialization Wizard

Integration with Cisco Unified CME is simplified by using the GUI initialization wizard. This and the following sections describe the process of using the initialization wizard:

Step 1   Log in to Cisco Unity Express.

Step 2   Initiate the Cisco Unity Express Initialization Wizard.

Step 3   Set the Cisco Unified CME HTTP access parameters.

Step 4   Select the Cisco Unified CME users to import.

Step 5   Set user mailbox defaults.

Step 6   Set call handling parameters.

Step 7   Review integration options and set the save configuration backup.

Step 8   View the initialization wizard results with imported users' passwords and PINs.

A screen-by-screen walk-through is the best way to understand the Cisco Unity Express Initialization Wizard process.

Step 1: Log In to Cisco Unity Express

From a workstation, use the appropriate browser to access the Cisco Unity Express web interface using the following URL: http://<ip address of the CUE module>. Enter the username and password created during the Cisco Unity Express module initialization (see Figure 11.1).

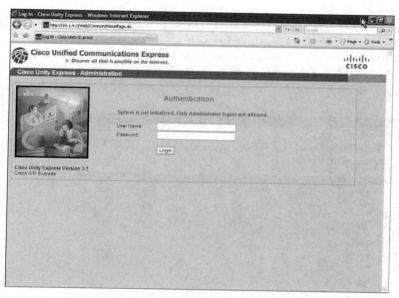

FIGURE 11.1 Logging in to Cisco Unity Express for the first time.

Step 2: Initiate the Cisco Unity Express Initialization Wizard

After logging in to the Cisco Unity Express web page, you have several choices. The recommended choice is the Initialization Wizard (see Figure 11.2).

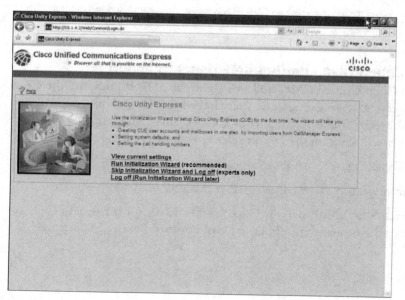

FIGURE 11.2 Starting the Cisco Unity Express Initialization Wizard.

Step 3: Set Cisco Unified CME HTTP Access Parameters

After you have started the wizard, enter the Cisco Unified CME IP address and web administrator username and password in the first screen, and then click **Next** (see Figure 11.3). If the address or credentials are not correct, you will be denied further access.

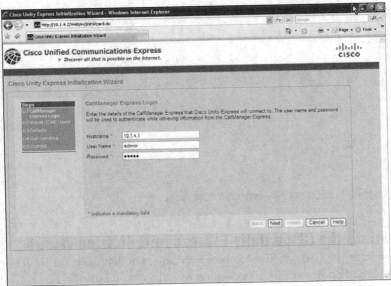

FIGURE 11.3 Entering the Cisco Unified CME IP address or host name and web administrator credentials.

Step 4: Select Cisco Unified CME Users to Import

Using the Cisco Unified CME credentials and the HTTP interface, the Cisco Unity Express module extracts the usernames from Cisco Unified CME and presents the users found for import in Cisco Unity Express. There are three important check boxes on the import screen, as shown in Figure 11.4:

▶ **Mailbox:** Creates a mailbox for each user

▶ **Administrator:** Determines whether this user is an administrator

▶ **Set CFNA/CFB:** Programs Cisco Unified CME for the default Call Forward No Answer (CFNA) and Call Forward Busy (CFB) settings.

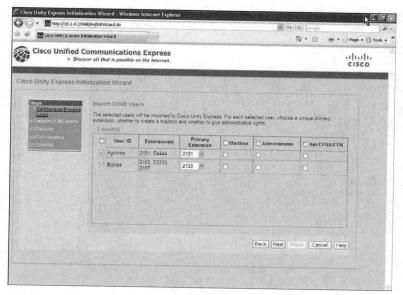

FIGURE 11.4   Select users to be imported.

When the users have been selected and their options have been checked, click **Next**.

Step 5: Set User Mailbox Defaults

The next screen is where you set the default settings for creating user mailboxes. After they are created, the individual user and group General Delivery Mailboxes (GDMs) can be individually modified. On this screen, you define the following fields, as shown in Figure 11.5:

- ▸ The default language
- ▸ Generated or blank passwords and PINs
- ▸ Total mailbox size
- ▸ Maximum message length
- ▸ Message expiry time in days

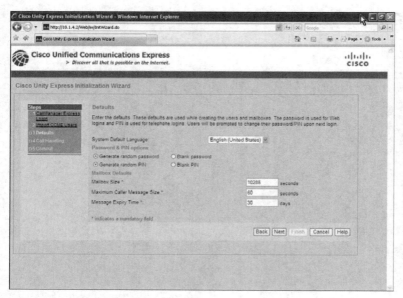

FIGURE 11.5 Set user mailbox defaults.

Step 6: Set Call Handling Parameters

The last entry screen is where you define the default directory numbers used to access voicemail, the voicemail operator extension, the Auto Attendant, the Auto Attendant operator extension, the Administration via Telephone (AVT) number, and the SIP notification method (see Figure 11.6). The SIP notification methods are as follows:

▶ **Subscribe-notify:** Registered users constantly poll and receive the status of the MWI.

▶ **Unsolicited-notify:** Contacts the user using the extension number to turn the MWI on or off.

CAUTION

The unsolicited-notify option might require periodical manual resynchronization.

▶ **Outcall:** This option uses the MWI on-and-off mechanism, where changes to the MWI indicators are sent through the MWI ephone-dn mechanism. If this option is selected, the wizard opens the MWI on and off fields.

When you have completed this screen, click **Next** to go to the review screen.

CAUTION

The outcall option might require periodical manual resynchronization.

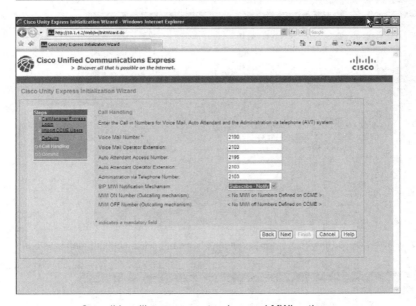

FIGURE 11.6 Set call handling access extensions and MWI options.

Step 7: Review Integration Options and Set the Save Configuration Backup

All the settings have been entered and are presented for review, as shown in Figure 11.7. At the bottom of the screen is a check box that when selected, causes the running configurations to be copied to NVRAM. This occurs for the Cisco Unity Express module and the Cisco Unified CME router when the wizard has completed the updates.

EXAM ALERT

The review screen is where you trigger configuration backups after the Cisco Unity Express Initialization Wizard completes.

Step 8: View the Initialization Wizard Results

After the Initialization Wizard has completed all the updates and saved the configurations, a final screen is presented, as shown in Figure 11.8. This screen contains a list of imported users with generated passwords and PINs, if those options were selected.

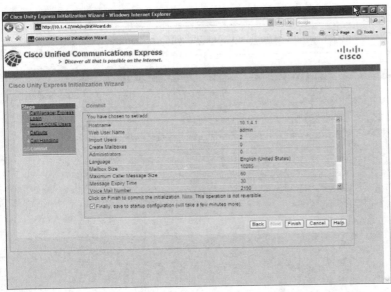

FIGURE 11.7 Review Cisco Unity Express integration options and select configuration save option.

FIGURE 11.8 Initialization Wizard report.

CAUTION

You should capture and save the information on this final screen for future reference so that users can log in to voicemail and user web pages.

Using Cisco Auto Attendant

The Cisco Unity Express module has a powerful built-in Auto Attendant (AA). It is activated by default when the Cisco Unity Express module is installed and can be accessed after the pilot number is configured and reachable from Cisco Unified CME.

Activating the Auto Attendant

To activate the AA, place a call to the pilot number for the AA and respond to the prompts. The default AA allows a user to enter an extension, search for a user by name, and be connected to the AA operator. Figure 11.9 shows the AA main screen.

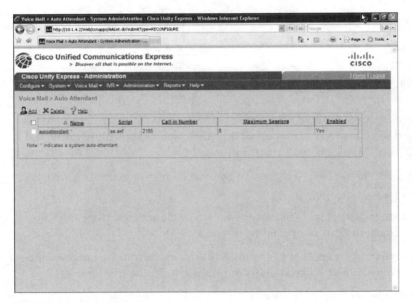

FIGURE 11.9 Main AA screen.

To disable and enable the default AA, choose **Voice Mail > Auto Attendant**.

The default AA actions cannot be modified, but there are several parameters that you can change and update to modify the basic functionality. Click `autoattendant` to edit these operational parameters.

The top half of the AA edit screen, which is shown in Figure 11.10, allows an administrator to set the call-in number, the script (upload a new one if developed offline), the language for this AA, the maximum sessions (should be approximately 60 to 75 percent of the total integration ports), and whether the AA script is enabled or disabled.

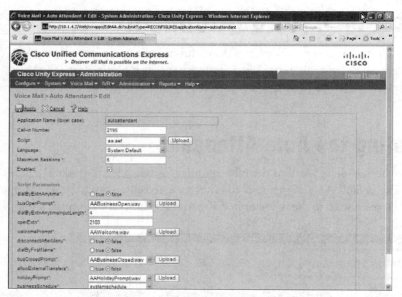

FIGURE 11.10 Top section of the AA Edit screen.

The bottom section of the AA screen lists the operational parameters that can be modified to change the operation of this AA script, as shown in Figure 11.11. The fields that can be changed are as follows:

- `dialByExtnAnytime`: Sets the dial by extension anytime to true or false (default).

- `busOpenPrompt`: The business open prompt identifies the organization and directs the call to normal operation.

- `dialByExtnAnytimeInputLength`: If dial by extension is true, this field sets the maximum entered digits during the welcome prompt.

- `operExtn`: Sets the AA operator extension when the caller presses 0.

- `welcomePrompt`: Sets the AA welcome prompt.

- `disconnectAfterMenu`: Disconnects after menu if no user input is detected; true or false (default).

- `dialByFirstName`: Sets dial by first name to true or false (default is last name).

- `busClosedPrompt`: The closed business prompt lets the caller know that the office is closed and directs the call to the after-hour process.

- `allowExternalTransfers`: Sets external transfers (PSTN calls) to true or false (default).

▶ `holidayPrompt`: Sets holiday prompt based on the holiday schedule.

▶ `businessSchedule`: Sets the business schedule used (triggers business open versus business closed prompts).

▶ `MaxRetry`: Defines the number of mistakes the caller can make before the AA plays the good-bye prompt.

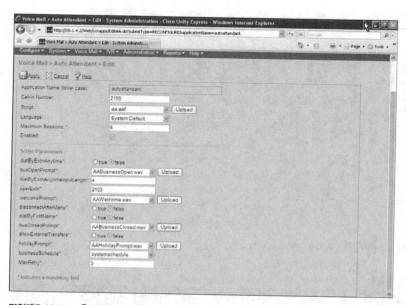

FIGURE 11.11 Bottom section of the AA Edit screen—parameters that can be modified.

EXAM ALERT

The default Auto Attendant script cannot be downloaded, modified, or deleted; it can only be enabled and disabled.

Managing Prompts with the GUI and AVT (TUI)

An administrator can log in using the Administration via Telephone (AVT) pilot number, also referred to as the Telephony User Interface (TUI), and can change the global alternate greeting for weather conditions, business closings, and so on. Another AVT option is to create and manage nonstandard AA prompts.

When recorded through AVT, the filename that gets created on the Cisco Unity Express module is `UserPrompt_mmddyyyyhhmmss.wav`, for example, `UserPrompt_09112008090500.wav`.

Prompts can be managed from the **System > Prompts** menu, and the default recording filename can be renamed to be more meaningful (see Figure 11.12).

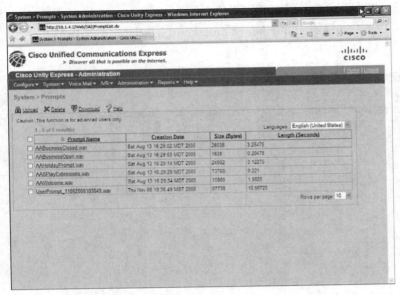

FIGURE 11.12   Prompts management screen.

EXAM ALERT

The filename format is important to remember both for the test and for production. If you record multiple prompts, write down the prompts recorded so that they can be changed to a more meaningful name after the recording session.

Figure 11.13 displays the list of available prompts that can be used with the default AA busClosedPrompt parameter. There is a good reason why the prompt names should be changed. Unless you have perfect memory recall, you probably wouldn't be able to remember what is recorded on the UserPrompt_01022008111256.wav (date and time stamp) file. A name such as BBbusinessClosed.wav is more appropriate.

There are two methods that can be used to create custom AA scripts: the Cisco Unity Express Editor Express, built into the Cisco Unity Express GUI, and an external JavaBeans development tool, the Cisco Unity Express Editor.

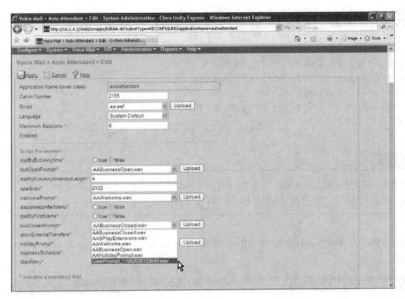

FIGURE 11.13 Using AVT recorded prompts.

Troubleshooting Cisco Unity Express

You can use some basic CLI commands to verify Cisco Unified CME and Cisco Unity Express operation and integration.

EXAM ALERT

Basic CLI troubleshooting commands in this section, especially formats and options, are important to remember for the exam.

Host Router CLI Tools

From the host router CLI, the administrator can verify the current status using the `service-module service-engine 1/0 status` command, as shown in Listing 11.5. The service module normal operational state is the Steady state.

Listing 11.5 Verifying Current Status

```
CME# service-module service-engine 1/0 status

Service Module is Cisco Service-Engine1/0
Service Module supports session via TTY line 33
Service Module is in Steady state
Getting status from the Service Module, please wait..
cisco service engine 1.0
```

NOTE

> Two other commands that can verify that the service module is present or active are
> show version and show ip interface brief.

On the host router, there are many ephone debug options, which are shown in
Listing 11.6.

Listing 11.6 debug ephone **Options**

```
CME# debug ephone ?
```

```
    alarm                   Enable ephone alarm message debugging
    detail                  Enable ephone detail debugging
    error                   Enable ephone error debugging
    keepalive               Enable ephone keepalive debugging
    loopback                Enable ephone loopback debugging
    moh                     Enable ephone music-on-hold debugging
    mwi                     Enable ephone mwi debugging
    pak                     Enable ephone packet debugging
    qov                     Enable ephone voice quality debugging
    raw                     Enable ephone raw protocol debugging
    register                Enable ephone registration debugging
    state                   Enable ephone state debugging
    statistics              Enable ephone statistics debugging
    vm-integration          Enable ephone vm-integration debugging
```

One of the easiest Cisco Unified CME and Cisco Unity Express integration
tools is the mwi option, used to troubleshoot MWI status.

The vm-integration option is used to troubleshoot a plain old telephone service (POTS)–connected voicemail system.

TIP

> After using Cisco IOS debug tools, make sure that you issue the undebug all or the
> no debug all command to turn off all debug options.

Because SIP is used for integrating Cisco Unified CME with Cisco Unity Express, the debug ccsip commands are often used to check call setup messages between Cisco Unified CME and Cisco Unity Express, as shown in Listing 11.7.

Listing 11.7 debug ccsip **Commands**

```
CME# debug ccsip ?

  all         Enable all SIP debugging traces
  calls       Enable CCSIP SPI calls debugging trace
  error       Enable SIP error debugging trace
  events      Enable SIP events debugging trace
  info        Enable SIP info debugging trace
  media       Enable SIP media debugging trace
  messages    Enable CCSIP SPI messages debugging trace
  preauth     Enable SIP preauth debugging traces
  states      Enable CCSIP SPI states debugging trace
```

There are three additional Cisco IOS debug commands that are useful:

▶ debug tftp: Assists in troubleshooting phone registration problems

▶ debug ip http: Troubleshoots webpage problems

▶ debug voice ccapi inout: Displays calls being set up to a Skinny Client Control Protocol (SCCP) IP phone

CAUTION

Use the debug voice ccapi inout command carefully because it can cause a large volume of output and high overhead.

Exam Prep Questions

1. What is the maximum number of users that Cisco Unity Express platforms can support?

   - ○ **A.** 8
   - ○ **B.** 100
   - ○ **C.** 250
   - ○ **D.** 500
   - ○ **E.** 3000
   - ○ **F.** 7500

2. Which Cisco Unity Express module can support up to a maximum of 100 mailboxes?

   - ○ **A.** Cisco Unity Express AIM
   - ○ **B.** Cisco Unity Express Network Module
   - ○ **C.** Cisco Unity Express Slot Module
   - ○ **D.** Cisco Unity Express Network Module 2V
   - ○ **E.** Cisco Unity Express Network Module Enhanced Capacity

3. How many hours of voicemail storage are available in the Cisco Unity Express AIM module?

   - ○ **A.** 8
   - ○ **B.** 14
   - ○ **C.** 100
   - ○ **D.** 250
   - ○ **E.** 300

4. The AVT or TUI interface can be used to accomplish which of the following three tasks?

   - ○ **A.** To restart the system
   - ○ **B.** To initiate a backup of the system
   - ○ **C.** Prompt management
   - ○ **D.** To allow an end user to have an email read to him
   - ○ **E.** To activate an Emergency Alternate Greeting (EAG)
   - ○ **F.** To add a new user to the system
   - ○ **G.** To delete a mailbox

5. What are the main differences between the memory and storage of the Cisco Unity Express Network Module and Cisco Unity Express AIM? (Choose two.)

   ○ **A.** Cisco Unity Express AIM uses flash-based storage, and Cisco Unity Express Network Modules use hard drive–based storage.

   ○ **B.** Cisco Unity Express Network Modules can store more hours of messages than Cisco Unity Express AIM.

   ○ **C.** Cisco Unity Express AIM and Cisco Unity Express Network Modules use different operating systems.

   ○ **D.** Cisco Unity Express AIM and Cisco Unity Express Network Modules use different installation packages for the various modules.

6. When do you need the software files for Cisco Unity Express?

   ○ **A.** To install a new module

   ○ **B.** Only for upgrades

   ○ **C.** To recover from a failure

   ○ **D.** To either upgrade or recover from a failure

7. Which components must be configured on the host router for proper functionality of the Cisco Unity Express module? (Choose three.)

   ○ **A.** Proper IP addressing of the service-engine interface

   ○ **B.** Proper IP addressing of the service module

   ○ **C.** Proper IP addressing of the router Cisco Unity Express interface

   ○ **D.** Static host route to the module

   ○ **E.** Static route to the external Ethernet port of the module

   ○ **F.** Ephone-dns for the pilot of Cisco Unity Express voicemail

8. Which dial peer properties does the host router need to have to connect to the Cisco Unity Express module? (Choose four.)

   ○ **A.** No VAD

   ○ **B.** Codec G.729

   ○ **C.** Codec G.711

   ○ **D.** SIP version 1

   ○ **E.** SIP version 2

   ○ **F.** H.323

   ○ **G.** DTMF relay using Sip Notify

   ○ **H.** DTMF relay disabled

9. Which Cisco Unified Communications Manager Express configuration is necessary to integrate with Cisco Unity Express and have MWI outcall work properly?

   ○ **A.** One ephone-dn with a number that starts with a unique value

   ○ **B.** One ephone-dn with a number that starts with a unique value followed by a number plus periods equal to the length of the extensions

   ○ **C.** Two ephone-dns, one for on and one for off, and each must have a unique number equal to the length of the extensions

   ○ **D.** Two ephone-dns, one for on and one for off, and each must have a unique number plus periods equal to the length of the extensions

   ○ **E.** Two ephone-dns, one for on and one for off, and their numbers must start with a common value followed by a number plus periods equal to the length of the extensions

10. Which items are configured during the Cisco Unity Express module initial setup? (Choose three.)

    ○ **A.** Host name

    ○ **B.** IP address

    ○ **C.** Voicemail pilot number

    ○ **D.** Auto Attendant pilot number

    ○ **E.** Users

    ○ **F.** Web administrator user and password

    ○ **G.** IP address of the Cisco Unified Communications Manager Express system

    ○ **H.** DHCP

11. Which statement best describes how to connect to the Cisco Unity Express module to perform the initial configuration?

    ○ **A.** Use Telnet to connect to the default IP address of 10.1.10.1.

    ○ **B.** Connect a crossover cable to the external Ethernet port on the module and use DHCP.

    ○ **C.** Connect a console cable to the Cisco Unity Express module.

    ○ **D.** Go across the backplane of the router to the Cisco Unity Express module.

    ○ **E.** Use the wireless connection to attach to the Cisco Unity Express module.

12. Which of the following items does the Initialization Wizard configure? (Choose three.)

    ○ **A.** Host name

    ○ **B.** IP address of the Cisco Unity Express module

    ○ **C.** Voicemail pilot number

    ○ **D.** Auto Attendant pilot number

    ○ **E.** Users

     ○ **F.** Web administrator username and password

     ○ **G.** IP address of the Cisco Unified Communications Manager Express system

     ○ **H.** DHCP

13. Which command do you use to view the status of the Cisco Unity Express module from the host router?

     ○ **A.** `Router# `**`service-module service-engine mod/port status`**

     ○ **B.** `Router# `**`service-engine service-module mod/port status`**

     ○ **C.** `Router(config)# `**`service-module service-engine mod/port status`**

     ○ **D.** `Router(config)# `**`service-engine service-module mod/port status`**

     ○ **E.** `Router(config)# `**`service-engine mod/port status`**

     ○ **F.** `Router# `**`service-engine mod/port status`**

14. Which command do you use to troubleshoot MWI problems on the phone?

     ○ **A.** `Router# `**`debug ephone vm-integration`**

     ○ **B.** `Router# `**`debug ephone mwi`**

     ○ **C.** `Router#(config)# `**`debug ephone vm-integration`**

     ○ **D.** `Router(config)# `**`debug ephone mwi`**

Answers to Exam Prep Questions

1. C. The NM-CUE-EC supports up to 250 users. The other answers are incorrect.

2. B. NM-CUE supports up to 100 mailboxes. AIM CUE supports up to 50 mailboxes and is incorrect. Answer E, 250, is the limit for the NM-CUE, so both these answers are incorrect. None of the other answers are valid Cisco Unity Express platforms.

3. B. Fourteen hours of storage are available. Answer C is valid for the NM-CUE, answer D is valid for the NM-CUE-EC, and answers A and D do not match any Cisco Unity Express platforms, so these answers are incorrect.

4. C, D, and E. A user with administrator rights can manage prompts (answer C), any user can retrieve voicemail (answer D), and a user with administration rights can activate the Emergency Alternate Greeting (EAG) (answer E). Answer A is incorrect; a restart is activated with the CLI or GUI. Answer B is incorrect because backups are started with the CLI or GUI. Answer F is incorrect because adding a new user is performed using the CLI or GUI. Answer G is incorrect because deleting a mailbox is initiated from the CLI or GUI.

5. **A and B.** Cisco Unity Express AIM uses flash-based storage, and Cisco Unity Express Network Modules use hard drive–based storage. Cisco Unity Express Network Modules can store more hours of messages than Cisco Unity Express AIM. Answer C is incorrect because all Cisco Unity Express platforms use the Linux operation system, and answer D is incorrect because the NM-CUE and AIM-CUE use the same installation file set.

6. **D.** You need the software files for Cisco Unity Express for upgrades and restores. Answer A is incorrect because new modules come with the software installed. Software installation files are required for upgrades and restores, not just upgrades and not just failures, so answers B and C are incorrect.

7. **A, B, and D.** Associate an IP address for the service-engine interface, assign an IP address to Cisco Unity Express, and create a static route pointing to the IP address of the Cisco Unity Express module. There is no Cisco Unity Express interface on the router, so answer C is incorrect. Static routes to other than the Cisco Unity Express IP address are ineffective, so answer E is incorrect. There are no ephone-dns associated with the voicemail pilot number, so answer F is incorrect.

8. **A, C, E, and G.** VAD must be disabled, the G.711 codec is incompatible with Cisco Unity Express recordings, SIP version 2, and DTMF relay is required. Answer B is incorrect; G.729 is not compatible with Cisco Unity Express recordings. Answer D is incorrect; SIP version 1 is not supported. Answer F is incorrect; H.323 is not used for Cisco Unity Express integration. Answer H is incorrect; DTMF relay must be enabled.

9. **D.** Two ephone-dns with unique activation numbers plus wildcard periods equal to the extension length are necessary. Answers A and B are incorrect because two ephone-dns are required, one for MWI on and one for MWI off. Answer C is incorrect because there is no specific length for the MWI activation numbers. Answer E is incorrect because the MWI activation number definition is wrong.

10. **A, B, and F.** Host name, IP address, and web administrator credentials are configured during the Cisco Unity Express module initial setup. Answer C, voicemail pilot; answer D, AA pilot; answer E, users; answer G, the Cisco Unified CME IP address; and answer H, DHCP, are not required during the initial setup process.

11. **D.** A virtual console connection through the host router backplane. Answer A is incorrect; there is no Telnet access to Cisco Unity Express preinstallation. Answer B is incorrect because module external ports cannot be used. Answer C is incorrect; there is no external console port. Answer E is incorrect; there is no wireless access.

12. **C, D, and G.** The Initialization Wizard configures voicemail pilot, Auto Attendant pilot, and the Cisco Unified Communications Manager IP address. Answer A, host name, configured during the initial CLI session, is incorrect. Answer B, Cisco Unity Express IP address, is incorrect. Users are not configured, but they can optionally be imported, so answer E is incorrect. Answer F is incorrect because the web administrator for both the host router and the Cisco Unity Express platform are configured prior to using the initialization wizard. Answer H is incorrect because DHCP is not used in Cisco Unified Communications Manager Express and Cisco Unity Express integration.

13. **A.** Answers B and F have sequence or missing field errors, and answers C, D, and E are in configuration mode and are incorrect.

14. **B.** Answer A is used for POTS voicemail system integrations, and answers C and D are in the wrong command mode.

Implementing Business Features

Terms you need to understand:

✓ Call forwarding

✓ Call transfer

✓ Call park

✓ Call pickup

✓ Intercom

✓ Paging

✓ Music on Hold (MOH)

✓ Call blocking

Techniques you need to master:

✓ Use the configuration commands for call forwarding and call transfer

✓ Understand the function and configuration of call park and call pickup groups

✓ Configure intercoms and modify them to meet the customer's needs

✓ Configure paging and MOH

✓ Implement call blocking and accounting

In this chapter, you explore how to configure a number of Cisco Unified Communications Manager Express (CME) features. Some features, such as hold, don't require any configuration. Others, such as call transfer, might work without configuration but have parameters that you can configure to better control how the feature will function. There are still others that will not work until you configure them.

Configuring Common Features

The following sections explore features that are commonly found on most phones. These sections do not cover common features that do not need configuration, such as hold, but rather focus on features that might require configuration.

Call Forward

The call forward feature simply allows you to forward an incoming call to a destination different than the one that was dialed. There are three types of call forward:

► Call forward all

► Call forward busy

► Call forward no answer

When call forward all is enabled, all incoming calls are forwarded to the number that was defined as the target. The end user can configure call forward all by pressing the CFwdAll softkey and then entering the target number followed by the pound sign (#). An end user can remove call forward all by pressing the CFwdAll softkey again.

The administrator can configure call forward options from the command-line interface (CLI) of the Cisco Unified CME. All three types of call forward can be configured from the CLI using the call-forward command. A keyword is used after the call-forward command to define which call forward is being configured. This command is issued in ephone-dn configuration mode. To configure call forward all, the keyword all is used and is followed by the number of the extension that calls will be forwarded to. The following commands show how to set up call forwarding for all incoming calls on ephone-dn 101 to extension 2000:

```
Router(config)# ephone-dn 101
Router(config-ephone-dn)# call-forward all 2000
```

> **NOTE**
>
> Most of the examples in this section assume that you are starting from global configuration mode. If you are already in ephone-dn configuration mode of the ephone you want to configure (for these examples, ephone-dn 101), the first command (`ephone-dn 101`) is not needed.

To configure where a call should be routed if the number that was dialed is busy, use the `call-forward` command followed by the keyword `busy` and the target number. The following commands show how to set up call forward busy on ephone-dn 101 to extension 2000:

```
Router(config)# ephone-dn 101
Router(config-ephone-dn)# call-forward busy 2000
```

The last type of call forward is no answer. Call forward no answer determines where the call should be routed if the dialed number does not answer.

The following commands show how to set up call forward no answer on ephone-dn 101 to extension 2000:

```
Router(config)# ephone-dn 101
Router(config-ephone-dn)# call-forward noan 2000
```

You can restrict where an end user can forward her calls by using the `call-forward max-length` and `call-forward pattern` commands. The `call-forward max-length` command sets the maximum number of digits that can be set using the CFwdAll softkey. By setting this to 8, you can make sure that users can only forward calls to local numbers (unless, of course, you are an area that requires 10- or 11-digit dialing). To set the maximum digits to 8 for ephone-dn 101, enter the following commands:

```
Router(config)# ephone-dn 101
Router(config-ephone-dn)# call-forward max-length 8
```

You can also set a pattern that restricts where calls can be forwarded to by using the `call-forward pattern` command. For example, to configure the pattern so that calls can only be forwarded to numbers within the 248 area code, use the following command:

```
Router(config-telephony)# call-forward pattern 91248.......
```

Notice that this command is not issued in ephone-dn configuration mode. It is issued in telephony-service mode, which means it is a global telephony command that affects all the phones in the system.

EXAM ALERT

By default, Cisco Unified CME only allows a call to be forwarded to other Skinny Client Control Protocol (SCCP) devices registered to itself. In other words, if you do not specify a call forward pattern, calls cannot be forwarded to any external destination.

Call Transfer

Another common feature is call transfer. This is simply the ability to transfer a call to another destination. Call transfer is initiated by pressing the Transfer softkey on the phone and then entering the destination number.

The two types of transfer are blind and consultative. A *blind* transfer is when you transfer a call without speaking to the party you are transferring the call to. A *consultative* transfer is when you speak to the party that you are transferring the call to before the transfer is complete. By using consultative transfers, you can let the party you are transferring the call to know who is calling.

The type of transfer that will be used is a global telephony setting. This is configured using the `transfer-system` command followed by one of the keywords shown in Table 12.1.

TABLE 12.1 Keywords for the `transfer-system` Command

Keyword	Function
`blind`	Calls will be transferred blindly using a single line and a Cisco-proprietary method.
`full-blind`	Calls will be transferred blindly using a supported standard method (H.450.X).
`full-consult`	Calls will be transferred with consultation using a supported standard method (H.450.X). This is the default setting.
`local-consult`	Local calls will be transferred with consultation, but transfers to non-local numbers will be blind.

The `transfer-system` command is issued at telephony-service configuration mode. To set the system transfer to full-blind, issue the following command:

```
Router(config-telephony)# transfer-system full-blind
```

In addition to being able to set the transfer type at a global level, you can also set it on a per-ephone-dn basis and override the transfer-system setting. When setting at the ephone-dn, the `transfer-mode` command is used with either of the keywords found in Table 12.2.

TABLE 12.2 Keywords for the `transfer-mode` **Command**

Keyword	Function
blind	Calls will be transferred blindly using a single line.
consult	Calls will be transferred with consultation using a second line if one is available.

> **NOTE**
>
> When `transfer-mode` is configured on the ephone-dn, the ITU-T H.450.2 protocol is used.

To set the call transfer mode to `blind` for ephone-dn 101, use the following command:

```
Router(config)# ephone-dn 101
Router(config-ephone-dn)# transfer-mode blind
```

Just as with call forward, you can determine what destination numbers a call can be transferred to. The command to configure where calls can be transferred to is similar to the `call-forward pattern` command. For example, to allow calls to be transferred to numbers within the 248 area code, use the following command:

```
Router(config-telephony)# transfer-pattern 91248.......
```

> **EXAM ALERT**
>
> By default, calls can be transferred only to local SCCP phones. To define other numbers that calls can be transferred to, use the `transfer-pattern` command.

You can also use the keyword `blind` at the end of the `transfer-pattern` command, which forces transfers to numbers that match patterns to be done as blind transfers. This overrides both the `transfer-system` and `transfer-mode` settings. To set the transfer pattern of 91248....... to blind, use the following command:

```
Router(config-telephony)# transfer-pattern 91248....... blind
```

Call Park

Call park is a feature that allows a caller to place a call on hold that can be retrieved from another phone. Normally when you place a call on hold, you can only retrieve the call from the same line. To use the call park feature, the user presses the Park softkey followed by the number he wants to park it at. To retrieve a parked call, a user can retrieve the call by pressing the PickUp softkey and entering the number the call was parked at. To pick up a parked call from the same phone that the call was parked on, the user presses the PickUp softkey followed by the star (*) button.

EXAM ALERT

Phones do not display the Park softkey until a call park slot is configured and the phones are reset.

For call park to work, you need to configure ephone-dns as call park slots. This is done in ephone-dn configuration mode using the park-slot command. There are a number of keywords that you can use with the park-slot command, but before going into all of them, let's look at a simple park-slot example. The following is an example of the commands required to create a call park slot:

```
Router(config)# ephone-dn 121
Router(config-ephone-dn)# number 5510
Router(config-ephone-dn)# park-slot timeout 10 limit 10
```

The first command creates the ephone that will be configured as a call park slot. The second command assigns the extension of 5510 to ephone-dn 121. The third command is where the call park slot configuration is done. The first part of the command, park-slot, configures ephone-dn 121 as a call park slot. The next portion of the command, timeout 10, sets the number of seconds before a reminder ring will play in the phone that placed the call on hold. The last portion of the command, limit 10, determines the amount of times the reminder ring will occur. In other words, based on the preceding example, the reminder ring will occur 10 seconds after the call has been parked and will repeat every 10 seconds, for a total of 10 times.

The other keywords that can be used with the park-slot command are listed in Table 12.3. The italicized words are the variables that you enter.

TABLE 12.3 Keywords for the park-slot Command

Keyword	Function
reserved-for *extension number*	Reserves this park slot for the extension number that follows this keyword
timeout *seconds*	Determines the number of seconds before a reminder ring will play in the phone that placed the call on hold
limit *count*	Determines the amount of time the party that placed the call on park will be reminded that the call is still on park

TABLE 12.3 *Continued*

Keyword	Function
notify *extension number*	Sets additional extensions that will receive the reminder ring
only	Causes the reminder ring to ring only the extension defined by the notify keyword
recall	Causes the call to be returned to the phone that placed it on park after the limit count has been reached
transfer *extension number*	Defines the extension to send the call to after the limit count has been reached
alternate *extension number*	Defines the extension to send the call to after the limit count has been reached if the recall number or number set with the transfer is busy
retry *seconds*	Determines how long the delay will be before trying to recall or a transfer is attempted if the first attempt fails

Consider the following commands:

```
ephone-dn 121
number 5510
park-slot timeout 12 limit 7 notify 2002 transfer 2010 alternate 2012
```

By using the preceding commands, you configure a call park slot with the following characteristics:

- ▶ Extension 5510.

- ▶ Reminder is played every 12 seconds.

- ▶ Reminder is played seven times.

- ▶ Extension 2002 and the extension that places the call on park receive the reminder.

- ▶ The call is transferred to extension 2010 after the limit count has been reached, and if 2010 is busy, the call is transferred to 2012.

Call Pickup Groups

Call pickup allows a person to answer a call that is coming in to a line other than his own. The following three types of call pickup can be configured:

▶ **Local Group Pickup:** Allows a user to answer a call that is ringing another phone within her pickup group. If two phones within the same group are ringing, the one that has been ringing the longest is the one that will be routed. To initiate local call pickup, the user presses the PickUp softkey followed by the *.

▶ **Group Pickup (different group):** Allows a user to answer a call coming in to a phone that is not in the same call pickup group. If two phones within the same group are ringing, the one that has been ringing the longest is the one that will be routed to the phone that initiated the call pickup. To initiate local call pickup, the user presses the GPckUp softkey followed by the other group pickup number.

NOTE

If only one pickup group is defined in Cisco Unified CME, this feature can be initiated by simply pressing the PickUp softkey. The user initiating the group pickup does not need to be a member of a group.

▶ **Directed Call Pickup:** Allows a user to answer a call that is coming in on another phone. User does not need to be a member of a pickup group. This is the default configuration.

Call pickup groups are configured at ephone-dn configuration mode. To assign a call pickup group to an end user, the `pickup-group` command followed by the group number is used. The pickup-group numbers do not need to be defined separately. The group is automatically created when a group pickup number is assigned to an ephone-dn.

The following commands show how to assign the pickup group 808 to ephone-dn 101:

```
Router(config)# ephone-dn 101
Router(config-ephone-dn)# number 1000
Router(config-ephone-dn)# pickup-group 808
```

In Listing 12.1, you can examine how the different types of group pickup work.

Listing 12.1   Pickup Group Configuration

```
Router(config)# ephone-dn 101
Router(config-ephone-dn)# number 1000
Router(config-ephone-dn)# pickup-group 808
Router(config)# ephone-dn 201
Router(config-ephone-dn)# number 2000
Router(config-ephone-dn)# pickup-group 908
```

Listing 12.1 *Continued*

```
Router(config)# ephone-dn 301
Router(config-ephone-dn)# number 3000
Router(config-ephone-dn)# pickup-group 908
Router(config)# ephone-dn 401
Router(config-ephone-dn)# number 1000
```

If ephone-dn 101 wants to pick up an incoming call for ephone-dn 201, the user would have to press the GPckUp softkey followed by 908. This is because ephone-dn 101 and ephone-dn 201 are not part of the same group.

If ephone-dn 301 wants to pick up an incoming call for ephone-dn 201, the user would have to press the PickUp softkey followed by the *. This works because they are both part of the same pickup group.

If ephone-dn 401 wants to pick up an incoming call for any other ephone-dns, the user has to press the GPckUp softkey and enter the pickup group number assigned to the ephone-dn she wants to answer. This example shows that the ephone-dn does not have to be member of a pickup group to use this feature.

If ephone-dn 301 started to ring, then 201 started ringing, and ephone-dn 101 did a group pickup for group 908, the call that was ringing to ephone-dn 301 would be routed to ephone-dn 401 because the call to ephone-dn 301 arrived first.

Intercom

The Intercom feature sets up a call between two Cisco Unified CME endpoints with the press of a single button. The feature is commonly configured so that the called party's phones will autoanswer through the speaker phone; the called party's phone is also automatically muted. The audio will only be one way until the called party presses the Mute button on the phone. The intercom is assigned to a button on the phone, and that button can only be used for the Intercom function. Intercoms are commonly used between executives and their assistants. Each phone has a button configured as an Intercom button. When the button is pressed, it automatically calls the intercom line of the other phone.

The intercom configuration is done in ephone-dn configuration mode using the intercom command. This command must be followed by the extension number of the intercom on the other phone. The keywords listed in Table 12.4 can be used with the intercom command to modify its behavior.

TABLE 12.4 Keywords for the `intercom` Command

Keyword	Function
barge-in	If the called party's line is in use, the call will be forced to a hold condition and the intercom call will be connected.
no-auto-answer	Disables the Autoanswer feature for intercom lines.
label	Assigns an alphanumeric label to the line (up to 30 characters).
no-mute	Does not activate the Mute feature when on the inbound call.

Listing 12.2 shows an intercom configuration.

Listing 12.2 Intercom Configuration

```
Router(config)# ephone-dn 701
Router(config-ephone-dn)# number 4466
Router(config-ephone-dn)# intercom 5577
Router(config)# ephone-dn 702
Router(config-ephone-dn)# number 5577
Router(config-ephone-dn)# intercom 4466
Router(config)# ephone 10
Router(config-ephone)# mac-address 00CC.0001.A123.1ABF
Router(config-ephone)# button 1:101 2:701
Router(config)# ephone 20
Router(config-ephone)# mac-address 00CC.0001.A123.1ADD
Router(config-ephone)# button 1:102 2:702
```

The second button on ephone 10 is assigned the extension number of 4466 and is configured as an intercom line that will dial 5577. The second button on ephone 20 is assigned the extension number of 5577 and is configured as an intercom line that will dial 4466. Because no additional keywords were used when either party presses the Intercom button, the other party's phone will autoanswer with mute enabled. When the called party presses the Mute button (to deactivate muting), the audio will be two way.

Listing 12.3 shows a more advanced intercom configuration.

Listing 12.3 Advanced Intercom Configuration

```
Router(config)# ephone-dn 701
Router(config-ephone-dn)# number A466
Router(config-ephone-dn)# intercom B577 no-auto-answer
Router(config)# ephone-dn 702
Router(config-ephone-dn)# number B577
Router(config-ephone-dn)# intercom A466 barge-in no-mute
Router(config)# ephone 10
Router(config-ephone)# mac-address 00CC.0001.A123.1ABF
Router(config-ephone)# button 1:101 2:701
Router(config)# ephone 20
Router(config-ephone)# mac-address 00CC.0001.A123.1ADD
Router(config-ephone)# button 1:102 2:702
```

With this configuration, when the user of ephone 10 presses the second button, a two-way audio call will be set up between itself and ephone 20. If ephone-dn 702 was already in use, the active call would be placed on hold and the intercom call would be connected because the barge-in keyword is assigned to the intercom line on ephone 20. If ephone 20 pressed the second button, the call would not connect until the user of ephone 10 went off-hook because the intercom line on ephone 10 has the no-auto-answer keyword. Also, notice that the numbers assigned to the intercom ephone-dns begin with an A or a B, which makes them nondialable.

Configuring Additional Features

The following sections discuss additional features that can be configured in Cisco Unified CME but are not necessarily found in all deployments.

Paging

The Paging feature offers the ability to send a one-way audio stream to a number of ephone-dns at once. This stream is played over the speaker of the phone. The stream is sent either multicast or unicast. Multicast is preferred because it requires less total bandwidth. Keep in mind that if multicast is used, additional network configuration might be required.

Paging is configured by creating paging ephone-dns. A paging ephone-dn can be assigned to one or more ephones. The paging command is used to configure an ephone-dn as a paging ephone-dn, and the paging-dn command is used to assign a paging ephone-dn to ephones. A group of ephones that have a common paging ephone-dn are referred to as a *paging set*. For example, Listing 12.4 shows how to create a unicast paging ephone-dn with the extension number 9090 and assign ephone 10, 12, and 14 to it.

Listing 12.4   Paging Configuration

```
Router(config)# ephone-dn 901
Router(config-ephone-dn)# number 9090
Router(config-ephone-dn)# paging
Router(config)# ephone 10
Router(config-ephone)# mac-address 00CC.0001.A123.1ABF
Router(config-ephone)# button 1:101
Router(config-ephone)# paging-dn 901
Router(config)# ephone 12
Router(config-ephone)# mac-address 00CC.0001.A123.1ADD
Router(config-ephone)# button 1:102
Router(config-ephone)# paging-dn 901
Router(config)# ephone 14
Router(config-ephone)# mac-address 00CC.0001.A123.CCDD
Router(config-ephone)# button 1:103
Router(config-ephone)# paging-dn 901
```

Based on this example, when a user dials 9090, this causes ephones 10, 12, and 14 to autoanswer on the speaker phone and creates a one-way audio stream.

As mentioned previously, the paging stream can be unicast or multicast. To configure multicast, you need to define the IP address and port number on the paging command. When doing this, keep in mind that the Cisco IP phones do not support multicast to 224.x.x.x.

Paging groups can also be created. A paging group is a group of paging ephone-dns. By creating a paging group, you can combine a number of paging sets into one larger group. For example, if you had ephones in three different paging sets, you could create one paging group that would send a page to all the ephones.

EXAM ALERT

Paging groups are configured in ephone-dn configuration mode using the paging-group command.

Listing 12.5 shows the configuration for two paging ephone-dns and one paging group ephone-dn. This listing is also using multicast.

Listing 12.5   Paging Group Configuration

```
Router(config)# ephone-dn 901
Router(config-ephone-dn)# number 9090
Router(config-ephone-dn)# paging 239.1.1.2 port 2000
Router(config)# ephone-dn 902
Router(config-ephone-dn)# number 9091
Router(config-ephone-dn)# paging 239.1.1.3 port 2000
Router(config)# ephone-dn 903
Router(config-ephone-dn)# number 9092
Router(config-ephone-dn)# paging 239.1.1.4 port 2000
Router(config-ephone-dn)# paging-group 901,902
Router(config)# ephone 10
Router(config-ephone)# mac-address 00CC.0001.A123.1ABF
Router(config-ephone)# button 1:101
Router(config-ephone)# paging-dn 901
Router(config)# ephone 12
Router(config-ephone)# mac-address 00CC.0001.A123.1ADD
Router(config-ephone)# button 1:102
Router(config-ephone)# paging-dn 902
Router(config)# ephone 14
Router(config-ephone)# mac-address 00CC.0001.A123.CCDD
Router(config-ephone)# button 1:103
Router(config-ephone)# paging-dn 902
```

Based on this example, if a user dials 9090, the page is sent to ephone 101. If a caller dials 9091, the page is sent to ephones 102 and 103. If a caller dials 9092, the page is sent to ephones 101, 102, and 103.

MOH

Music on Hold (MOH) is a feature that allows callers to hear an audio stream while they are on hold. MOH does not play music for local devices, that is, a phone that is registered to the Cisco Unified CME. These callers simply hear a tone repeated at intervals. The audio source that is played is a .wav or .au file that is in flash. The file format must be 8-bit 8kHz a-law or mu-law.

After the audio file is copied to flash, it is activated by using the moh command followed by the name of the audio file. For example, the moh companymusic.wav command would cause the file named companymusic.wav to serve as the audio callers heard when they are placed on hold. All MOH commands are entered in telephony-service configuration mode.

By default, unicast is used unless MOH is configured to use multicast. Multicast can be enabled by issuing the multicast moh command. The multicast IP address and port must follow this command. The following examples show how to configure a Cisco Unified CME to play the companymusic.wav file using multicast:

```
moh companymusic.wav
multicast moh 239.1.1.2 port 2000
```

You can specify an interface on the router that should transmit multicast packets by using the route keyword followed by the IP address of the interface. You can specify up to four interfaces on the line. To specify multiple interfaces, simply list them one after the other, with a space separating them.

The following commands set up MOH to use multicast on IP address 239.1.1.2 and port 2000. They also specify that the interfaces with 10.10.10.10 and 12.1.1.1 should transmit the multicast stream.

```
moh companymusic.wav
multicast moh 239.1.1.2 port 2000 route 10.10.10.10 12.1.1.1
```

To change the audio file, you need to copy the new one to the flash, disable MOH using the no moh command, and then enter the moh command with the name of the new file. The following example shows the commands used to change the MOH audio file to corpann.au:

```
no moh
moh coprann.au
```

Directory Services

Users on the Cisco Unified CME can look up the numbers of other users using the Directory button on the phone. For this to work, the administrator needs to ensure that names are associated with ephone-dns. This is done using the `name` command in ephone-dn configuration. The command is quite simple: You simply enter the command name followed by the name of the user. The following is an example of how the name Al McMorris would be added to ephone-dn 101:

```
Router(config)# ephone-dn 101
Router(config-ephone-dn)# number 7001
Router(config-ephone-dn)# name Al McMorris
```

After you have names associated with ephone-dns, you can define the order that the names will appear: first name first or last name first. The `directory` command is used to determine this. To have the first name listed first, use the `first-name-first` keyword. To have the last name listed first, use the `first-name-last` keyword. The default is `first-name-first`. Use the following command to set the directory to last name first:

```
Router(config-telephony)# directory first-name-last
```

> **NOTE**
>
> Make sure that when you associate names to the ephone-dn you use the same format that is selected using the `directory` command. So, if you selected `first-name-last`, make sure that you enter the last name first with the `name` command.

You can also add names and numbers to the directory that do not belong to phones in the system. This is useful for outside numbers that many users need to dial from time to time. The command to add an outside name and number to the directory is `directory entry`. This command is followed by a directory tag (also referred to as an entry tag), number, and name. The directory tag is similar to the tags assigned to ephones and ephone-dns, but the only numbers that can be used are 1–99. This means that you can only add 99 outside numbers to the directory. The following is an example of the command used to add and outside number:

```
Router(config-telephony)# directory entry 12 2485470903 name ACME
```

In this example, the number 12 is the directory tag and 2485470903 is the number that is assigned the ACME name in the directory. The `name` keyword is required before the actual name, that is, the only keyword in this command.

Call Blocking

It is common to want to restrict certain types of calls from being placed by all or some phones or during certain times of the day. For example, you might want to prevent long-distance calls from being placed after hours to prevent any after-hours workers from placing this type of call. The call blocking feature allows you to configure this.

Call blocking is configured from telephony-service configuration mode using the `after-hours` command. Call blocking is configured by first defining the time of day and the days of the week or the date that you want to have the calls blocked. Then you define the types of calls that are blocked by defining patterns.

To block international calls on Saturday from 2:00 p.m. until midnight and all day Sunday, use the following commands:

```
Router(config-telephony)# after-hours day sat 14:00 23:59
Router(config-telephony)# after-hours day sun 00:00 00:00
Router(config-telephony)# after-hours block pattern 1 9011
```

The last line defines the pattern. The 1 following the `pattern` keyword is a tag. Each pattern must have a unique tag. This example assumes that a 9 must be dialed to make an outside call. So, because a 9 must be dialed and 011 is dialed to make international calls, 9011 matches international calls. The first two lines of this example define the time and days that this pattern will be blocked.

The day/times you define as after hours apply to all the patterns. That is, you cannot apply different day/times to different patterns. The one exception to this is that you can block specific patterns all hours/all days by adding 7-24 to the end of the `after-hours block` command. To block 11-digit calls Saturday from 2:00 p.m. until midnight and all day Sunday and international calls all days/all hours, use the following commands:

```
Router(config-telephony)# after-hours day sat 14:00 23:59
Router(config-telephony)# after-hours day sun 00:00 00:00
Router(config-telephony)# after-hours block pattern 1 91.......... 7-24
Router(config-telephony)# after-hours block pattern 2 9011
```

You can also configure some phones to override call blocking. There are two ways to configure this, as follows:

▶ Configure an ephone as exempt from call blocking.

▶ Configure an override code for an ephone.

To configure after-hours exemption, use the `after-hours exempt` command at ephone configuration mode. Any ephone that this command is applied to is exempt from call blocking configuration. Typically, this is only used on phones that are in secure locations.

For phones that are in less secure locations, a personal identification number (PIN) can be applied to the ephone. Call blocking can then be overridden by entering the PIN. PINs do not override patterns that have the `7-24` keyword applied. To use this feature, the caller must press the Login softkey and enter the PIN assigned to the ephone. If the correct PIN is entered, call blocking is overridden. PINs are configured on ephones by using the `pin` command. The following example shows how to configure a PIN to ephone 12:

```
Router(config)# ephone 12
Router(config-ephone)# mac-address 00CC.0001.A123.1ADD
Router(config-ephone)# button 1:102
Router(config-ephone)# pin 3371
```

Based on this example, if the user at ephone 12 wants to place a call that is blocked due to after-hours call blocking, he can override the call blocking by pressing the Login softkey and entering 3371. By default, call blocking override remains active for 60 minutes after the PIN is entered, or midnight, whichever comes first. This time can be adjusted by defining a login timeout value. The login timeout is defined at telephony-service configuration mode using the `login` command. You can set a timeout value and a time of day that all logins are cleared. To set a timeout value of 30 minutes and set all logins to be cleared at 5:00 p.m., issue the following command:

```
Router(config-telephony)# login timeout 30 clear 1700
```

Notice in this example that the clear time is set using the 24-hour clock format. So, based on this example, when a user logs in using the PIN assigned to the ephone, call blocking will be overridden for 30 minutes or until 5:00 p.m., whichever comes first.

Call Accounting

Some companies like to track calls placed by client codes or account numbers. This is often done for cost-accounting purposes. Cisco Unified CME allows you to assign an account number to calls. The user can assign an account number to a call by pressing the Acct softkey followed by the number she wants to assign and then pressing the # key. Doing this causes the account number to be assigned to this call in the call detail records (CDRs).

NOTE

When the Acct softkey is pressed, the call is placed on hold while the account code is being entered.

Exam Prep Questions

1. Which of the following call forwarding configurations is incorrect?

   ○ **A.** `Router(config)# ephone-dn 101`

      `Router(config-ephone-dn)# call-forward busy 2000`

   ○ **B.** `Router(config)# ephone-dn 101`

      `Router(config-ephone-dn)# call-forward all 2000`

   ○ **C.** `Router(config)# ephone-dn 101`

      `Router(config-ephone-dn)# call-forward no-answer 2000`

   ○ **D.** None of the call forwarding configurations provided is incorrect.

2. Which command sets call transfer to transfer blindly using a single line and a Cisco-proprietary method?

   ○ **A.** `Router(config-telephony)# transfer-system full-blind`

   ○ **B.** `Router(config-telephony)# transfer-system blind`

   ○ **C.** `Router(config-telephony)# transfer-system blind-only`

   ○ **D.** `Router(config-telephony)# transfer-system local-blind`

3. Which of the following statements about call pickup is correct?

   ○ **A.** Directed Call Pickup allows a user to answer a call that is coming in on another phone.

   ○ **B.** Group Pickup allows a user to answer a call coming into a phone that is in the same call pickup group.

   ○ **C.** Local Group Pickup allows a user to answer a call that is ringing another phone within his pickup group. If two phones within the same group are ringing, the user will be prompted to select either of them.

   ○ **D.** Ephones can have only one pickup group assigned.

4. A customer wants an intercom line set up between a manager and assistant. When the manager presses the Intercom button, the customer wants two-way audio set up, regardless of the status of the assistant's phone. How would you configure this?

   ○ **A.** Using the `auto-mode` command in the intercom configuration.

   ○ **B.** Using the `no-auto-answer` feature.

   ○ **C.** By enabling barge-in on the manager's phone.

   ○ **D.** None of the options provided is correct.

5. Which statements about paging are correct? (Choose two.)

- ○ **A.** The paging stream can be unicast or multicast.
- ○ **B.** Additional configuration is required for unicast.
- ○ **C.** Multicast is preferred because it requires less total bandwidth.
- ○ **D.** Paging groups are configured in ephone configuration mode using the `paging-group` command.

6. A customer has the following requirements for MOH:

- ▶ The current sales specials are played to all calls that are on hold.
- ▶ The audio source file must be in `.wav` format.
- ▶ The stream must be sent using multicast.
- ▶ Two router interfaces must be configured to transmit the stream.

Based on these requirements, which of the following statements is true?

- ○ **A.** All requirements can be met.
- ○ **B.** Because MOH must be sent using both unicast and multicast, all the requirements cannot be met.
- ○ **C.** The stream can only be transmitted out one interface, so all the requirements cannot be met.
- ○ **D.** The source file must be in `.au` format, so all the requirements cannot be met.
- ○ **E.** None of the provided answer options is true.

7. A customer wants to be able to add outside names and numbers to the directory and wants to know whether any limitations exist. What would you tell the customer?

- ○ **A.** The only limitation is that the names can be 8 characters long.
- ○ **B.** There are no limitations.
- ○ **C.** You can only add 50 outside names and numbers to the directory.
- ○ **D.** You can only add 99 names and numbers.

8. When implementing call blocking, how do you allow a phone to override call blocking?

- ○ **A.** Assign a PIN to the ephone-dn.
- ○ **B.** Use the `override` keyword at the end of the `after-hours pattern` command.
- ○ **C.** Assign the `after-hours exempt` command on the ephone.
- ○ **D.** Set the call blocking privileges so that the override is allowed.

9. Which statement about call accounting is incorrect?

   ○ **A.** When the Acct softkey is pressed, the call is placed on hold.

   ○ **B.** The user can assign an account number to a call by pressing the Acct softkey.

   ○ **C.** Cisco Unified CME allows you to assign an account number to calls.

   ○ **D.** Account codes are preconfigured by the administrator.

10. Which of the following sets of commands would be used to create a paging ephone-dn?

    ○ **A.** Router(config)# **ephone 901**

    　　　Router(config-ephone)# **number 9090**

    　　　Router(config-ephone)# **paging**

    ○ **B.** Router(config)# **ephone-dn 901**

    　　　Router(config-ephone-dn)# **number 9090**

    　　　Router(config-ephone-dn)# **paging**

    ○ **C.** Router(config)# **ephone-dn 901**

    　　　Router(config-ephone-dn)# **number 9090**

    　　　Router(config-ephone-dn)# **paging-dn**

    ○ **D.** Router(config)# **ephone-dn 901**

    　　　Router(config-ephone-dn)# **number 9090**

    　　　Router(config-ephone-dn)# **paging-group**

Answers to Exam Prep Questions

1. **C.** The no-answer keyword is not valid for call forwarding. Answers A and B are valid commands for call forwarding. Answer D is incorrect.

2. **B.** The blind keyword sets the call transfer to transfer blindly using a single line and a Cisco-proprietary method. Answer A is incorrect because the full-blind keyword sets the call transfer to transfer blindly using supported standard methods. Answer C is incorrect because blind-only is an invalid keyword. Answer D is incorrect because local-blind is an invalid keyword.

3. **A.** Directed Call Pickup allows a user to answer a call that is coming in on another phone. Answer B is incorrect because Group Pickup allows a user to answer a call coming in to a phone that is not in the same call pickup group. Answer C is incorrect because if two phones within the same group are ringing, the one that has been ringing the longest will be routed. Answer D is incorrect because pickup groups are assigned ephone-dns, not ephones.

4. **D.** Answer A is incorrect because `auto-mode` is not a valid command. Answer B is incorrect because `no-auto-answer` would disable autoanswer and autoanswer needs to be enabled for the intercom to work as the customer desires. Answer C is incorrect because `barge-in` should be enabled on the assistant's phone.

5. **A and C.** The paging stream can be unicast or multicast, and multicast is preferred because it requires less total bandwidth. Answer B is incorrect because it is multicast that might require additional configuration. Answer D is incorrect because the `paging-group` command is issued in ephone-dn configuration mode, not ephone configuration mode.

6. **E.** None of the answer options is true. Answer A is incorrect because MOH will not be played to all phones because it does not play to internal phones. Answer B is incorrect because MOH can use unicast or multicast; it does not have to use both. Answer C is incorrect. The stream can be transmitted out up to four interfaces. Answer D is incorrect because the file can be a `.wav` or `.au` file.

7. **D.** You can only add 99 names and numbers. Answer A is incorrect because names do not have an 8-character limit. Answer B is incorrect because the directory does have some limitations. Answer C is incorrect because you can have up to 99 outside names and numbers.

8. **C.** You assign the `after-hours exempt` command on the ephone to allow a phone to override call blocking. Answer A is incorrect because a PIN is assigned to an ephone, not an ephone-dn. Answer B is incorrect because `override` is not a valid keyword. Answer D is incorrect because you do not set call blocking privileges.

9. **D.** Account codes are not preconfigured by the administrator. Answers A, B, and C are all incorrect because they are valid statements.

10. **B.** Answer A is incorrect because a paging ephone-dn must be created in ephone-dn configuration mode, not ephone configuration mode. Answer C is incorrect because the command to make an ephone-dn a paging ephone-dn is `paging`, not `paging-dn`. Answer D is incorrect because the command to make an ephone-dn a paging ephone-dn is `paging`, not `paging-group`.

Suggested Reading and Resources

1. Search Cisco.com for "Cisco Unified Communications Manager Express Reference."

CHAPTER THIRTEEN

Maintaining and Troubleshooting Cisco Unified CME

Terms you need to understand:

✓ Command-line interface (CLI)

✓ Trivial File Transfer Protocol (TFTP)

✓ File Transfer Protocol (FTP)

✓ Dial peers

Techniques you need to master:

✓ Set up Cisco Unified CME to provide TFTP and FTP backup and restore capabilities

✓ Activate, deactivate, and view Cisco Unified CME CLI debug commands

✓ Use show commands to verify call-agent operation

After Cisco Unified CME is installed and operating, administrators must be able to identify and correct problems incurred for adds, moves, and changes. This chapter describes the protocols used to back up the Cisco Unified CME configuration.

This chapter also describes the use of show and debug commands. Using the CLI debug commands can impact call processing and should be used during low-call-volume periods and disabled when the troubleshooting issue is resolved.

Backup and Restore

There are two different protocols that you can use to back up Cisco Unified Communications Manager Express (CME): TFTP and FTP. Figure 13.1 is a typical setup for maintaining configuration backups.

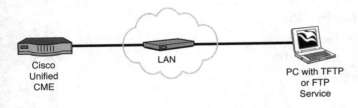

FIGURE 13.1   Maintain and manage Cisco Unified CME configurations.

There are several TFTP and FTP freeware packages available to provide the TFTP and FTP services on a local PC. Listing 13.1 shows the interactive back-up process.

Listing 13.1   Interactive Backup Process

```
CUCME# copy running-config tftp

Address or name of remote host []? 192.168.10.148
Destination filename [cucme-confg]?
!!
16123 bytes copied in 2.776 secs (5808 bytes/sec)
CUCME#
```

Listing 13.2 shows a single command to back up the configuration. This is useful for building configuration backup scripts for multiple devices. Make sure that you add two extra carriage return/line feed (CR/LF) combinations after the single line to bypass the host name and filename verifications.

Listing 13.2   Back Up the Configuration with a Single Command

```
srvrsw# copy running-config tftp://192.168.10.148/cucme-config-11-11-2008

Address or name of remote host [192.168.10.148]?
Destination filename [cucme-config-11-11-2008]?
!!
4553 bytes copied in 0.792 secs (5749 bytes/sec)
srvrsw#
```

You can use FTP to back up Cisco Unified CME configurations. As shown in Listing 13.3, the file transfer fails if you do not create an FTP username and password before attempting a transfer.

Listing 13.3   Failed FTP Backup

```
CUCME# copy running-config ftp

Address or name of remote host []? 192.168.10.148
Destination filename [cucme`-confg]?
%Error opening ftp://192.168.10.148/cmex-confg (Incorrect Login/Password)
```

You must create a valid FTP username and password and run it again, as shown in Listing 13.4.

Listing 13.4   Successful FTP Backup

```
CUCME (config)# ip ftp user backup
CUCME(config)# ip ftp password backup00!
CUCME(config)# ^Z
CUCME# copy running-config ftp

Address or name of remote host []? 192.168.10.148
Destination filename [cucme-confg]?
Writing cucme-confg !
16130 bytes copied in 8.460 secs (1907 bytes/sec)
CUCME#
```

TIP

Use the FTP service when you are uploading new IOS versions; the upload time is greatly reduced.

EXAM ALERT

Remember to use the FTP username and password for backing up and restoring configurations.

Troubleshooting the Cisco Unified CME Installation

Cisco Unified CME tends to operate without intervention after the appropriate installation features and functions have been configured, tested, and verified. In this section, we cover tools that you can use to make troubleshooting the installation much easier.

Initial IP Phone Activation and Registration Issues

One of the most common issues is to complete all the correct setups for telephony service, add the correct ephone-dns and ephones, and copy all the appropriate IP phone operating files to flash—and the phones still won't operate. The `debug tftp events` command is one of the clearest methods for tracking the initial registration process. Listing 13.5 shows the output generated by an IP phone attempting and failing to retrieve its configuration file.

Listing 13.5   Debug TFTP Events

```
CUCME# terminal monitor
CUCME# debug tftp events

TFTP Event debugging is on
Sep 20 20:37:47.887: TFTP: Looking for CTLSEP00036BAAC71D.tlv
Sep 20 20:37:47.959: TFTP: Looking for SEP00036BAAC71D.cnf.xml
Sep 20 20:37:48.055: TFTP: Looking for XMLDefault.cnf.xml
Sep 20 20:37:49.399: TFTP: Opened system:/its/XMLDefault.cnf.xml, fd 7,
➥size 2679 for process 65
Sep 20 20:37:49.419: TFTP: Finished system:/its/XMLDefault.cnf.xml, time
➥00:00:00 for process 65
Sep 20 20:37:49.555: %IPPHONE-6-REG_ALARM: 13: Name=SEP00036BAAC71D
➥Load=8.0(9.0) Last=CM-aborted-TCP
CUCME# no debug all
```

EXAM ALERT

If you telnet into the Cisco Unified CME router, don't forget to use the `terminal monitor` command before entering your debug command. Use the `terminal no monitor` command and either the `no debug all` command or the `undebug all` command when you have solved the issue.

The four most common issues that prevent the IP phones from registering relate to the omitting the following commands, which are covered in more detail in Chapter 10, "Configuring Cisco Unified CME to Support Endpoints":

- ▶ The `load` command under `telephony-service`
- ▶ The `ip source` command under `telephony-service`
- ▶ The `create cnf-files` command under `telephony-service`
- ▶ The `tftp-server` global commands for *all* the files required to activate the IP phone

The `show telephony-service` command can be used to verify the first three of the preceding issues, and the `show run` command can be used to verify the last issue.

EXAM ALERT

Verify these four issues because they typically are responsible for 80 percent of all IP phone registration errors when installing a Cisco Unified CME platform, either through omission or incorrect configuration.

The `load` command identifies the IP phone software image that is compatible with the current version of IOS software on the router:

```
telephony-service
. . .
 load 7931 SCCP31.8-3-3S
 load 7961 SCCP41.8-3-3S
```

CAUTION

These `load` commands reference a `.loads` file that must be configured to initiate the synchronization of the Cisco Unified CME IOS and the IP phone.

The `ip source` command creates the contact point for all TFTP and registration requests on the Cisco Unified CME host:

```
telephony-service
. . .
 ip source-address 10.6.150.1 port 2000
```

The `create cnf-files` and `cnf-file perphone` commands should be used to create a specific file for each phone to simplify troubleshooting a specific IP phone:

```
telephony-service
. . .
 cnf-file perphone
 create cnf-files
```

The `tftp-server` command activates the Cisco Unified CME TFTP process for a specific file. The newer Cisco IP phones have complex operating system files that are downloaded individually based on the instructions in the `.loads` file. Listing 13.6 shows the files required for a Cisco 7931 IP Phone.

Listing 13.6   Files Required for a Cisco 7931 IP Phone

```
tftp-server flash:/apps31.8-3-2-27.sbn alias apps31.8-3-2-27.sbn
tftp-server flash:/cnu31.8-3-2-27.sbn alias cnu31.8-3-2-27.sbn
tftp-server flash:/cvm31sccp.8-3-2-27.sbn alias cvm31sccp.8-3-2-27.sbn
tftp-server flash:/dsp31.8-3-2-27.sbn alias dsp31.8-3-2-27.sbn
tftp-server flash:/jar31sccp.8-3-2-27.sbn alias jar31sccp.8-3-2-27.sbn
tftp-server flash:/SCCP31.8-3-3S.loads alias SCCP31.8-3-3S.loads
tftp-server flash:/term31.default.loads alias term31.default.loads
```

NOTE

Verify these files using the release notes on Cisco.com for the Cisco Unified CME IOS version.

Common show Commands Used to Verify CUCME Operations

The following are samples of show commands used to troubleshoot and verify Cisco Unified CME operation.

show ephone

The show ephone command can provide basic or detailed information about an individual phone, all phones of a specific type, just the registered phone, and many other options. In Listing 13.7, not all phone types are shown to reduce the list of options for this command. Listings 13.7 through 13.9 show variations of the show ephone command.

Listing 13.7   The show ephone Command Option Output

```
CME# show ephone ?

. . .
  7911                  Cisco IP Phone 7911
. . .
  7941                  Cisco IP Phone 7941
. . .
  7961                  Cisco IP Phone 7961
  7961GE                Cisco IP Phone 7961GE
  7962                  Cisco IP Phone 7962
  7965                  Cisco IP Phone 7965
. . .
```

Listing 13.7 *Continued*

```
CIPC                      Cisco IP Communicator
H.H.H                     mac address
anl                       SCCP Gateway (AN)
ata                       ATA  phone emulation for analog phone
attempted-registrations   Attempted ephone list
bri                       SCCP Gateway (BR)
cfa                       registered ephones with call-forward-all set
dn                        Dn with tag assigned
dnd                       registered ephones with do-not-disturb set
login                     phone login status
offhook                   Offhook phone status
overlay                   registered ephones with overlay DNs
phone-load                Ephone phoneload information
registered                Registered ephone status
remote                    non-local phones (with no arp entry)
ringing                   Ringing phone status
sockets                   Active ephone sockets
summary                   Summary of all ephone
tapiclients               Ephone status of tapi client
telephone-number          Telephone number assigned
unregistered              Unregistered ephone status
vgc-phone                 vg248 phone emulation for analog phone
|                         Output modifiers
<cr>
```

Listing 13.8 **The** show **ephone Command Output**

CME# **show ephone**

```
ephone-1[0] Mac:001E.7AC3.9460 TCP socket:[1] activeLine:0 REGISTERED in
➥SCCP ver 12/9
mediaActive:0 offhook:0 ringing:0 reset:0 reset_sent:0 paging 0 debug:0
➥caps:8
IP:10.1.3.34 49759 7961  keepalive 14383 max_line 6
button 1: dn 1   number 2101 CH1    IDLE          CH2    IDLE
Preferred Codec: g711ulaw
Username: abrown Password: cisco

ephone-3[2] Mac:001B.D508.6693 TCP socket:[3] activeLine:0 REGISTERED in
➥SCCP ver 12/9
mediaActive:0 offhook:0 ringing:0 reset:0 reset_sent:0 paging 0 debug:0
➥caps:9
IP:10.1.3.32 52326 7931  keepalive 14457 max_line 24
button 1: dn 3   number 2103 CH1    IDLE
Preferred Codec: g711ulaw
Username: asmith Password: 123
```

Listing 13.8 *Continued*

```
ephone-4[3] Mac:4000.0000.1234 TCP socket:[-1] activeLine:0 UNREGISTERED
mediaActive:0 offhook:0 ringing:0 reset:0 reset_sent:0 paging 0 debug:0
➥caps:0
IP:0.0.0.0 0 Unknown 0  keepalive 0 max_line 0
Preferred Codec: g711ulaw
```

Listing 13.9 The show ephone registered **Command Output**

```
CME# show ephone registered

ephone-1[0] Mac:001E.7AC3.9460 TCP socket:[1] activeLine:0 REGISTERED in
➥SCCP ver 12/9
mediaActive:0 offhook:0 ringing:0 reset:0 reset_sent:0 paging 0 debug:0
➥caps:8
IP:10.1.3.34 49759 7961  keepalive 14385 max_line 6
button 1: dn 1  number 2101 CH1    IDLE           CH2    IDLE
Preferred Codec: g711ulaw
Username: abrown Password: cisco

ephone-3[2] Mac:001B.D508.6693 TCP socket:[3] activeLine:0 REGISTERED in
➥SCCP ver 12/9
mediaActive:0 offhook:0 ringing:0 reset:0 reset_sent:0 paging 0 debug:0
➥caps:9
IP:10.1.3.32 52326 7931  keepalive 14459 max_line 24
button 1: dn 3  number 2103 CH1    IDLE
Preferred Codec: g711ulaw
Username: asmith Password: 123
```

show ephone-dn

The show ephone-dn command provides detailed information on the configuration of each directory number assigned in the Cisco Unified CME to phones and features. Listings 13.10 through 13.12 show variations of the show ephone-dn command.

Listing 13.10 The show ephone-dn **Command Options Output**

```
CME# show ephone-dn ?

  <1-144>     dn tag
  callback    Show ephone-dn with pending callback set
  conference  Show ephone-dn in conference mode
  loopback    Show ephone-dn in loopback mode
  park        Show ephone-dn configured as park-slots
  statistics  Show ephone-dn most recent call statistics
  summary     Summary of all ephone-dn
  |           Output modifiers
  <cr>
```

Listing 13.11 The show ephone-dn Command Output

```
CME# show ephone-dn

50/0/1 CH1    IDLE          CH2    IDLE

EFXS 50/0/1 Slot is 50, Sub-unit is 0, Port is 1
Type of VoicePort is EFXS
Operation State is DORMANT
Administrative State is UP
No Interface Down Failure
Description is not set
Noise Regeneration is enabled
Non Linear Processing is enabled
Non Linear Mute is disabled
Non Linear Threshold is -21 dB
Music On Hold Threshold is Set to -38 dBm
In Gain is Set to 0 dB
Out Attenuation is Set to 0 dB
Echo Cancellation is enabled
Echo Cancellation NLP mute is disabled
Echo Cancellation NLP threshold is -21 dB
Echo Cancel Coverage is set to 8 ms
Echo Cancel worst case ERL is set to 6 dB
Playout-delay Mode is set to adaptive
Playout-delay Nominal is set to 60 ms
       . . .
```

Listing 13.12 The show ephone-dn statistics Command Output

```
CME1# show ephone-dn 1 statistics

DN 1 chan 1 incoming 1 answered 0 outgoing 19 answered 14 busy 0
Far-end disconnect at: connect 1 alert 0 hold 0 ring 1
Last 64 far-end disconnect cause codes
0 16 28 19 0 0 0 0 0 0 0 0 0 0 0 0
0 0 0 0 0 0 0 0 0 0 0 0 0 0 0 0
0 0 0 0 0 0 0 0 0 0 0 0 0 0 0 0
0 0 0 0 0 0 0 0 0 0 0 0 0 0 0 0
local phone on-hook
```

The following URL defines cause codes:

http://www.quintum.com/support/xplatform/ivr_acct/webhelp/Disconnect_
Cause_Codes.htm

show telephony-service

The show telephony-service command is used to verify the operation of the Cisco Unified CME call-agent. Listings 13.13 through 13.15 show variations of the show telephony-service command.

Listing 13.13 The show telephony-service Command Options Output

```
CME# show telephony-service ?

  admin                 Show telephony-service admin username and password
  all                   Show telephony-service details
  bulk-speed-dial       Show Bulk Speed dial Info
  conference            Show telephony-service conferences
  dial-peer             Show telephony-service dialpeers
  directory-entry       Show telephony-service directory-entry
  ephone                Show ephone configuration
  ephone-dn             Show ephone-dn configuration
  ephone-dn-template    Show ephone-dn-template configuration
  ephone-template       Show ephone-template configuration
  fac                   Show Feature Access Code List
  tftp-bindings         Show telephony-service tftp-server bindings
  user-defined-locale   Show User Defined Locales
  voice-port            Show telephony-service voice ports
  |                     Output modifiers
  <cr>
```

Listing 13.14 The show telephony-service voice-port Command Output

```
CME# show telephony-service voice-port

voice-port 50/0/1
! Slot 50 is used to create EFXS ports to
 station-id number 2101
! represent ephone-dns.
 timeout ringing 10
!
voice-port 50/0/3
 station-id number 2103
 timeout ringing 10
!
voice-port 50/0/4
 station-id number 2104
!
```

Listing 13.15   The `show telephony-service` Command Output

```
CME# show telephony-service

CONFIG (Version=4.3(0))
=====================
Version 4.3(0)
Cisco Unified Communications Manager Express
For on-line documentation please see:
www.cisco.com/univercd/cc/td/doc/product/access/ip_ph/ip_ks/index.htm

ip source-address 10.1.150.1 port 2000
no auto-reg-ephone
load 7931 SCCP31.8-3-3S
load 7961 SCCP41.8-3-3S
max-ephones 42
max-dn 100
max-conferences 8 gain -6
dspfarm units 0
dspfarm transcode sessions 0
conference software
privacy
no privacy-on-hold
hunt-group report delay 1 hours
hunt-group logout DND
max-redirect 5
voicemail 2190
 —More—
```

EXAM ALERT

Use the `show telephony-service` command to verify the Cisco Unified CME version number because the additional phone image files and scripting files must be synchronized to this version.

Exam Prep Questions

1. Which of the following commands is used to generate configuration files for the IP phones connected to a Cisco Unified CME host?

   ○ **A.** `config-generate`

   ○ **B.** `create-cnf`

   ○ **C.** `cnf-file perphone`

   ○ **D.** `tftp-server <url>`

   ○ **E.** `load <phone type> <filename>`

2. Which of the following protocols can be used to back up a Cisco Unified CME configuration to an external device? (Choose two.)

   ○ **A.** FTP

   ○ **B.** SCCP

   ○ **C.** SMTP

   ○ **D.** SIP

   ○ **E.** TFTP

3. If you turn on debugging from the CLI of the Cisco Unified CME and no output appears on the screen, which of the following commands could help?

   ○ **A.** `show debug output`

   ○ **B.** `terminal monitor`

   ○ **C.** `debug ephone`

   ○ **D.** `show ephone`

4. Which of the following commands provides a list of all the Cisco Unified CME–registered IP phones?

   ○ **A.** `show ephone registered`

   ○ **B.** `terminal monitor`

   ○ **C.** `debug ephone registration`

   ○ **D.** `show debug output`

5. Which of the following IOS CLI commands displays the Cisco Unified CME version number?

   O **A.** show debug output

   O **B.** show version

   O **C.** show ephone

   O **D.** show telephony-service

   O **E.** show ephone-dn

6. Which of the following commands are used to verify features programmed on ephone-dns? (Choose two.)

   O **A.** show ephone-dn feature

   O **B.** show ephone-dn park

   O **C.** show ephone park

   O **D.** show telephony-service

   O **E.** show ephone-dn conference

7. Which of the following commands can be used to verify three of the most common issues encountered during IP phone registration problems?

   O **A.** show ephone-dn

   O **B.** show voice-port

   O **C.** show ephone registered

   O **D.** show telephony-service

   O **E.** show ephone unregistered

8. Which of the following commands permits the user to view debug output over a Telnet connection the Cisco Unified CME device?

   O **A.** telnet

   O **B.** terminal no monitor

   O **C.** tftp

   O **D.** terminal monitor

Answers to Exam Prep Questions

1. **B.** The `create-cnf` command under telephony-service generates configuration files for the IP phones connected to a Cisco Unified CME host. Answer A is an invalid command, answer C defines the type of configuration files generated, answer D provides access to the phone image files stored in flash, and answer E directs phones to the correct image control file that defines which image files should be downloaded, so these answers are incorrect.

2. **A and E.** You can use FTP and TFTP to back up a Cisco Unified CME configuration to an external device. Answer C is incorrect because SMTP is an email protocol. Answers B and D, SCCP and SIP, are used for IP phone call control and are incorrect.

3. **B.** The `terminal monitor` command helps you determine why no output appears on-screen. Answer A is an invalid command; answer C is used to troubleshoot ephone registration operations, and answer D is used to verify current ephone operational status as well as many other options and are incorrect.

4. **A.** The `show ephone registered` command provides a list of all the Cisco Unified CME–registered IP phones. Answer D is an invalid command, answer B activates console message output for Telnet sessions, and answer C is used to troubleshoot ephone registration operations and are incorrect.

5. **D.** The `show ephone-dns` command displays the Cisco Unified CME version number. Answer A is an invalid command, answer B displays the IOS version but not the Cisco Unified CME version, answer C displays the current information on all configured ephones, and answer E displays the information for all configured ephone-dns and are incorrect.

6. **B and E.** These commands display the ephone-dns assigned to the conference and park features. Answers A and C are invalid commands, and answer D is used for an overview of all features, so these answers are incorrect.

7. **D.** This command highlights the source IP address, phone load information, and the configuration file generation status. Answer A shows directory numbers, answer B is used for PSTN connections, answer C shows registered ephones, and answer E is an invalid command and they are all incorrect.

8. **D.** The `terminal monitor` command is correct. Answer A is incorrect because it is used to establish the connection, answer B is incorrect because it is used to initiate a file transfer, and answer C is incorrect because it disables displaying debug output on a Telnet session.

PART IV

Cisco Smart Business Communications System

CHAPTER FOURTEEN

Introducing the Smart Business Communications System

Terms you need to understand:

✓ Smart Business Communications System

✓ Cisco Configuration Assistant

Techniques you need to master:

✓ Understand the features of Cisco Unified Communications 500 series devices

✓ Understand the features of the Cisco Configuration Assistant

As you know by now, Cisco Unified Communications Manager Express (CME) supports up to 250 users, which is ideal for a medium-size office. But what about offices with less than 50 users? While the Cisco Unified CME would work for small offices, these offices often desire a compact all-in-one solution. This is where the Smart Business Communications System (SBCS) comes in. The SBCS provides telephony, wireless, and security features to up to 50 users.

SBCS Overview

The SBCS provides a cost-effect, easy-to-deploy and -manage communications solution for small offices. The aim is to offer a complete communications solution that is not just voice. The SBCS offers switching, routing, wireless, and security services in addition to acting as a full-featured voice solution that includes voicemail.

The equipment required for this solution can be as simple as a Cisco Unified Communications 500 (UC500) series device and a few phones. Depending on the number of phones and types of features you require, other equipment, such as a Cisco Catalyst Express 520 series switch, a Cisco 521 Wireless Express access point, or third-party phones, could be necessary.

The following is a brief summary of the features that the Cisco Unified Communications 500 series devices can offer:

- ▶ Call processing (Communications Manager Express, built in)
- ▶ Voice messaging (Cisco Unity Express, built in)
- ▶ Auto Attendant (Cisco Unity Express, built in)
- ▶ Data routing
- ▶ LAN switching—Power over Ethernet (PoE)
- ▶ Support for Skinny Client Control Protocol (SCCP), Session Initiation Protocol (SIP), and wireless IP phones
- ▶ Virtual Private Network (VPN) capabilities
- ▶ Firewall
- ▶ GUI-based configuration—Cisco Configuration Assistant
- ▶ Integrated wireless LAN (WLAN) capability (optional and not available on all models)

Cisco Unified Communications 500 Series Platform

The primary hardware that is required in SBCS is a Cisco Unified Communications 500 series device. This device comes in two models:

- The Cisco Unified Communications 500 series 8/16-user device

- Unified Communications series 32/48-user device

The 500 series 8/16-user is a 1.5U-high device and is available in two models: the UC520-8U-2BRI-K9 and UC520-8U-4FXO-K9. Both models offer similar features; the main difference is that the UC520-8U-2BRI-K9 has two Basic Rate Interface (BRI) ports and the UC520-8U-4FXO-K9 has four Foreign Exchange Office (FXO) ports.

NOTE

The UC500 includes eight Ethernet ports and supports eight users. When purchasing the 16-user version, an additional 8-port external switch is included.

The UC500 includes the following components:

- **Console port:** This port can be used as a console or auxiliary port. It can automatically detect a modem.

- **Compact flash:** 1GB compact flash is installed by default for Unity Express.

- **Music on Hold (MOH) audio jack:** This jack allows you to plug in an external device to provide the MOH audio source. An audio file can also be loaded on the compact flash, but this should only be used as a secondary fallback source. It can take up to 30 seconds for fallback to occur.

- **PoE:** There are eight 10/100 switch ports. Each supports PoE, which powers the attached phones. The maximum amount of power that the 500 can support is a total of 80W.

- **Expansion port:** This is a 10/100 Ethernet port that is used to connect to a switch when more port density is required. The Catalyst Express 520-24PC is the recommended switch.

- **WAN port:** This port is used to connect to a router or broadband device such as a cable or digital subscriber line (DSL) modem.

- **Built-in Foreign Exchange Station (FXS) ports:** Analog phones can be connected to these ports.

▶ **PSTN connectivity:** Four FXO ports or two BRI ports.

▶ **Voice interface card (VIC) slot:** This is an expansion slot that allows you to plug in any of the following VICs: VIC2-2FXO, VIC2-4FXO, VIC2-2FXS, VIC-4FXS/DID, VIC3-2FXS/DID, VIC3-4FXS/DID, VIC2-2BRI-NT/TE, or VWIC2-1MFT-T1/E1.

▶ **Wi-Fi:** This is an optional feature. It is an integrated AP that supports 802.11b and 802.11g. This provides wireless access for both voice and data devices.

The Unified Communications series 32/48-user device is used for 24-, 32-, and 48-user configurations. This device is a 2U-high device and comes in two base configurations. The first configuration includes a T1/E1 port. The other configuration includes a 4-port FXO instead of the T1/E1 port. Other components found in this device include four FXS ports, four FXO ports, eight PoE switch ports, one WAN port, one expansion port, one console port, and one VIC slot.

> **EXAM ALERT**
>
> The Unified Communications series 32/48 device cannot have an internal wireless access point. If wireless services are required, the Cisco 521 Wireless Access Point or the Cisco 526 Wireless Express Mobility Controller is recommended.

Catalyst Express Switches

If more than eight ports are needed, an external switch needs to be attached to the UC500 series device. Certain Catalyst Express 520 series switches are recommended for this purpose. Of course, you can use other switches, but the benefit of using one of these switches is that you can use the Cisco Configuration Assistant to deploy and maintain them. While all the Catalyst Express 520 series switches are not recommended for use with the Cisco Unified Communications 500 series device, you should be familiar with the following five 520 series switches:

▶ **Cisco Catalyst Express 520-8PC switch:** Eight 10/100 PoE ports and one 10/100/1000 or a small-form-factor pluggable (SFP) port.

▶ **Cisco Catalyst Express 520-24TT switch:** Twenty-four 10/100 ports and two 10/100/1000 ports or an SFP port. It is an unmanaged switch that supports some advanced features, such as quality of service (QoS) and VLANs.

▶ **Cisco Catalyst Express 520-24LC switch:** Twenty-four 10/100 PoE ports and two 10/100/1000 ports or an SFP port. Supports PoE for a small number of phones or other PoE devices.

▶ **Cisco Catalyst Express 520-24PC switch:** Twenty-four 10/100 PoE ports and two 10/100/1000 ports or an SFP port. Can support a larger number of PoE devices than the 520-24LC.

> **EXAM ALERT**
>
> The Cisco Catalyst Express 520-24PC switch is the recommended switch for 32/48-user deployments.

▶ **Cisco Catalyst Express 520G-TC switch:** Twenty-four 10/100/1000 ports and two 10/100/1000 ports or an SFP port. This is a good choice for a server or backbone connectivity.

Supported Endpoints

The endpoints supported within the SBCS are extensive. Table 14.1 offers a brief overview of the supported models.

TABLE 14.1 Endpoints Supported Within the SBCS

Model	Lines	Protocol	Features
7605/06	1	SCCP/SIP	—
7911/12	1	SCCP/SIP	10/100 switch
7921/20	1	SCCP	Wireless phone, speakerphone (21 only)
7931G	24	SCCP	Speakerphone
7936	1	SCCP	10/100 switch, speakerphone
7940G	2	SCCP/SIP	10/100 switch, speakerphone
7941G / G-GE	2	SCCP/SIP	10/100 (1000 GE only) switch, speakerphone
7942G/45G	2	SCCP/SIP	10/100 (1000 45G only) switch, speakerphone, (color screen 45G only)
7960G/61G	6	SCCP/SIP	10/100 switch, speakerphone
7961G-GE	6	SCCP/SIP	10/100/1000 switch, speakerphone
7962G	6	SCCP/SIP	10/100 switch, speakerphone
7965G	6	SCCP/SIP	10/100/1000 switch, speakerphone, color screen
7970G	8	SCCP/SIP	10/100 switch, speakerphone, color touch screen
7971G-GE	8	SCCP/SIP	10/100/1000 switch, speakerphone, color touch screen
7975G	8	SCCP/SIP	10/100/1000 switch, speakerphone, color touch screen
7985G	1	SCCP	10/100 switch, speakerphone, video

Using Additional SBCS Features

As mentioned previously, the SBCS not only offers telephony services but also other services that are critical to the small business. This adds function to the product and helps make the purchase more attractive to the customer. The following sections take a brief look at these additional features.

SBCS Wireless Features

As mentioned earlier, the 8/16-user model of the UC500 offers an optional integrated wireless access point. In addition, you can expand the wireless coverage by installing Cisco 521 Wireless Access Points. You can then use a Cisco 526 Wireless Express Mobility Controller to create a unified wireless network. These devices support wireless VLANs.

The Cisco 521 Wireless Access Points support the following security protocols:

▶ Wired Equivalent Privacy (WEP)

▶ Wi-Fi Protected Access (WPA) and WPA2

▶ Lightweight Extensible Authentication Protocol (LEAP)

▶ Protected Extensible Authentication Protocol (PEAP)

SBCS Security Features

The SBCS has the following built-in security features:

▶ **Network Address Translation (NAT):** A single public IP address is required to for the entire LAN infrastructure.

▶ **Standard IEEE 802.1X on switch:** Requires 802.1X applications to provide valid access credentials. This helps prevent unauthorized access to resources.

▶ **Cisco IOS Firewall:** Provides stateful and application-based filtering (context-based access control [CBAC]) as well as per-user authentication and authorization, transparent firewall, and real-time alerts.

▶ **Cisco Easy VPN Remote and Server support:** Easily managed point-to-point VPNs.

Understanding the Cisco Configuration Assistant

The Cisco Configuration Assistant (CCA) eases the configuration and maintenance of the SBCS. This is a GUI-based tool that is installed on a PC that has connectivity to the SBCS. The main purpose of this feature is to allow the telephony services to be quickly deployed. This tool offers a visual display of the topology as well as a graphical view of the front of the UC500, which allows you to see the status of ports.

Cisco Smart Assist is the part of the Cisco Configuration Assistant that allows quick and easy configuration of devices and applications. The features that can be configured using Cisco Smart Assist are

- ▶ Phone extensions

- ▶ Assignment of phone extensions

- ▶ Dial plan

- ▶ Cisco Unified Communications 500 private branch exchange (PBX) configuration

- ▶ Autodiscovery of supported devices

- ▶ Password and VLAN synchronization

- ▶ VLANs

- ▶ Firewall

- ▶ QoS

EXAM ALERT

In the correct environment, using CCA makes expanding the telephony system as easy as adding the appropriate switch and plugging the phones in. The phones are automatically discovered and configured.

Exam Prep Questions

1. Which of the following protocols does the UC 500 support? (Choose two.)

○ **A.** SCCP

○ **B.** SIP

○ **C.** SMDI

○ **D.** VLAN

2. Which statement about the UC520-8U-2BRI-K9 is true?

○ **A.** The UC520-8U-2BRI-K9 has two T1 ports.

○ **B.** The UC520-8U-2BRI-K9 has four built-in FXO ports.

○ **C.** By default, the UC520-8U-2BRI-K9 has an integrated wireless access point.

○ **D.** The UC520-8U-2BRI-K9 has two BRI ports.

3. Which of the following switches is recommended to be used with the UC 500 when you need to expand beyond eight phones?

○ **A.** Cisco Catalyst Express 520-24PC

○ **B.** Cisco Catalyst Express 520-24LC

○ **C.** Cisco Catalyst Express 520-24TT

○ **D.** Cisco Catalyst Express 520G-TC

4. Which of the following wireless security protocols does the Cisco 521 Wireless Access Point support? (Choose all that apply.)

○ **A.** WEP

○ **B.** WPA

○ **C.** LEAP

○ **D.** PEAP

5. Which of the following does the Cisco Configuration Assistant not provide?

○ **A.** Visual view of topology

○ **B.** Graphical display of the back of the UC 500

○ **C.** Ability to monitor port status

○ **D.** Ease of telephony services configuration

6. What is the maximum number of users supported by the UC500?

   ○ **A.** 10

   ○ **B.** 48

   ○ **C.** 58

   ○ **D.** 50

   ○ **E.** 100

7. Which of the following endpoints are not supported by the UC500?

   ○ **A.** 7960

   ○ **B.** 7940

   ○ **C.** 7931

   ○ **D.** 7971

   ○ **E.** None of the options provided is correct.

8. Which of the following statements about the UC500 security features is true?

   ○ **A.** Provides stateful and application-based filtering

   ○ **B.** Public Address Translation

   ○ **C.** SSL-encrypted hypertunneling

   ○ **D.** Enhanced IEEE 802.1X

9. Which of the following features can be configured using CCA?

   ○ **A.** Create phone extensions

   ○ **B.** Assign phone extensions

   ○ **C.** Dial plan

   ○ **D.** All the options provided are true.

10. Which of the following statements about endpoint support is correct?

   ○ **A.** The UC500 supports SCCP and SIP on all Cisco IP phones.

   ○ **B.** The UC500 supports SCCP and SIP on all the Cisco 7936 and 7940G IP Phones.

   ○ **C.** The UC500 supports SCCP and SIP on all the Cisco 7960G and 7970G IP Phones.

   ○ **D.** All endpoints registered to a UC500 must use the same protocol.

Answers to Exam Prep Questions

1. **A and B.** UC500 supports SCCP and SIP. Answer C is incorrect because SMDI is a voicemail signaling protocol that is not supported. Answer D is incorrect because VLAN is not a protocol.

2. **D.** The UC520-8U-2BRI-K9 has two BRI ports. Answer A is not correct because the UC520-8U-2BRI-K9 does not have two T1s built in; it has two BRIs. Answer B is incorrect because the UC520-8U-2BRI-K9 does not have four built-in FXO ports; it has built-in FXS ports. Answer C is incorrect because the integrated wireless access point is an option and is not installed by default.

3. **A.** The Cisco Catalyst Express 520-24PC switch is the recommended switch. Answers B, C, and D are incorrect.

4. **A, B, C, and D.** WEP, WPA, LEAP, and PEAP are all supported wireless security protocols.

5. **B.** The Cisco Configuration Assistant does not offer a graphical view of the back of the UC500; it offers a graphical view of the front of it. Answer A is incorrect because the UC500 offers a visual view of topology. Answer C is incorrect because the UC500 offers the ability to monitor port status. Answer D is incorrect because the UC500 offers ease of telephony services configuration.

6. **D.** The maximum number of phones that are supported by the UC500 is 50. Answers A, B, C, and E are incorrect.

7. **E.** The 7960, 7940, 7931, and the 7971 are all supported by the UC500.

8. **A.** The UC500 includes a Cisco IOS Firewall that provides stateful and application-based filtering (context-based access control [CBAC]) as well as per-user authentication and authorization, transparent firewall, and real-time alerts. Answer B is incorrect because the UC500 supports Network Address Translation. There is no such thing as Public Address Translation. Answer C is incorrect; there is no such feature. Answer D is incorrect because the UC500 offers standard IEEE 802.1X.

9. **D.** Creation of phone extensions, assignment of phone extensions, and dial plan configuration are all supported by the CCA.

10. **C.** The UC500 supports SCCP and SIP on all the Cisco 7960G and 7970G IP Phones. Answer A is incorrect; not all phones can use SIP and SCCP. Answer B is incorrect; the 7936 does not support SIP. Answer D is incorrect; all endpoints do not need to use the same protocol.

Suggested Reading and Resources

1. Cisco.com. Search for "Cisco Unified Communications 500 Series for Small Business Data Sheet."

15

Implementing the Smart Business Communications System

Terms you need to understand:

✓ Cisco Configuration Assistant (CCA)

✓ Hunt group

✓ PBX mode

✓ Key system mode

Techniques you need to master:

✓ Install CCA

✓ Configure DHCP on the UC500 using CCA

✓ Configure a dial plan on the UC500 using CCA

✓ Configure speed dials on the UC500 using CCA

✓ Add users and phones to the UC500 using CCA

✓ Configure voice features on the UC500 using CCA

✓ Configure voicemail and Auto Attendant pilot numbers on the UC500 using CCA

The Cisco Configuration Assistant (CCA) is a useful tool that allows basic configuration of the UC500. You must become familiar with the various functions that it can perform. This chapter takes you through the use of the CCA application to install and manage the Small Business Communications System (SBCS).

Installing CCA and Managing the SBCS

CCA is an application that is installed on a PC. The installation process is fairly simple. You need to acquire a copy of CCA, which you can find on the Cisco website (http://www.cisco.com/go/configassist). After the software is downloaded, you need to install it on a PC that meets the following minimum specifications:

▶ 1GHz processor

▶ 512MB RAM (1GB recommended)

▶ 150MB free hard disk space (300MB recommended)

▶ 1024 × 768 display resolution

▶ Vista Ultimate, Windows XP SP1, or Windows 2000 SP3 operating system

To start the installation, simply execute the file that you downloaded. The installation process requires only basic information from you. First, it asks whether you agree to the license agreement. After you accept the agreement, you are asked to confirm or change the directory in which the program will be installed. A status bar appears, showing the progress of the installation. When the installation is complete, you can begin configuration setup.

Setup

After the installation completes, an icon for CCA will be on the desktop. Click the icon to launch CCA. After CCA has started, run the setup wizard. To begin, select **Setup > Device Setup Wizard**. From the drop-down menu that appears on the next screen, select the UC500. Next, power up the UC500 and make sure that the PC is connected to one of the Power over Ethernet (PoE) ports on the UC500. The UC500 will have an IP address of 192.168.10.1 and a subnet mask of 255.255.255.0. The PC will automatically receive an IP address on the same network because DHCP is enabled by default on the UC500.

CCA verifies that the UC500 is connected and prompts you to enter a new host name, username, and password. Next, you are prompted to configure the time. This can be done by manually selecting the time and date or by synchronizing with the PC's clock. The last step is to set up the WAN link IP address and select the local settings such as region, phone language, and voicemail language.

Device Properties

After you attach to the UC500, you will probably want to change some of the default settings. You can access the core settings by choosing **Configure > Device Properties**, as shown in Figure 15.1.

FIGURE 15.1 Device properties.

As you can see from Figure 15.1, you can set a number of parameters in this area. Each is listed in Table 15.1.

TABLE 15.1 Voice Device Configuration Parameters

Parameter	Description
IP address	Configure IP addresses, domain name, and DNS
Host name	Configure host name
System time	Set up NTP, sync time to PC, or manually set time
HTTP port	Set HTTP port (80 by default)
Users and password	Set admin username and password
Device access	Enable or disable Telnet and SSH
SMNP	Configure SMNP settings

Graphical Views

There are two graphical views you can access from within CCA:

▶ The topology view, which presents a topological representation of the Cisco devices that CCA is aware of

▶ A graphical view of the front panel of the UC500

The topology view is created from the information that the CCA learns from Cisco Discovery Protocol (CDP). CDP is a Cisco-proprietary protocol that is used to share information about other Cisco devices. From this view, you can right-click the devices shown and configuration options appear. The options that are available depend on the device you have selected.

Figure 15.2 shows the graphical view of the front of a UC500. From this view, you can see which ports are installed in the UC500 and view the status of the PoE ports. You can also configure the settings such as speed, duplex, and power of the PoE ports by right-clicking one and selecting **Port Settings**.

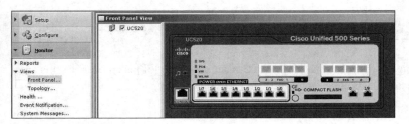

FIGURE 15.2 Front view.

Upgrading

CCA allows you to easily upgrade the system files without having to access the command-line interface (CLI). Choose **Maintenance** > **Software Upgrade**. A screen appears that shows the version of the Cisco IOS Software currently installed. To upgrade the IOS version, click the **Upgrade Status** button. A small window appears that prompts you for the name of the image file you want to upgrade to. Click the **Browse** button and navigate to the location on your PC in which the file is stored.

The UC500 has two operating systems, the Cisco IOS and the Cisco Unity Express OS. When using CCA to upgrade the system files, you can choose to upgrade one or both of these. If you choose to upgrade both, you need to make sure that the `.zip` file you select contains both sets of required files. The language selection is used for Unity Express, and additional languages can be downloaded from Cisco.com. Click **OK** to begin the upgrade. You can click the **Status** button in the Software Upgrade window to monitor the progress of the upgrade.

File Management

CCA can also assist you in maintaining the files in the UC500 flash. To view the files that are in flash, choose **Maintenance** > **File Management**. In the new window that appears, click the **files** tab and then click the arrow that is next to **flash**. The flash memory content is displayed. You can delete files from flash by selecting the Delete check box next to the file you want to remove and clicking **Apply** or **OK**.

New files can be copied to flash using the drag-and-drop method. To do this, simply drag a file from your PC and place it on the UC500 on the topology view. You will be prompted to confirm that you want to copy the file. Select **Upload** and the file will be uploaded to flash. The previous topic, upgrading, explains how to upgrade the IOS using the Software Upgrade feature. You can also use this drag-and-drop method to upload a new IOS to flash.

Cisco Configuration Assistant: Voice Configuration

One of the most important parts of the CCA in terms of the exam is the voice configuration area. Because you need to be familiar with the graphical interface, a figure showing each screen and a definition for each parameter that appears on the screen are provided. To begin voice configuration, choose **Configure** > **Telephony** > **Voice**.

Device

The first area of configuration is Device. The majority of the information found on the Device screen is automatically populated based on what CCA learned during its discovery phase. CCA uses CDP to identify and map directly connected neighbors, such as an external Cisco switch, and add them to the device list and topology view. In Figure 15.3, you see that CCA learned that the device is a UC520 with Unity Express with four Foreign Exchange Station (FXS) ports, four Foreign Exchange Office (FXO) ports, and eight switch ports built in. All other slots in this device are empty. You need to determine whether to configure the voice system to operate in private branch exchange (PBX) or keysystem mode.

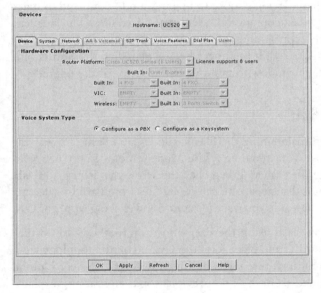

FIGURE 15.3 Voice device configuration.

EXAM ALERT

PBX mode is the default. In this configuration, incoming calls are routed to an Auto Attendant or operator and then routed to the desired party. In the keysystem mode, most phones are configured the same, and incoming calls can be answered on any phone.

System

The System configuration screen is used to configure locale settings and speed dials. In Figure 15.4, you see all the parameters that you can configure from this screen. Table 15.2 briefly defines each parameter.

FIGURE 15.4 Voice system configuration.

TABLE 15.2 Voice System Configuration Parameters

Parameter	Description
Region	Determines the default cadence and call progress tones
Call Progress Tone	Determines the subset of the tones defined by the region
Date Format	Determines how the date will be formatted on the phone
Time Format	Determines whether a 12- or 24-hour clock is used
Phone Language	Determines the language that appears on the phone
System Message	The message that appears in the corner of the phone
Voicemail Language	Determines the language for the voicemail system

The location of the language files also appears on this screen as do speed dials that are configured on this system. To add a speed dial, click the **Add** button at the bottom of this screen. A row will be added in the System Speed Dial box. Enter the name and number in the row and click **Apply**.

Network

The Network section is where you configure IP and VLAN information. In Figure 15.5, you can see the various parameters that need to be configured.

The first parameter is the VLAN Number. Select the VLAN that is going to be used for voice, that is, the voice VLAN. The DHCP IP Address Pool, Subnet Mask, Excluded Address From, and Excluded Address To parameters allow you to configure a DHCP pool for the voice VLAN. The IP address and subnet mask define the scope of all available subnet addresses, and the exclusion range blocks IP addresses within that range from being assigned to end devices.

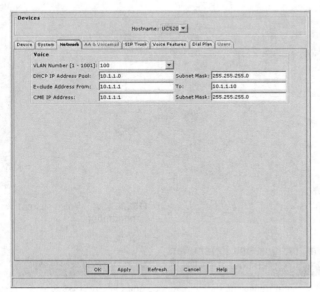

FIGURE 15.5 Voice network configuration.

Make sure that the IP address and subnet mask of the interface that will be servicing SCCP requests are configured and operational.

Auto Attendant and Voicemail

This section describes the AA & Voicemail tab. In Figure 15.6, you see that there are 16 fields that can be configured here, but by default, only four are required. Table 15.3 offers a description of these four fields.

TABLE 15.3 Voice AA and Voicemail Configuration Parameters

Parameter	Description
Auto Attendant Extension	The extension number that triggers the Auto Attendant. This is typically the main extension number of the company.
Auto Attendant PSTN Number	The number that when dialed from outside the system (over the PSTN), triggers the Auto Attendant.
Voicemail Access Extension	The extension that triggers the voicemail welcome greeting.
Voicemail Access PSTN Number	The extension that triggers the voicemail welcome greeting when calling from the outside (over the PSTN).

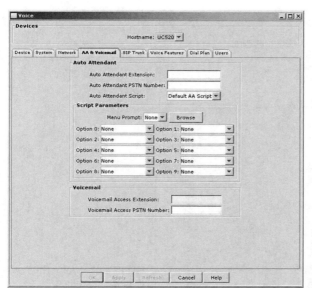

FIGURE 15.6 Voice AA and voicemail configuration.

In addition to these four parameters, there are also script-related parameters. If the default script is selected for the Auto Attendant, these parameters are not used. However, if you choose to use a script other than the default, you might need to configure these additional parameters.

To select a script, click the down arrow on the Auto Attendant Script drop-down box and select the desired script. When a nondefault script is selected, the script parameters will be accessible. Select the audio file that you want to play when the Auto Attendant answers from the Menu Prompt drop-down box. The 10 Option parameters (labeled Option 0 through Option 9) allow you to configure where a call is transferred to when a user presses a touchtone during the greeting. You can select an extension from the drop-down list or simply type in the desired extension.

SIP Trunk

If you are using a SIP trunk, you need to configure the SIP trunk parameters. Figure 15.7 shows the SIP trunk configuration page.

When configuring a SIP trunk, select the service provider from the Service Provider drop-down list. This list has three choices: AT&T, Cbeyond Communications, and Generic SIP Trunk Provider. The service provider will provide you with the information for the rest of the fields on the screen. In some cases, the service provider might not require all parameters to be configured. Keep in mind that SIP trunks are not supported when the system is configured in keysystem mode.

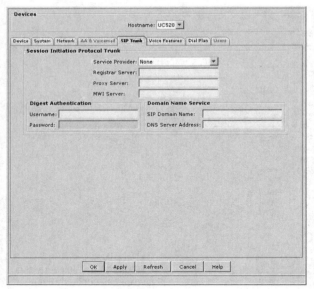

FIGURE 15.7 Voice SIP trunk configuration.

Voice Features

The Voice Features section is where you configure features such as paging and hunt groups. In Figure 15.8, you can see that nine features can be configured here. However, when configured in keysystem mode, only intercom and paging can be configured on this page. Let's look at each feature individually.

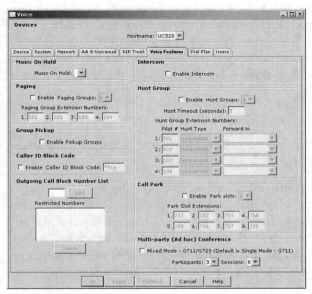

FIGURE 15.8 Voice features configuration.

Music on Hold

The Music on Hold (MOH) feature is simple to configure. From the drop-down list, select the audio source file you want to use for MOH. The file must be in the flash on the UC500 for it to appear in this list. Use this feature when there is no external MOH source connected to the UC500.

Paging

By default, paging is disabled. To enable paging, select the Enable Paging Groups check box. You can configure up to four paging groups with three directory numbers (DNs) each from this page. Select the paging group number from the Paging Group drop-down list, and then enter the DNs under the Paging Group Extension Numbers label.

Group Pickup

Group Pickup allows one person in an office to enter a code on her phone and answer someone else's phone in the same pickup group. To enable Group Pickup, select the Enable Pickup Groups check box. Up to eight pickup groups can be configured.

Caller ID Block Code

The Caller ID Block Code feature allows the user to dial a number that starts with a star (*) before dialing the destination number to block his caller ID. To enable this feature, select the Enable check box and enter the code in the Caller ID Block Code field. The code should be four digits, starting with a *.

Outgoing Call Block Number List

You can configure numbers that you do not want internal calls to be able to dial. This is accomplished by adding the numbers to the outgoing call block number list. To add a number, enter it in the field to the left of the Add button and then click the **Add** button. The numbers you add will appear in the Restricted Numbers box.

Intercom

To allow phones to be configured with intercoms, select the Enable Intercom check box.

Hunt Group

You can configure up to four hunt groups from this screen. To configure a hunt group, select the Enable check box and select the number of hunt groups you want to configure from the Hunt Groups drop-down list. Configure the Hunt Timeout value, which determines the number of seconds each DN in the group will ring. Now configure the pilot number for each hunt group. The pilot is the number of the first DN in the hunt group. This is the number that will be dialed to reach this hunt group. Now configure the hunt type.

Call Park

You can configure up to eight call park numbers from this screen. To configure call park numbers, select the Enable check box and select the number of call park numbers you want to configure from the Park Slots drop-down list. Now simply enter the numbers you want to use as call park numbers in the Park Slot Extensions fields.

Multi-party (Ad hoc) Conference

By default, eight ad hoc conferences with three participants are supported. All three calls must be G.711 or G.729. To have more participants or to run mixed mode (G.711 and G.729) with more than three participants, you must have available digital signal processor (DSP) resources. If DSPs are available, you can increase the number of conference participants using both G.711 and G.729 codecs.

Dial Plan

The Dial Plan section allows you to define the following:

- ▶ **Number of Digits Per Extension:** Determines the number of digits an extension will be. The default is three.

- ▶ **Outgoing Call Dial Plan Locale:** Determines whether the North America dial plan will be used. If so, the most common settings are predefined. When Other is chosen, no predefined settings exist.

- ▶ **Number of Digits in Area Code:** Determines the length of the area code for the country that the system is installed in.

- ▶ **Number of Digits in Local Number:** Determines the number of digits for a local call in the country that the system is installed in.

- ▶ **Digits for Placing Long Distance Call:** Determines the digits that must be dialed when placing a long-distance call.

- **Digits for Placing International Call:** Determines the digits that must be dialed when placing an international long-distance call.

- **Access Code:** Determines the number that must be dialed to place an outbound call.

- **Emergency Numbers:** Determines the number that can be dialed for emergency service in the country in which the system is installed.

- **FXO Trunks:** Determines when inbound FXO calls are sent. The choices are Operator, Hunt Group, and Custom Configuration. If Operator is selected, enter the operator extension. If Hunt Group is selected, choose the appropriate hunt group from a drop-down list. If Custom Configuration is selected, configure the destination number for each port.

- **Direct Inward Dial:** You can configure mapping for Direct Inward Dial (DID) by clicking the Configure button. You can then configure one-to-one DID translations or many-to-one DID translations.

Users

The Users section not only allows you to create users but also phones as well. In Figure 15.9, you see the 7971 phone with extension 2001 assigned to user Helen Costew.

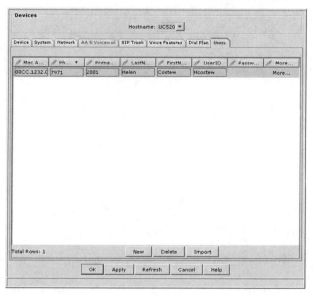

FIGURE 15.9 Voice user configuration.

To add a phone, click the **New** button. This adds a line below the last phone listed with a MAC address of all 0s. Enter the MAC address of the phone in the first field. From the drop-down list in the second field, select the phone model. Enter the primary DN in the next field. Enter the last and first name in the fourth and fifth fields and the user ID in the sixth field. The password should be entered in the next field. The last field is a link to phone-specific configuration. Depending on what type of phone you are adding, you can configure such things as button settings, forwarding, intercom, pickup groups, and so on.

Cisco Configuration Assistant: System Configuration

In the Configuration section of CCA, you can access the port, security, and wireless settings.

Configure Port Settings

To access the Ethernet port settings, choose **Configure** > **Ports** > **Port Settings**, as shown in Figure 15.10.

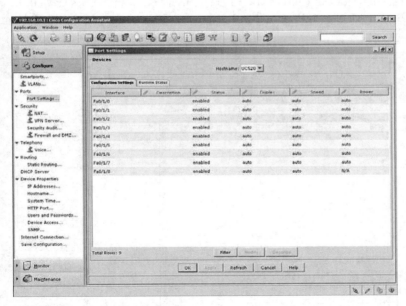

FIGURE 15.10 Port settings selection.

Figure 15.11 shows the Port Configuration Settings screen. You can use this screen to review physical connectivity.

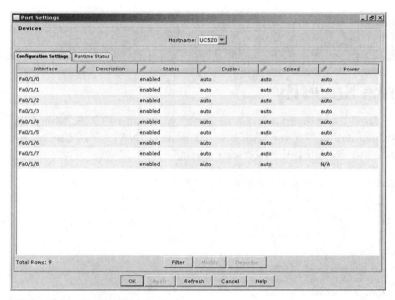

FIGURE 15.11 Port settings by device.

Figure 15.12 shows the Runtime Status screen. You can use this screen to review the PoE power consumption.

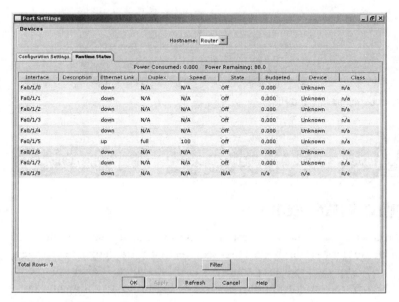

FIGURE 15.12 Port runtime status.

Configure Security

Figure 15.13 provides an overview of the Security section of CCA, where the administrator can define Network Address Translation (NAT), VPN server for remote access, and firewall and DMZ settings.

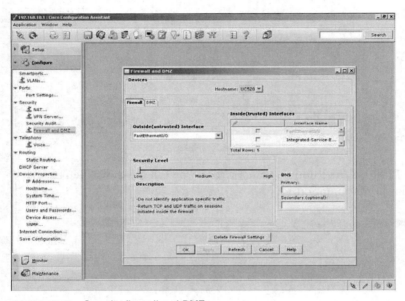

FIGURE 15.13 Security firewall and DMZ.

Configure Wireless

SBCS supports wireless connectivity for small businesses, and you should treat voice and data services similarly to LAN connectivity. Implement a wireless VLAN (WVLAN) for data and a separate WVLAN for voice. Make sure to create the VLANs before configuring the WVLANs. Figure 15.14 shows an example of data and voice WVLANs.

FIGURE 15.14   Wireless configuration.

Configure Routing

Routing is typically not a major issue with an SBCS installation because all networks terminate at the router component. To connect to the Internet, you need to create a static route that directs all unknown IP addresses, except for RFC 1918 private addresses, to the Internet interface. No dynamic routing protocols are supported.

Monitoring SBCS with CCA

CCA does not just configure the SBCS; it can also monitor both internal and external resources. Figure 15.15 shows the menu location on CCA that provides access to Health, Event Notification, and System Messages.

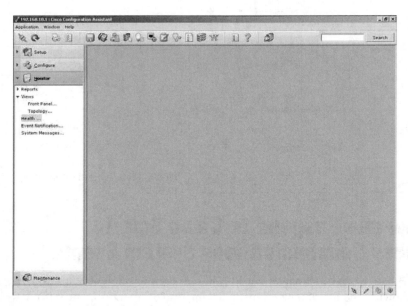

FIGURE 15.15   Monitoring selection.

After the installation is complete, the SBCS should run for years with no trouble. As system features and phones are added, the SBCS could be taxed to provide the same level of service that the users received after the initial installation. Use the tools described in the following sections to monitor the effectiveness, identify critical events, and note system information messages.

View the Health of a Cisco Smart Business Communications System

Figure 15.16 provides a look at the six standard graphical displays used to monitor SBCS: Bandwidth Utilization, Packet Error Rate, PoE Utilization, Temperature, CPU Utilization, and Memory Utilization.

EXAM ALERT

There are six standard graphs that CCA supplies for monitoring SBCS environments.

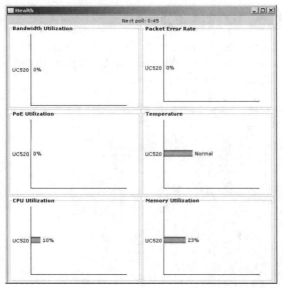

FIGURE 15.16 Health-monitoring example.

Review and Respond to Cisco Smart Business Communications System Events

With CCA active on the management PC, system events will generate a pop-up window showing the list of new events. Clicking one of the pop-up events takes you to the Event Notification screen.

Figure 15.17 displays a mechanism for reviewing and acknowledging all events that the UC500 and its associated devices generate during normal and failed conditions.

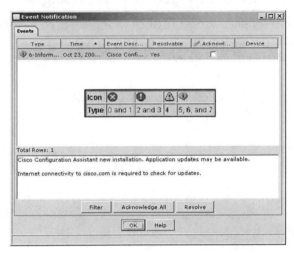

FIGURE 15.17   Event notification
example.

There are four categories of event types that are identified by unique icons, and each event type is matched to standard syslog levels as follows:

- ▶ **Critical error:** Syslog level (type) 0 and 1 events are identified with a red circled X icon.

- ▶ **Error:** Syslog level (type) 2 and 3 events are identified with a red circled exclamation point icon.

- ▶ **Warning:** Syslog level (type) 4 events are identified by the exclamation point within a yellow triangle icon.

- ▶ **Informational:** Syslog level (type) 5, 6, and 7 events are identified by the blue i bubble icon.

Always take care of the more critical errors and then go back to review and acknowledge the warnings and information messages.

EXAM ALERT

Remember the four event levels defined by icons and their associated standard syslog levels 0–7.

Review and Respond to Cisco Smart Business Communications System Messages

Rather than maintaining an active Telnet or Secure Shell (SSH) connection to the UC500, the CCA provides a mechanism to view or save the current console message output. Figure 15.18 shows an example of the System Messages screen.

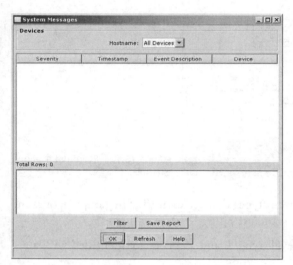

FIGURE 15.18 System message example.

Maintaining SBCS with CCA

The following sections cover several maintenance options for SBCS. Figure 15.19 shows the following five functions: Software Upgrade, File Management, Configuration Archive, Restart/Reset, and License Management.

Software Upgrade

CCA allows you to easily upgrade the system files without having to access the command-line interface (CLI). The current version of IOS can be found by choosing **Maintenance** > **Software Upgrade**. A line appears that shows the name of the IOS that is currently installed. To upgrade the operating systems, click the **Upgrade Settings** button. A small window appears that prompts you for the name of the upgrade image file. Click the **Browse** button and navigate to the location on your PC in which the file is stored. See Figure 15.20 for a sample of this process.

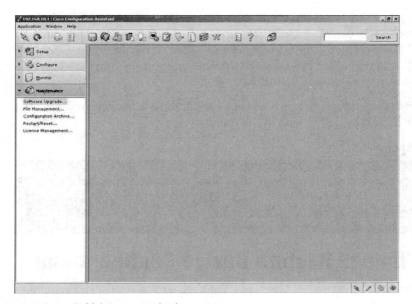

FIGURE 15.19 Maintenance selection screen.

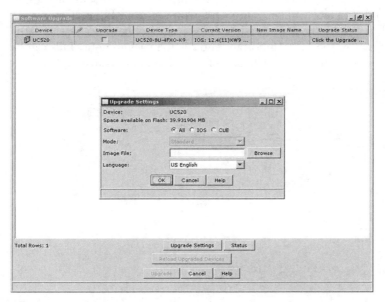

FIGURE 15.20 Software upgrade screen.

The UC500 has two operating systems, the Cisco IOS and the Cisco Unity Express (CUE) OS. When using CCA to upgrade the system files, you can choose to upgrade one or both of these. If you choose to upgrade both, make sure that the .zip file you select contains both sets of required files. The language selection is used for Unity Express and additional languages must be downloaded from Cisco.com as required and added to the .zip file. Click **OK** to begin the upgrade. You can click the **Status** button in the Software Upgrade window to monitor the progress of the upgrade.

Don't forget the other option, which is to copy and paste the updated .zip file from your PC to the device icon in the topological view.

> **EXAM ALERT**
>
> There are two methods to upgrade operating system files on the SBCS: drag and drop a .zip file onto the topological view icon or choose **Maintenance > Software Upgrade** at the CCA graphical user interface (GUI).
>
> When upgrading, there are three upgrade choices: just UC500, just CUE, or both.

Back Up and Restore Device Configurations

In the Maintenance section of CCA, you can back up and restore device configurations. Cisco Unified Communications Manager Express configurations can be backed up without service interruption. Cisco Unity Express backups are always performed by taking voicemail and Auto Attendant services offline. Restores are performed offline for both call processing and voicemail. Figure 15.21 shows the backup screen, where the most important entry is the backup note. This can be used to clearly identify the "what, when, and why" backup information.

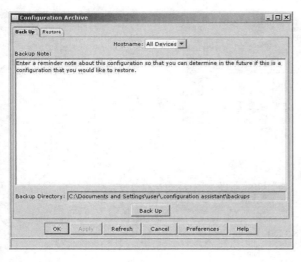

FIGURE 15.21 Configuration backup screen.

Individual device backups or all devices can be associated with a specific backup job, so documentation of the contents is important. Backup filenames are built from the host name, date and time, and MAC address for easier identification.

The backup screen allows you to scan restore files for the specific device, the specific device type, or all backed up configurations, as shown in Figure 15.22.

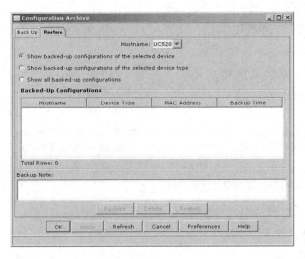

FIGURE 15.22 Configuration restore screen.

Reset a Cisco Smart Business Communications System to a Factory Default State

If you need to clear an existing SBCS to go back to the initial factory defaults, select the Reset to Factory Default check box in the **Maintenance > Restart/ Rest** section, as shown in Figure 15.23.

FIGURE 15.23 Restart and reset factory defaults screen.

> **NOTE**
>
> A complete configuration backup should be taken prior to resetting any device to factory default.

Exam Prep Questions

1. Which of the following statements about the UC500 default configuration is correct?

   ○ **A.** DHCP is enabled by default.

   ○ **B.** The default password is 1cisco23.

   ○ **C.** The default IP address is 10.10.10.1.

   ○ **D.** The SSID is UCCISCO.

2. You are instructed to update the Cisco IOS and the Cisco Unity Express version on the UC500. You decide to use the CCA upgrade feature to do this. Which of the following do you need to do?

   ○ **A.** Upload the needed files to flash using the CLI.

   ○ **B.** Create a `.zip` file that contains all the required software.

   ○ **C.** Issue the `upgrade prep` command.

   ○ **D.** None of the options is correct because you cannot upgrade both operating systems from CCA.

3. Which of the following statements about PBX mode are true? (Choose two.)

   ○ **A.** PBX mode is the default mode.

   ○ **B.** In PBX mode, calls can be routed to an operator or Auto Attendant.

   ○ **C.** Most phones are configured the same in PBX mode.

   ○ **D.** PBX mode is only used when integrating the UC500 with a traditional PBX.

4. Your company has recently installed a UC500. Because the company used to have a keysystem, you decide to configure the UC500 in keysystem mode. You just had a SIP trunk installed and are tasked with configuring it on the UC500. Which of the following information is needed?

   ○ **A.** Proxy server IP address

   ○ **B.** MWI server IP address

   ○ **C.** SIP provider ID

   ○ **D.** SIP trunk SPID

   ○ **E.** None of the options is correct.

5. Which of the following statements best describes sequential hunting?

○ **A.** The call is sent to the first DN in the hunt group. If that DN does not answer, the call is then forwarded to other DNs in the order they appear in the hunt group.

○ **B.** The call is sent to the first DN in the hunt group. If that DN does not answer, the call is then forwarded to other DNs based on their idle time.

○ **C.** The call is sent the least recently used DN in the hunt group. If that DN does not answer, the call is then forwarded to other DNs in the order they appear in the hunt group.

○ **D.** The call is sent to the first DN in the hunt group. If that DN does not answer, the call is then forwarded to other DNs in random order.

6. Which security features are available on the SBCS? (Choose all that apply.)

○ **A.** NAT

○ **B.** VPN

○ **C.** Encrypted RTP

○ **D.** Encrypted call control signaling

○ **E.** Firewall features

○ **F.** Windows XP firewall plug-in

7. How many monitoring graphs are displayed by default with the Health Monitoring feature?

○ **A.** 2

○ **B.** 4

○ **C.** 6

○ **D.** 8

8. Which of the following device selections are valid for software upgrades? (Choose three.)

○ **A.** UC500 only.

○ **B.** Cisco Unity Express only.

○ **C.** Cisco 1841 ISR.

○ **D.** Catalyst 500 Express switch.

○ **E.** Both: Combined UC500 and Cisco Unity Express.

○ **F.** All the options are correct.

9. Which of the following answers correctly maps the standard syslog message priorities 0–7 to the four event types displayed on the CCA Event Notification screen?

   ○ **A.** Critical error to levels 0 through 3, error to level 4, warning to level 5, and informational to levels 6 through 7

   ○ **B.** Critical error to level 0, error to levels 1 through 3, warning to levels 4 through 5, and informational to levels 6 through 7

   ○ **C.** Critical error to levels 0 to 2, error to levels 3 through 4, warning to level 5, and informational to levels 6 through 7

   ○ **D.** Critical error to levels 0 to 1, error to levels 2 to 3, warning to level 4, and informational to levels 5 through 7

10. Which of the following provides a one-step backup and restore process for the integrated SBCS?

    ○ **A.** Use the `backup all` CLI command on the UC 500.

    ○ **B.** Drag and drop the UC500 icon to a local PC directory.

    ○ **C.** Use the **CCA** > **Maintenance** > **Configuration Archive** section.

    ○ **D.** Browse to the UC500 from Windows and copy the disks to a PC directory.

Answers to Exam Prep Questions

1. **A.** DHCP is enabled by default. The following answers are incorrect: B (actual default password is cisco), C (actual default IP address is 192.168.1.1), and D (actual default SSIDs are uc520-data and uc520-voice).

2. **B.** Create a `.zip` file that contains all the appropriate operating system and application files for Cisco Unified Communications Manager and Cisco Unity Express. Answer A is incorrect because the files will be uploaded using CCA. Answer C is incorrect because there is no such command as `upgrade prep`. Answer D is incorrect because you can upgrade both operating systems using CCA.

3. **A and B.** PBX mode is the default, and calls can be routed to an attendant or Auto Attendant. Answer C is incorrect because most phones are configured the same in keysystem mode, not PBX mode. Answer D is wrong because PBX mode has nothing to do with integrating to a PBX.

4. **E.** You cannot use SIP trunks when UC500 systems are configured in keysystem mode. Answers A, B, C, and D are incorrect for the same reason.

5. **A.** Sequential hunting hunts sequentially down the list of directory numbers. Answer B is incorrect because sequential hunting does not use idle time. Answer C is incorrect because sequential hunting does not send the call to the least recently used DN. Answer D is incorrect because sequential hunting does not send the call to DNs in a random order.

6. **A, B, and E.** These are device security features. Answers C and D are about communications security, not device security. Answer F is used to secure PCs.

7. **C.** Six health-monitoring graphs are provided by default. Answers A, B, and D list incorrect values.

8. **A, B, and E.** UC500 only, Cisco Unity Express only, or both components. Answers C and D are for devices not supported by CCA; therefore answer F, all devices, is incorrect.

9. **D.** This answer correctly maps the syslog levels 0 to 7 to the four event icons used in Cisco Configuration Assistant, and answers A, B, and C are incorrect.

10. **C.** This answer correctly identifies the process for backing up the UC500 platform. Answer A is not a valid CLI command. Answers B and D require Windows networking support, which is not a supported protocol with the UC500 series and is incorrect.

PART V

Practice Exams and Answers

16

Practice Exam 1

The 58 multiple-choice questions provided here help you determine how prepared you are for the actual exam and what topics you need to review further. Write down your answers on a separate sheet of paper so that you can take this exam again if necessary. Compare your answers against the answer key that follows this exam.

1. Your customer has a Cisco Unified Communications Manager and is using both Cisco IP phones and third-party phones such as the Grandstream. He also wants to use SCCP for all phones. Which of the following statements would be true about his environment?

   ○ **A.** This is the preferred configuration.

   ○ **B.** This will not work because SCCP only works with third-party phones.

   ○ **C.** This will not work because Cisco phones require SIP.

   ○ **D.** This will not work because SCCP does not work with most third-party phones.

2. Looking at the following configuration, which of the following statements is true?

```
dial-peer voice 15 pots
destination-pattern 5551100
 port 0/0/1

dial-peer voice 16 pots
destination-pattern 5551100
 port 0/1/0
```

   ○ **A.** An incoming call to 5551100 will match dial peer 15 first.

   ○ **B.** An incoming call to 5551100 will match dial peer 16 first.

   ○ **C.** An incoming call to 5551100 will match dial peer 15 first and will fail over to dial peer 16 if dial peer 15 is not registered.

   ○ **D.** An incoming call to 5551100 will randomly match dial peer 15 and 16.

3. How do you configure an intercom DN so that it is not dialable?

   ○ **A.** Use the `intercom nond` command.

   ○ **B.** Use an extension number that contains an A, B, C, or D.

   ○ **C.** Use the `intercom nodial` command.

   ○ **D.** Use an extension number that contains a *.

4. When configuring a dial plan from CCA, which of the following statements is true?

   ○ **A.** The emergency numbers are automatically populated if the North American Number Plan locale is selected.

   ○ **B.** You should manually enter the emergency numbers in the Emergency Numbers fields.

   ○ **C.** The emergency numbers are set to 911 and 9911 and cannot be changed.

   ○ **D.** The emergency numbers can only be three digits.

5. Which features can be configured using Smart Assist?

   ○ **A.** Phone extensions.

   ○ **B.** Dial plans.

   ○ **C.** Autodiscovery of supported devices.

   ○ **D.** VLANs.

   ○ **E.** All answer options are correct.

6. Which of the following statements is correct?

   ○ **A.** MGCP and H.323 are peer-to-peer protocols.

   ○ **B.** SIP and SCCP are client/server protocols.

   ○ **C.** H.323 and SCCP are client/server protocols.

   ○ **D.** H.323 and SIP are peer-to-peer protocols.

   ○ **E.** MGCP and SCCP are client/peer protocols.

7. A button that has three extensions assigned to it is what kind of button?

   ○ **A.** Multiline

   ○ **B.** Shared

   ○ **C.** Overlay

   ○ **D.** Monitor

   ○ **E.** Dual-number

8. Which of the following statements about paging are true? (Choose two.)

   ○ **A.** Multicast or unicast can be used for paging.

   ○ **B.** If configured properly, paging can allow two-way audio.

   ○ **C.** Paging groups are a collection of ephone-dns that have been configured as paging dns.

   ○ **D.** Multicast paging requires an address in the 224.0.0.0 network.

9. When using the User Configuration feature in CCA, which of the following can be configured? (Choose all that apply.)

   ○ **A.** Users

   ○ **B.** Phones

   ○ **C.** Extensions

   ○ **D.** Forwarding

   ○ **E.** Intercoms

10. A customer has decided to deploy Cisco Unified CME and her network engineer wants to know what protocols would be used. She is adamant about only allowing open-standard protocols. Based on this, what would you tell her?

   ○ **A.** We can use H.323 and SIP as the primary protocols with no feature loss.

   ○ **B.** We can use H.323 and SIP as the primary protocols, and the only feature that we will lose is automatic devices discovery.

   ○ **C.** We can use H.323 and SIP as the primary protocols but will not be able to use certain Cisco phones and will lose a number of features.

   ○ **D.** We must use CDP and SCCP, which are both proprietary.

   ○ **E.** CME does not support any proprietary protocols.

11. When looking at the following configuration in terms of outgoing dial peers, which of the following statements is true?

```
dial-peer voice 50 VOIP
 destination-pattern 555.
 session target ipv4:10.10.11.1

dial-peer voice 60 VOIP
 destination-pattern 5551...
 session target ipv4:10.10.11.1

dial-peer voice 70 VOIP
 destination-pattern 55512..
 session target ipv4:10.10.11.1
```

   ○ **A.** When a call is placed to 5551200, it will match dial peer 70.

   ○ **B.** When a call is placed to 5551200, it will match dial peer 50.

   ○ **C.** When a call is placed to 5551200, it will match dial peer 60.

   ○ **D.** When a call is placed to 5551200, it will match dial peer 0.

12. The following configuration is an example of what kind of line?

```
Router(config)# ephone-dn 101 dual-line
Router(config-ephone-dn)# number 2000
Router(config)# ephone 10
Router(config-ephone)# mac-address 00CC.0001.A123.1ABF
Router(config-ephone)# button 1:101
Router(config)# ephone 12
Router(config-ephone)# mac-address 00C0.0011.A145.1DDA
Router(config-ephone)# button 1:101
```

○ **A.** Multiline

○ **B.** Shared

○ **C.** Overlay

○ **D.** Monitor

○ **E.** Dual-number

13. What will the following configuration accomplish?

```
Router(config-telephony)# after-hours day sat 11:00 23:59
Router(config-telephony)# after-hours day sun 00:00 00:00
Router(config-telephony)# after-hours block pattern 1 9011
```

○ **A.** It will block calls to numbers that begin with 1 9011 all day Sunday and from 11:00 a.m. to 11:59 p.m. Saturday.

○ **B.** It will allow calls to extension 9011 all day Sunday and from 11:00 a.m. to 11:59 p.m. Saturday.

○ **C.** It will block calls to extensions that begin with 90 all day Sunday and from 11:00 a.m. to 11:59 p.m. Saturday.

○ **D.** It will block calls to 911 all day Sunday and from 11:00 a.m. to 11:59 p.m. Saturday.

○ **E.** It will block international calls all day Sunday and from 11:00 a.m. to 11:59 p.m. Saturday.

14. A customer is currently using a keysystem but is upgrading to Cisco Unified Communications Manager Express. When the topic of configuring the Cisco Unified Communications Manager Express in keysystem mode comes up, the customer is hesitant. He thinks he might want to use PBX mode. What are you going to tell the customer?

○ **A.** Don't worry. If we configure it as a keysystem, it can be changed to PBX mode by selecting PBX mode from the Device tab in CCA.

○ **B.** If you choose to use PBX mode, you will need to purchase the PBX mode license.

○ **C.** PBX and keysystem mode are pretty much the same, so it doesn't matter what you pick.

○ **D.** I need to decide before I configure the system because after I select the mode, I cannot change it in CCA.

15. From the graphical view of the front panel on the UC500, which of the following config-urations can be accessed? (Choose all that apply.)

- ○ **A.** Speed
- ○ **B.** Duplex
- ○ **C.** Power
- ○ **D.** IP address

16. What do you do in CCA to enable the ability to add intercom lines to phones?

- ○ **A.** Choose **Telephony** > **Voice** > **Voice Features** and select the **Enable Intercom** check box.
- ○ **B.** Choose **Telephony** > **Voice** > **User Features** and select the **Enable Intercom** check box.
- ○ **C.** Choose **Telephony** > **Voice** > **Voice Features** and select the **Intercom** check box.
- ○ **D.** Choose **Telephony** > **Voice Features** and select the **Intercom** check box.

17. A customer is interested in the Caller ID Block Code feature. What would you tell her about it?

- ○ **A.** It is a 4-digit number that must begin with a *. When a user dials this code followed by a 10-digit number, the 10-digit number he entered will be sent as the caller ID.
- ○ **B.** It is a 4-digit number that must begin with a *. When a user dials this code, his caller ID will be blocked.
- ○ **C.** It is a 4-digit number that must begin with a *. When a user dials this code, his caller ID is blocked on local calls.
- ○ **D.** It is a 4-digit number that must begin with a *. When a user dials this code, his caller ID is blocked if the dialed number is in the outgoing Call Block Number List.

18. What information is configured on the Network tab under **Telephony** > **Voice** in CCA? (Choose two.)

- ○ **A.** Cisco Unity Express IP address
- ○ **B.** Cisco Unified Communications Manager Express IP address
- ○ **C.** DHCP scope
- ○ **D.** TFTP address
- ○ **E.** DNS

19. When configuring the Auto Attendant from CCA, when do the script parameters need to be configured?

- ○ **A.** When the Default AA Script is selected
- ○ **B.** When the Default AA Script is not selected
- ○ **C.** When the Main AA Script is selected
- ○ **D.** When the Main AA Script is not selected

20. How is signaling accomplished by the CO to ring the phone in loop start?

- ○ **A.** Contact closure
- ○ **B.** Switch hook
- ○ **C.** AC ring voltage
- ○ **D.** M-lead

21. What type of phone configuration causes the phone to call a predetermined number when off-hook?

- ○ **A.** PLAR
- ○ **B.** E&M
- ○ **C.** Loop Start
- ○ **D.** Ground Start

22. What type of E&M signaling is not supported on Cisco routers?

- ○ **A.** Type I
- ○ **B.** Type II
- ○ **C.** Type III
- ○ **D.** Type IV

23. Which of the following commands is part of a pickup group configuration?

- ○ **A.** `ephone-pickup 101`
- ○ **B.** `pickup-number 1000`
- ○ **C.** `pickup-group 808`
- ○ **D.** `group-pickup 809`

24. What are the valid line-coding formats for T1 circuits? (Choose two.)

    ◯   **A.**   AMI

    ◯   **B.**   HDB3

    ◯   **C.**   B8ZS

    ◯   **D.**   CRC4

25. What is the speed of a T1 CAS circuit?

    ◯   **A.**   64Kbps

    ◯   **B.**   2.048Mbps

    ◯   **C.**   144Kbps

    ◯   **D.**   1.544Mbps

26. The PSTN and service provider environment is made up of physical devices, communications circuits, and communications protocols. Which of the following answers are considered PSTN components? (Choose two.)

    ◯   **A.**   Telephones

    ◯   **B.**   CO switches

    ◯   **C.**   SS7

    ◯   **D.**   PBX

27. Which of the following statements best describe the differences between keysystems and PBX systems? (Choose two.)

    ◯   **A.**   PBX systems have additional advanced features not found in keysystems.

    ◯   **B.**   PBX systems are used in smaller organizations, and keysystems are found in larger organizations.

    ◯   **C.**   PBX systems are only used in organizations that have at least 1,000 users.

    ◯   **D.**   Keysystems typically provide all line appearances on each phone; PBX systems use internal extensions.

    ◯   **E.**   Key systems are only used in organizations that have 10 or fewer users.

28. DTMF is used to provide telephone keypad digits using which of the following methodologies?

    ◯   **A.**   Generating a unique analog frequency for each digit

    ◯   **B.**   Generating 100ms pulses 10ms apart

○ **C.** Changing frequencies to indicate the digit dialed

○ **D.** Generating four low and four high frequencies, with each digit represented by a combination of one low and one high frequency

29. The analog-to-digital conversion process follows which of the following sequences?

○ **A.** Compress the signal, quantize the signal, sample the signal, and encode the value

○ **B.** Sample the signal, encode the value, quantize the signal, and compress the signal

○ **C.** Sample the signal, quantize the signal, encode the value, and compress the signal

○ **D.** Quantize the signal, compress the signal, sample the signal, and encode the value

30. Voice gateway DSP resources provide media termination points to enhance voice services and functions. Which of the following features are provided over and above standard analog and digital voice termination? (Choose two.)

○ **A.** Conversion of G.729 to PAM

○ **B.** Conferencing

○ **C.** Speakerphone

○ **D.** Transcoding

○ **E.** Routing of call signaling to the correct phone number

○ **F.** Voice media splicing

31. Which protocol is responsible for packetizing incoming digital or analog voice traffic into IP packets for transport over the IP network?

○ **A.** IP

○ **B.** cRTP

○ **C.** UDP

○ **D.** RTP

○ **E.** Frame Relay

○ **F.** Ethernet

32. Which of the following protocols is used to provide QoS feedback to the media stream source about an RTP stream?

- ○ **A.** SMTP
- ○ **B.** RADIUS
- ○ **C.** RTCP
- ○ **D.** cRTP

33. VoIP samples are encapsulated in RTP, UDP, and IP headers. Assuming that there are no optional header fields, how many bytes of information are required for these three headers?

- ○ **A.** 4
- ○ **B.** 12
- ○ **C.** 20
- ○ **D.** 40
- ○ **E.** 48
- ○ **F.** 64

34. Why is 802.1Q trunking used to connect two Ethernet switches? (Choose two.)

- ○ **A.** Standards-based multi-VLAN trunking
- ○ **B.** To allow clients to see the 802.1Q header
- ○ **C.** To provide inter-VLAN communications over a bridge
- ○ **D.** To load-balance traffic between parallel links using STP
- ○ **E.** To provide voice and data VLANs on a shared physical connection

35. Excessive traffic levels on Layer 2 switches impact voice quality. Which of the following is most likely to create excessive Layer 2 traffic?

- ○ **A.** Flood storm
- ○ **B.** Broadcast storm
- ○ **C.** Loop overload
- ○ **D.** Broadcast overload

36. Which of the following commands correctly configures a router's FastEthernet or GigabitEthernet subinterface to process VLAN 50 traffic across an 802.1Q trunk connection to a switch?

○ **A.** Router(config)# **encapsulation 50 dot1Q**

○ **B.** Router(config-if)# **encapsulation 50 802.1Q**

○ **C.** Router(config)# **encapsulation 802.1Q 50**

○ **D.** Router(config-if)# **encapsulation dot1Q 50**

37. Which of the following IP addressing schemes provides security and data separation?

○ **A.** Statically apply IP addresses to IP phones to ensure stability.

○ **B.** Apply public IP addresses to IP phones so that they can be reached from the PSTN.

○ **C.** Use DHCP to provide separate voice and data subnets with private IP addresses.

○ **D.** Deploy IP phones on the same subnet as data devices.

38. When is the IP DHCP relay feature not required?

○ **A.** If the DHCP server does not have a local interface on the network with the DHCP clients

○ **B.** When the DHCP request-and-response process is not broadcast

○ **C.** To relay the proprietary DHCP request of an IP phone to the standard DHCP request understood by the Cisco IOS Software

○ **D.** If IP phones, data devices, and the DHCP server all reside on the same subnet

39. The ITU-T specifies which of the following values as an acceptable one-way, end-to-end delay for voice transmission?

○ **A.** 15ms

○ **B.** 150ms

○ **C.** 200ms

○ **D.** 300ms

40. Which of the following transport layer protocols is used to carry real-time IP traffic?

○ **A.** UDP

○ **B.** TCP

○ **C.** XNS

○ **D.** HTTP

41. Which of the following transport protocols is used to carry IP traffic that is not sensitive to potential packet drops and retransmissions?

   ○　**A.** UDP

   ○　**B.** TCP

   ○　**C.** XNS

   ○　**D.** HTTP

42. Which of the following voice components is connected to an FXS port?

   ○　**A.** CO analog trunk

   ○　**B.** Tie line

   ○　**C.** Fax machine

   ○　**D.** ISDN line

   ○　**E.** Q.931 line

43. Which statement best describes voice gateway call legs?

   ○　**A.** A logical connection between two devices

   ○　**B.** A voice gateway map between incoming and outgoing call terminations

   ○　**C.** Instructions on how to route the call

   ○　**D.** Connection across a VoIP network to the IP address of a voice gateway

   ○　**E.** Signaling mechanism used in VoIP

44. Which properties are defined on VoIP dial peers? (Choose three.)

   ○　**A.** Frequency range

   ○　**B.** Codec

   ○　**C.** DSP function

   ○　**D.** Fax rate

   ○　**E.** VAD

   ○　**F.** Sampling rate

45. VoIP dial peers send calls to which of the following targets?

   ○　**A.** Port number

   ○　**B.** IP address

   ○　**C.** Call leg

   ○　**D.** Virtual voice port

46. What is the maximum number of users that a Cisco Unity Express Network Module platform can support?

- ○ **A.** 8
- ○ **B.** 100
- ○ **C.** 250
- ○ **D.** 500
- ○ **E.** 3000
- ○ **F.** 7500

47. Which Cisco Unity Express platform can support up to a maximum of 100 user mailboxes?

- ○ **A.** Cisco Unity Express AIM
- ○ **B.** Cisco Unity Express Network Module
- ○ **C.** Cisco Unity Express Slot Module
- ○ **D.** Cisco Unity Express Network Module 2V
- ○ **E.** Cisco Unity Express Network Module Enhanced Capacity

48. Which Cisco Unity Express module supports up to 14 hours of messages?

- ○ **A.** Cisco Unity Express AIM
- ○ **B.** Cisco Unity Express Network Module
- ○ **C.** Cisco Unity Express Slot Module
- ○ **D.** Cisco Unity Express Network Module 2V
- ○ **E.** Cisco Unity Express Network Module Enhanced Capacity

49. AVT or TUI can be used to accomplish which of the following tasks by dialing in either locally or from the PSTN?

- ○ **A.** To restart the system
- ○ **B.** To initiate a backup of the system
- ○ **C.** To activate an EAG
- ○ **D.** To manage system or user prompts
- ○ **E.** To allow an end user to have an email read to her

50. What is the main difference between the storage media of the Cisco Unity Express Network Module and the Cisco Unity Express AIM?

 ○ **A.** Cisco Unity Express AIM uses flash-based storage, and Cisco Unity Express Network Modules use hard drive–based storage.

 ○ **B.** Cisco Unity Express AIM uses hard drive–based storage, and Cisco Unity Express Network Modules use flash-based storage.

 ○ **C.** Cisco Unity Express AIM and Cisco Unity Express Network Modules use different operating systems.

 ○ **D.** Cisco Unity Express AIM and Cisco Unity Express Network Modules use different installation packages for the various modules.

51. Under which of the following instances would the original Cisco Unity Express installation software be required?

 ○ **A.** To install a new Cisco Unity Express platform

 ○ **B.** To upgrade a new Cisco Unity Express platform

 ○ **C.** After replacing a failed Cisco Unity Express platform

 ○ **D.** To delete Cisco Unity Express platform features

52. Proper configuration of the Cisco Unity Express host router is crucial to provide access to voicemail features. Which of the following functions must be configured on the host router? (Choose three.)

 ○ **A.** Proper IP addressing of the service-engine interface

 ○ **B.** Proper IP addressing of the router Cisco Unity Express interface

 ○ **C.** Valid Cisco Unity Express IP route propagation

 ○ **D.** Static route to the external Ethernet port of the module

 ○ **E.** Proper IP addressing of the Cisco Unity Express service module

 ○ **F.** Ephone-dns for the pilot of Cisco Unity Express voicemail

53. Which of the following `telephony-service` commands are required to generate individual configuration files for the SCCP IP phones connected to a Cisco Unified Communications Manager Express host? (Choose two.)

 ○ **A.** `config-generate`

 ○ **B.** `create-cnf`

 ○ **C.** `cnf-file perphone`

 ○ **D.** `tftp-server <url>`

 ○ **E.** `load <phone type> <filename>`

54. Backup and restore capabilities are crucial for long-term maintenance of any telephony system. Which two protocols can be employed by Cisco Unified Communications Manager Express and the Cisco UC500 series telephony systems for this purpose? (Choose two.)

- ○ **A.** SMTP
- ○ **B.** SCCP
- ○ **C.** FTP
- ○ **D.** SIP
- ○ **E.** TFTP

55. The UC520 powers up with a preconfigured default configuration. Which of the following are correct statements concerning the default configuration?

- ○ **A.** DHCP is not enabled by default.
- ○ **B.** The default credential is a username of cisco with a password of cisco.
- ○ **C.** The default IP address is 10.10.10.1.
- ○ **D.** Phones will be automatically detected and assigned extensions starting with 201.

56. New enhanced features have been released for your UC500 series installation, and you want to upgrade the Cisco IOS and the Cisco Unity Express version on the UC500. You decide to use the CCA Upgrade feature to do this. Which of the following must be performed to complete this task? (Choose two.)

- ○ **A.** Choose **Maintenance** > **Software Upgrade** from the Feature bar and use the Software Upgrade window.
- ○ **B.** Create a `.zip` file that contains all the required application software.
- ○ **C.** Drag the `.zip` file that contains the update files from a local folder and drop it on the UC500 icon in the Topology view.
- ○ **D.** None of these answers is correct, because you cannot upgrade both operating systems at the same time using CCA.

57. When the UC500 is activated, which of the following statements are true about the PBX operating characteristics? (Choose all that apply.)

- ○ **A.** PBX mode is the default mode.
- ○ **B.** Most phones are configured with the same directory numbers.
- ○ **C.** In PBX mode, calls can be routed to an operator or Auto Attendant.
- ○ **D.** PBX mode is only used when integrating the UC500 with a traditional PBX.

58. You just had a SIP trunk installed and are tasked with configuring it on the UC500. Which of the following information is needed?

   ❍ **A.** The SIP proxy server IP address

   ❍ **B.** The fully qualified domain names (FQDNs) provided by the service provider

   ❍ **C.** The SIP proxy domain name

   ❍ **D.** The SIP trunk SPID

   ❍ **E.** The MWI SIP server IP address

17

Practice Exam 1
Answer Key

1. D	21. A	41. B
2. D	22. D	42. C
3. B	23. C	43. B
4. B	24. A, C	44. B, D, E
5. E	25. D	45. B
6. D	26. B, C	46. C
7. C	27. A, D	47. B
8. A, C	28. D	48. A
9. A, B, C, D, E	29. C	49. C, D
10. C	30. B, D	50. A
11. B	31. D	51. B, C
12. B	32. C	52. A, C, E
13. E	33. D	53. C, E
14. D	34. A, E	54. C, E
15. A, B, C	35. B	55. B, D
16. A	36. D	56. A, C
17. B	37. C	57. A, C
18. B, C	38. D	58. B, C
19. B	39. B	
20. C	40. A	

Question 1

D. Most third-party phones use SIP, not SCCP. Answer A is incorrect because SIP is required for third-party phones. Answer B is incorrect because SCCP does not work with third-party phones. Answer C is not correct because while some Cisco phones will work with SIP, they do not require it.

Question 2

D. Because a preference is not defined, there is no predetermined order. Answers A and B are not correct because the `preference` command is required to determine priority dial peers. Answer C is incorrect because a dial peer does not "register" to a CME.

Question 3

B. Answers A, B, C, and D are valid DTMF tones but are not found on most phones, so they cannot be dialed. Answer A is incorrect because `intercom nond` is not a valid command. Answer C is incorrect because `intercom nodial` in not a valid command. Answer D in incorrect because * cannot be part of a DN.

Question 4

B. Emergency numbers must be entered manually. Answer A is incorrect because emergency numbers are not automatically populated. Answer C is incorrect because emergency numbers are entered by the engineer or administrator and can be modified. Answer D is incorrect because emergency numbers can be greater then three digits.

Question 5

E. Phone extensions, dial plans, autodiscovery, and VLANs are features that can be configured using Smart Assist.

Question 6

D. H.323 and SIP are peer-to-peer protocols. Answer A is incorrect because MGCP is a client/server protocol. Answer B is incorrect; SIP is a peer-to-peer protocol. Answer C is incorrect because H.323 is a peer-to-peer protocol. Answer E is incorrect because there is no such thing as a client/peer protocol.

Question 7

C. A line that has three or more extensions assigned to it is an overlay line. Answer A is incorrect because multiline is not a type of button. Answer B is incorrect because a shared line is the same DN on multiple phones. Answer D is incorrect because monitor is used to watch the status of another DN. Answer E is incorrect because dual-number only allows two extensions to be assigned to the same button.

Question 8

A and C. Paging can use multicast or unicast, and paging groups are a collection of ephone-dns. Answer B is incorrect because paging is only one-way audio. Answer D is incorrect because Cisco IP phones do not support the 224.0.0.0 network.

Question 9

A, B, C, D, and E. Users, phones, extensions, forwarding, and intercoms can all be set up using CCA.

Question 10

C. Because we are using only open-standard protocols, SCCP will not be used and we will end up with fewer features. Answers A and B are incorrect because if SCCP is not used, there is some feature loss. Answer D is incorrect because while CDP and SCCP are normally used in a CME environment, they are not required. Answer E is incorrect because CME does support SCCP, which is a proprietary protocol.

Question 11

B. Because CME analyzes numbers on a digit-by-digit basis, it routes the call as soon as a match is found, even if all the digits have not been analyzed yet. Answers A, C, and D are incorrect because CME will route a call as soon as a dial peer is matched, even as other dial peers are potential matches.

Question 12

B. Because the same ephone-dn is assigned to two ephones, it is a shared line. Answer A is incorrect because multiline is not a type of button. Answer C is incorrect because an overlay line allows multiple DNs to be assigned to a single button. Answer D is incorrect because monitor is used to watch the status of another DN. Answer E is incorrect because dual-number only allows two extensions to be assigned to the same button.

Question 13

E. The times specified are Saturday 11:00 a.m. to 11:59 p.m. and all day Sunday. The pattern is 9011. Because you must dial 9011 when dialing an international number, the configuration will block international calls all day Sunday and from 11:00 a.m. to 11:59 p.m. Saturday. Answer A is incorrect because 1 is not part of the pattern. Answer B is incorrect because calls are blocked, not allowed. Answers C and D are incorrect because calls that are blocked must match the 9011 pattern.

Question 14

D. PBX or keysystem can only be selected once; this is normally done at the beginning of the configuration. Answer A is incorrect because you can only choose PBX or keysystem mode once. Answer B is incorrect because there is no additional license for PBX mode. Answer C is not correct because PBX and keysystem mode are significantly different.

Question 15

A, B, and C. Speed, duplex, and power can all be configured from the front panel view. Answer D is incorrect because you can only view the IP address of the UC500 from the front panel view.

Question 16

A. The Enable Intercom check box is found by choosing **Telephony > Voice > Voice Features**. Answers B, C, and D are incorrect because they are not valid selections.

Question 17

B. The Caller ID Block Code is a 4-digit number that must begin with a * and prevents caller ID from being sent. Answer A is incorrect because the user does not enter the number that she wants to have displayed as her caller ID. Answer C is incorrect because the caller ID is blocked on all calls, not just local calls. Answer D is incorrect because the dialed number does not need to be listed in the Call Block Number List.

Question 18

B and C. The IP address and DHCP scope are configured on the **Telephony > Voice** tab. Answers A, D, and E are incorrect because they cannot be configured on the Voice tab.

Question 19

B. The script parameters are only configured when a script other than the Default AA Script is selected. Answer A is incorrect because when the Default AA Script is selected, the script parameters are not configurable. Answers C and D are incorrect because there is no Main AA Script.

Question 20

C. AC ring voltage supplied to the phone in loop start will cause the phone to ring. Answers A, B, and D are incorrect because neither option will provide signaling to the phone in loop start.

Question 21

A. Private line, automatic ringdown (PLAR) allows a phone to be configured to call a predetermined number when the phone is taken off-hook. Answers B, C, and D are incorrect. E&M, Loop Start, and Ground Start are analog signaling types.

Question 22

D. E&M Type IV signaling is not supported on Cisco routers. Answers A, B, and C are incorrect. Type I, II, and III are all supported on Cisco routers.

Question 23

C. The `pickup-group` command is used when configuring pickup groups. Answers A, B, and D are incorrect because they are not valid commands.

Question 24

A and C. AMI and B8ZS are valid line-coding formats for digital T1 circuits. Answers B and D are incorrect because HDB3 and CRC4 are line-coding types used for E1 circuits.

Question 25

D. The T1 CAS circuit has a speed of 1.544Mbps. Answers A, B, and C are incorrect. 64Kbps is the speed of a DS0 on a T1 circuit, 2.048Mbps is the speed of an E1 circuit, and 144Kbps is the speed of a BRI circuit.

Question 26

B and C. CO switches and SS7 are PSTN components. Answer A, telephones, and answer D, PBX, connect to the edge of the PSTN and are incorrect.

Question 27

A and D. PBX systems have advanced call-routing features, and each user is typically assigned an extension. Answers B and C are incorrect. There is no specific organization size limit on PBX or keysystems, although keysystems are typically used in organizations with 50 or fewer users.

Question 28

D. Each digit is represented with a combination of low- and high-frequency tones. Answers A and C are incorrect; two frequencies per digit, not one. Answer B refers to off-on pulses, not tones, and is incorrect.

Question 29

C. The analog-to-digital conversion sequence is sampling the raw analog signal with an 8-bit analog-to-digital converter (ADC), quantizing the 8 bits of raw data into a logarithmic scale, encoding the logarithmic value into a plus and minus value, and compressing the signal for digital transmission (codec format). Answers A, B, and D are incorrect sequences.

Question 30

B and D. Digital signal processors can provide enhanced hardware conferencing and transcoding. Answers A, C, E, and F are incorrect. Router DSPs do not convert G.729 to pulse amplitude modulation (PAM), control a speakerphone, or route calls, and voice media splicing is an incorrect term.

Question 31

D. The Real Time Protocol encapsulates the voice samples produced by a DSP and adds a sequence number, a time stamp, and a media type before handing the information to UDP for further processing. The other answers are Layer 2 through 4 protocols used in the delivery of RTP segments.

Question 32

C. The Real Time Control Protocol takes the receiving device measurements of packet loss, jitter, and delay and sends the information back to the sender using even ports between 16386 and 32768. This feedback information is used to identify quality of service voice network issues. Answer A is incorrect because SMTP is an email protocol, answer B is incorrect because RADIUS is an authentication and reporting protocol, and answer D is incorrect because cRTP is used to compress IP, UDP, and RTP headers for point-to-point circuits.

Question 33

D. The TCP/IP packet headers include IP (20 bytes), UDP (8 bytes), and RTP (12 bytes), for a total of 40 bytes. All other answers are incorrect default values.

Question 34

A and E. 802.1Q is an IEEE-standard trunking protocol supported by all current Cisco products, and Cisco products provide a mechanism (voice or auxiliary VLANs) to provide two VLANs on a single physical connection. Answer B is incorrect; client systems do not require access to the 802.1Q header. Answer C is incorrect; VLANs and their subnets are connected by Layer 3 routing. Answer D is incorrect; load balancing using STP is not tied to 802.1Q trunking.

Question 35

B. None of the other terms has meaning in the Ethernet switch environment.

Question 36

D. In interface mode, the `encapsulation dot1q 50` command terminates VLAN 50 on the router. Answers A and C are incorrect because they are in the wrong configuration mode, and answer B has the parameters of the `encapsulation` command backward.

Question 37

C. Use DHCP to deploy private addresses for both voice and data subnets. Answer A is incorrect; statically applying IP addresses is time consuming and error prone. Answer B is incorrect; using public IP addresses for phones opens a security threat. Answer D is incorrect; there is no separation of voice and data traffic.

Question 38

D. This answer is correct when all devices are on the same subnet. Answer A is incorrect because this would be a reason for using DHCP relay. Answer B is incorrect; the IP phone DHCP request is a broadcast. Answer C is incorrect because the Cisco IP phones use standard DHCP services.

Question 39

B. The ITU-T defines a one-way delay of 150ms as acceptable. Lower values such as 15ms work fine but are not a requirement, and higher values impact the quality of the call experience to the users, so answers A, C, and D are incorrect.

Question 40

A. TCP uses retransmission of dropped packets and the voice media traffic would sound bad, XNS is the Xerox Network Protocol, and HTTP is used for web browsing, so answers B, C, and D are incorrect.

Question 41

B. UDP does not retransmit dropped packets and the call setup would fail, XNS is the Xerox Network Protocol, and HTTP is used for web browsing, so answers A, C, and D are incorrect.

Question 42

C. Central office analog trunks are usually connected to FXO ports, tie lines are used to bridge a local CO connection to another CO or a PBX to another PBX, ISDN circuits are digital, and Q.931 is a signaling protocol, so answers A, B, D, and E are incorrect.

Question 43

B. Call legs are used to connect an incoming and outgoing call leg for signaling and media stream translation. Answer A is incorrect because call legs are locally significant to the voice gateway. Answer C is incorrect because call legs only exist after the call has been set up between two endpoints. Answer D is incorrect because call legs exist for both POTS and VoIP connections. Answer E is incorrect because, again, call legs are used to map an incoming to an outgoing call flow and are not a signaling mechanism.

Question 44

B, D, and E. Selecting a specific codec or negotiating a codec, activation or deactivation of VAD, and fax transmission rate settings can all be controlled using dial peer configuration commands. Frequency range, DSP functionality, and sampling rate cannot be configured on a dial peer, so answers A, C, and F are incorrect.

Question 45

B. All VoIP calls are directed to an IP address. Answer A refers to a POTS voice port, answer C refers to a call-mapping mechanism used by voice gateways, and answer D is virtually incorrect because it references an imaginary virtual voice port, so answers A, C, and D are incorrect.

Question 46

C. The NM-CUE-EC supports up to 250 users. The other answers—A, B, D, E, and F—are incorrect.

Question 47

B. 100 is the limit for the NM-CUE. Answers A, C, D, and E are incorrect.

Question 48

A. Answer C is valid for the NM-CUE, answer E is valid for the NM-CUE-EC, and answers B and D do not match any valid Cisco Unity Express platform, so these answers are incorrect.

Question 49

C and D. A user with administrator rights can manage prompts and change the system EAG usage, and any user can manage his own prompts using TUI or AVT. Answers A, B, and E are incorrect.

Question 50

A. Answers B, C, and D are incorrect.

Question 51

B and C. Upgrades and hardware-only replacements require installation software. Answer A is incorrect because new modules come with the software installed, and answer D is incorrect; feature deletions do not require the original distribution software.

Question 52

A, C, and E. The service-engine interface, valid IP routing, and proper IP addressing for the service or integration module are required. Answer B is incorrect; there is no Cisco Unity Express interface on the router. Answer D is incorrect because static routes to other than the Cisco Unity Express IP address don't count. Answer F is incorrect because ephone-dns are not defined for the voicemail pilot number.

Question 53

C and E. Answer C changes the default method of generating the configuration files from per-phone type to individual phone configuration files, and answer E provides the required load information for the individual configuration files. Answer A is an invalid command, answer B is automatically triggered when ephones or ephone-dns are modified, and answer D provides access to the phone image files stored in flash, so these answers are incorrect.

Question 54

C and E. Answer A is an email protocol, and answers B and D are used for IP phone call control, so these answers are incorrect.

Question 55

B and D. Use lowercase cisco for username and password, and automatically assign extensions starting with 201. Answers A and C are incorrect. DHCP is enabled by default, and the default IP address is 192.168.1.1.

Question 56

A and C. Answer B is incorrect because the files required include the operating system, not just the applications (a single .zip file is available on Cisco.com for complete platform upgrades). Answer D is incorrect because you can upgrade both operating systems using CCA.

Question 57

A and C. PBX is the default mode, and incoming calls can be routed to an operator or Auto Attendant. Answer B is incorrect because the default configuration assigns extensions to the phones. Answer D is incorrect because PBX mode doesn't having anything to do with integrating with a PBX.

Question 58

B and C. The FQDNs and the SIP proxy domain name are required. Answer A, the SIP proxy server address (not required), answer D (SPID is an ISDN term), and answer E (MWI SIP server does not apply for an external trunk) are incorrect.

18

Practice Exam 2

The 58 multiple-choice questions provided here help you determine how prepared you are for the actual exam and what topics you need to review further. Write down your answers on a separate sheet of paper so that you can take this exam again if necessary. Compare your answers against the answer key that follows this exam.

1. Which of the following are peer-to-peer signaling protocols?

   ○ **A.** H.323

   ○ **B.** MGCP

   ○ **C.** SIP

   ○ **D.** RTP

   ○ **E.** SCCP

2. Imagine there are two gateways connected to each other through IP and an analog phone is plugged into each gateway. If a call were set up between the analog phones, how many call legs would there be?

   ○ **A.** 1

   ○ **B.** 3

   ○ **C.** 4

   ○ **D.** 6

3. What is the maximum number of phones that Cisco Unified CME supports?

   ○ **A.** 100

   ○ **B.** 325

   ○ **C.** 175

   ○ **D.** 240

4. What command sets the maximum number of ephones?

   ○ **A.** `maximum-ephones`

   ○ **B.** `ephones-max`

   ○ **C.** `maxephones`

   ○ **D.** `max-ephones`

5. Which of the following sets of commands is not valid?

   ○ **A.** Router(config)# **ephone-dn 101**

     Router(config-ephone-dn)# **call-forward noan 2000**

   ○ **B.** Router(config)# **ephone-dn 101**

     Router(config-ephone-dn)# **call-forward busy 2000**

○ **C.** `Router(config)#` **`ephone-dn 101`**

        `Router(config-ephone-dn)#` **`call-forward all 2000`**

○ **D.** `Router(config)#` **`ephone-dn 101`**

        `Router(config-ephone-dn)#` **`call-forward noasw 2000`**

6. What two graphical views does CCA offer?

○ **A.** Topology

○ **B.** Current traffic volume

○ **C.** Front panel

○ **D.** Auto Attendant call flow

7. When configuring hunt groups using CCA, what effect does setting the second hunt group hunt type to sequential have on the other hunt groups?

○ **A.** It will cause calls sent to the second hunt group to forward to the third hunt group.

○ **B.** It will allow hunt groups to forward calls to other hunt groups.

○ **C.** Unanswered calls from the first hunt group will be forwarded to the second hunt group.

○ **D.** It will have no effect on the other hunt groups.

8. Which of the following statements about signaling protocols are true? (Choose two.)

○ **A.** H.323 is an open-standard, peer-to-peer protocol.

○ **B.** MGCP is an open-standard, peer-to-peer protocol.

○ **C.** H.323 is an open-standard, client/server protocol.

○ **D.** MGCP is an open-standard, client/server protocol.

9. Imagine there are two gateways connected to each other through IP and an analog phone is plugged into each gateway. Which type of dial peer would be configured to allow the gateways to route calls between each other?

○ **A.** POTS

○ **B.** VoIP

○ **C.** VOICE-IP

○ **D.** IP-VoIP

10. What is the maximum number of directory numbers that Cisco Unified CME supports?

  ○ **A.** 240

  ○ **B.** 480

  ○ **C.** 720

  ○ **D.** 960

11. Which of the following statements about full-consult transfers is most accurate?

  ○ **A.** Full-consult transfers will be transferred with consultation using a supported standard method.

  ○ **B.** Full-consult transfers will be transferred with consultation using a supported standard method but require a second line. If a second line is not available, the transfer will fail.

  ○ **C.** Full-consult transfers will be transferred with consultation using a supported standard method but require a second line. If a second line is not available, an H.450.12 transfer will be used.

  ○ **D.** Full-consult transfers will be transferred with consultation using a supported standard method but require a second line (dual-line). If a second line is not available, a blind transfer will be used.

12. Which port on a UC500 is used to connect the device to an Internet provider?

  ○ **A.** Expansion port

  ○ **B.** WAN port

  ○ **C.** DSL port

  ○ **D.** External port

13. Which of the following statements about keysystem mode are true?

  ○ **A.** Keysystem mode is the default mode.

  ○ **B.** In keysystem mode, calls are routed to an operator or Auto Attendant.

  ○ **C.** Most phones are configured the same in keysystem mode.

  ○ **D.** Keysystem mode is only used when integrating the UC500 with a traditional key system.

14. Which statement best describes MGCP?

  ○ **A.** The Media Gateway Control Protocol (MGCP) is an IETF-standard peer-to-peer protocol.

  ○ **B.** The Media Gateway Control Protocol (MGCP) is an IETF-standard client/server protocol. Unlike SCCP, MGCP does not need a server to instruct what action to perform.

    ◯ **C.** The Media Gateway Control Protocol (MGCP) is an IETF-standard client/server protocol and operates much the same way as H.323.

    ◯ **D.** The Media Gateway Control Protocol (MGCP) is an IETF-standard client/server protocol.

15. Which of the following statements about dial peers are correct? (Choose two.)

    ◯ **A.** A VoIP dial peer's session target is the IP address of the destination device.

    ◯ **B.** A POTS dial peer contains a `port` command to determine where to route the call.

    ◯ **C.** The dial peer tag number must be unique and within the range 100–1024.

    ◯ **D.** Dial peer 0 is used to match all inbound calls.

16. The maximum number of phones that can register to a Cisco Unified CME is determined by which of the following?

    ◯ **A.** License.

    ◯ **B.** Platform.

    ◯ **C.** Type of phones.

    ◯ **D.** All the options provided are correct.

17. Based on the following configuration, which statement is true?

```
Router# config t
Router(config)# ephone-dn 101
Router(config-ephone-dn)# number 2000
Router(config-ephone-dn)# exit
Router(config)# ephone 10
Router(config-ephone)# mac-address 00CC.0001.A123.1ABF
Router(config-ephone)# button 4m101
```

    ◯ **A.** Ephone-dn 101 would be assigned to the fourth button and would be used to monitor the status of the extension assigned to ephone-dn 101. This line could be used to place or receive calls.

    ◯ **B.** Ephone-dn 101 would be assigned to the fourth button and would be used to receive multiple (many) calls.

    ◯ **C.** Ephone-dn 101 would be assigned to the fourth button and configured as a multi-dn.

    ◯ **D.** Ephone-dn 101 would be assigned to the fourth button and would be used to monitor the status of the extension assigned to ephone-dn 101. This line could not be used to place or receive calls.

18. Which statement is true about the following call park configuration?

```
Router(config)# ephone-dn 121
Router(config-ephone-dn)# number 5510
Router(config-ephone-dn)# park-slot timeout 12 limit 7 notify 2002
➥transfer 2010 alternate 2012
```

- ○ **A.** The call park number is 121.

- ○ **B.** A reminder tone is played every 7 seconds.

- ○ **C.** Only extension 2002 receives a reminder.

- ○ **D.** The call is transferred to extension 2010 after the limit count has been reached, and if 2010 is busy, the call is transferred to 2012.

19. Which of the following features can be configured using CCA? (Choose all that apply.)

- ○ **A.** Dial plan

- ○ **B.** Cisco Unified Communications 500 PBX configuration

- ○ **C.** Autodiscovery of supported devices

- ○ **D.** VLANs

20. When configuring voicemail using CCA, where would you enter the internal pilot number for voicemail?

- ○ **A.** The Auto Attendant Extension field

- ○ **B.** The Auto Attendant PSTN Number field

- ○ **C.** The Voicemail Access Extension field

- ○ **D.** The Voicemail Access PSTN Number field

21. You are going to deploy gateways in a Cisco Unified Communications Manager Express environment, and your customer has requested that you use a signaling protocol that supports voice, video, and data. Furthermore, he would like a protocol that is an open standard. Based on these requirements, which protocol would you choose?

- ○ **A.** PIMG

- ○ **B.** DMTF

- ○ **C.** H.323

- ○ **D.** MGCP

- ○ **E.** SMDI

22. Which of the following lines would not be part of a POTS dial peer?

   ◯ **A.** `dial-peer voice 10 POTS`

   ◯ **B.** `destination-pattern 1...`

   ◯ **C.** `session target 10.10.1.2`

   ◯ **D.** `preference 0`

23. What type of CCS circuit supplies 2B+D?

   ◯ **A.** PRI

   ◯ **B.** BRI

   ◯ **C.** T1

   ◯ **D.** E1

24. When selecting an MOH file using CCA, which of the following statements is true?

   ◯ **A.** The audio file must be uploaded to the flash before selecting it in CCA.

   ◯ **B.** The audio file will be uploaded to the flash when it is selected in CCA.

   ◯ **C.** The file must be in RTP format.

   ◯ **D.** The file must be recorded in a-law au format.

25. Which of the following is not a security feature of SBCS?

   ◯ **A.** Network Address Translation.

   ◯ **B.** Standard IEEE 802.1X on switch.

   ◯ **C.** Cisco IOS Firewall.

   ◯ **D.** Cisco Easy VPN Remote and Server support.

   ◯ **E.** None of the options provided is correct.

26. Which of the following PSTN components communicate using SS7?

   ◯ **A.** Central office customer trunks

   ◯ **B.** Central office switches

   ◯ **C.** Central office private tie lines

   ◯ **D.** Central office channel banks

27. Numbering plans have an authority that regulates number distribution and which of the following items?

  ○ **A.** A numbering plan that mandates an international standard.

  ○ **B.** A numbering plan that is a set of rules used to construct numbers.

  ○ **C.** A numbering plan that is an internal set of rules configured on a PBX.

  ○ **D.** The NANP regulates all numbering plans.

28. A public telephone number consists of a country code, a national destination code, and a subscriber number. Which international standard requires these three components?

  ○ **A.** H.323

  ○ **B.** SIP

  ○ **C.** E.164

  ○ **D.** Q.931

  ○ **E.** QSIG

29. The Nyquist Theorem is best described by which of the following statements?

  ○ **A.** Sample at the same rate as the highest frequency to ensure that the signal can be accurately reconstructed at the receiver.

  ○ **B.** Sample at twice the rate of the highest frequency to ensure that the signal can be accurately reconstructed at the receiver.

  ○ **C.** Capture frequencies up to 4000Hz.

  ○ **D.** Capture frequencies up to 8000Hz.

30. Which of the following protocol headers contains a sequence number, a payload type, and a time stamp?

  ○ **A.** IP

  ○ **B.** TCP

  ○ **C.** UDP

  ○ **D.** RTP

  ○ **E.** FTP

31. Which codec variant provides voice activity detection (VAD) and comfort noise genera-tion (CNG)?

  ○ **A.** G.711 ulaw

  ○ **B.** G.711 alaw

○ **C.** Annex C

○ **D.** Annex B

32. G.711 and G.729 codecs are most commonly used in Cisco Unified Communications deployments. How much bandwidth is used for voice samples using these two codecs, respectively?

○ **A.** 64Kbps, 8Kbps

○ **B.** 8Kbps, 32Kbps

○ **C.** 16Kbps, 64Kbps

○ **D.** 8Kbps, 64Kbps

33. Which of the following is responsible for compressing the standard VoIP headers from 40 bytes to 2 bytes on Cisco point-to-point connections?

○ **A.** RTCP

○ **B.** RTP

○ **C.** cRTP

○ **D.** sRTP

34. Which IP protocol requires Cisco IOS configuration commands for each file used to provide IP phone images during the initial registration process?

○ **A.** HTTP

○ **B.** DHCP

○ **C.** FTP

○ **D.** TFTP

35. NTP services can be configured on many Cisco devices, but there is a best-practice method that should be used. Which of the following could be considered best practice? (Choose two.)

○ **A.** Reference a public NTP server from the Cisco Unified Communications Manager Express router.

○ **B.** Use the CLI clock set command on the Cisco Unified Communications Manager Express router.

○ **C.** Use the GUI to set the date and time on the Cisco Unified Communications Manager Express router.

○ **D.** Purchase an atomic or radio clock as an internal NTP source.

36. What information does `XMLDefault.cnf.xml` or `SEP001BD5086771.cnf` contain that is used by an IP phone to synchronize the operating image?

○ **A.** The default language

○ **B.** The NTP-synchronized time

○ **C.** The filename used to update phone images

○ **D.** The ring tones used in the installation

37. Which of the following command sequences would be used to deliver firmware file `SCCP41.8-3-3S.loads` at the request of a Cisco IP phone?

○ **A.** `ftp-server flash:/SCCP41.8-3-3S.loads`

   `telephony-service`

   `load 7941 SCCP41.8-3-3S.loads`

○ **B.** `tftp-server flash:/SCCP41.8-3-3S.loads`

   `telephony-service`

   `load 7941 SCCP41.8-3-3S`

○ **C.** `tftp-server flash:/SCCP41.8-3-3S`

   `telephony-service`

   `load 7941 SCCP41.8-3-3S`

○ **D.** `ftp-server SCCP41.8-3-3S.loads`

   `telephony-service`

   `load 7941 SCCP41.8-3-3S.loads`

38. What can be defined when the network topology, traffic types, and traffic levels have been gathered prior to a new Cisco Unified Communications Manager Express implementation?

○ **A.** Policy map

○ **B.** Class map

○ **C.** QoS policy

○ **D.** Link configuration options

39. How many different DSCP values are available for QoS classification?

○ **A.** 8

○ **B.** 16

○ **C.** 32

○ **D.** 64

40. Which of the following commands will provide dynamic QoS operation for Cisco IP phones plugged into a switch port (QoS enabled when the phone is plugged in, QoS disabled when the phone is not plugged in)?

- ❍ **A.** Switch(conf)# **auto qos voip trust**
- ❍ **B.** Switch(conf-if)# **auto qos voip cisco-phone**
- ❍ **C.** Switch(conf)# **auto qos voip cisco-phone**
- ❍ **D.** Switch(conf-if)# **auto qos voip trust**

41. What happens to an HDLC circuit when the bandwidth command on the interface is 768Kbps or less and AutoQoS is applied to the interface? (Choose three.)

- ❍ **A.** RTP header compression is automatically activated.
- ❍ **B.** A QoS policy is automatically generated.
- ❍ **C.** The encapsulation is changed from HDLC to PPPoE.
- ❍ **D.** The encapsulation is changed from HDLC to PPP.

42. Which of the following items are benefits of an ITSP? (Choose three.)

- ❍ **A.** Per-line cost is lower
- ❍ **B.** Uses Q.931
- ❍ **C.** Can be purchased in groups of 23
- ❍ **D.** Uses SIP or H.323
- ❍ **E.** Has unlimited number of simultaneous connections
- ❍ **F.** Never has long-distance charges
- ❍ **G.** Can be provisioned in increments of one circuit

43. After the voice gateway strips off the left-justified matched digits 0 through 9 on a POTS dial peer call, what are the remaining digits called?

- ❍ **A.** Leftover digits
- ❍ **B.** Wildcard digits
- ❍ **C.** Called digits
- ❍ **D.** Lucky digits

44. What command allows you to expand an extension into a full telephone number or replace one number with another?

⭕ **A.** `prefix`

⭕ **B.** `forward-digits`

⭕ **C.** `num-exp`

⭕ **D.** `expando`

45. A VoIP dial peer has the following properties: no vad, codec G711ulaw, DTMF relay using SIP Notify messages, and SIP version 2. This dial peer can be used to connect to which Cisco Unified Communications Express component?

⭕ **A.** Hardware conferencing

⭕ **B.** Cisco Unity Express

⭕ **C.** An Internet telephony service provider

⭕ **D.** A remote VPIM location

46. A VoIP dial peer with a destination pattern of `2199....` could be used to activate which phone features? (Choose two.)

⭕ **A.** MWI on

⭕ **B.** Call park

⭕ **C.** Group paging

⭕ **D.** Group Call pickup

⭕ **E.** MWI off

47. Which Cisco Unified Communications Express component requires the IP address and the web administrator to be configured prior to using the integrated administration GUI on the host router?

⭕ **A.** Cisco Unified Communications Manager Express

⭕ **B.** Cisco Unity Connection

⭕ **C.** Cisco Unity Express

⭕ **D.** Cisco IP Contact Center Express

48. Which of the following options can be used to connect to Cisco Unity Express during the installation and upgrade processes?

   ○ **A.** Use Telnet to connect to the default Cisco Unity Express IP address of 192.168.1.1.

   ○ **B.** Connect a PC using a crossover cable to the external Ethernet port on the module and use DHCP.

   ○ **C.** Connect a console cable to the Cisco Unity Express module.

   ○ **D.** Go across the backplane of the router to the virtual console port on the Cisco Unity Express module.

49. Which of the following items are configured with the Initialization Wizard? (Choose two.)

   ○ **A.** Host name

   ○ **B.** IP address of the Cisco Unity Express module

   ○ **C.** Call-in numbers

   ○ **D.** Users

   ○ **E.** Cisco Unified Communications Manager Express system credentials

50. You are sent to a customer for the first time to identify and correct a voicemail problem. Which of the following commands can be used to identify the version of software currently installed and running on the Cisco Unity Express module?

   ○ **A.** Router# `service-engine service-module` *mod/port* ➥`status`

   ○ **B.** Router(config)# `service-module service-engine` *mod/port* `status`

   ○ **C.** Router# `service-module service-engine` *mod/port* ➥`status`

   ○ **D.** Router(config)# `service-engine service-module` ➥*mod/port* `status`

   ○ **E.** Router(config)# `service-engine` *mod/port* `status`

   ○ **F.** Router# `service-engine` *mod/port* `status`

51. MWI indicators are not working when voicemail messages are left in user mailboxes. Which of the following commands can be used to identify outcall MWI problems? (Choose two.)

○ **A.** Router# `debug ephone voicemail`

○ **B.** Router# `debug ephone vm-integration`

○ **C.** Router# `debug ephone mwi`

○ **D.** Router# `debug voip dialpeer all`

52. Debugging output is being sent to the console display when connected to the console port of the Cisco Unified Communications Manager Express. Which of the following commands will turn off the debug commands? (Choose two.)

○ **A.** `show debug output`

○ **B.** `no debug all`

○ **C.** `debug ephone`

○ **D.** `undebug all`

53. When debugging a problem with Cisco Unity Communications Manager Express using a Telnet session, which of the following commands can be used to disable messages to the console port?

○ **A.** Router(config)# `no console logging`

○ **B.** Router# `show debug output`

○ **C.** Router# `terminal monitor`

○ **D.** Router(config)# `logging buffer 64000`

54. Which of the following IOS CLI commands displays the Cisco Unified Communications Manager Express IOS version number and feature set?

○ **A.** `show debug output`

○ **B.** `show version`

○ **C.** `show ephones`

○ **D.** `show telephony-service`

○ **E.** `show ephone-dns`

55. Which of the following options are available for ephone hunt groups? (Choose two.)

   ○ **A.** Sequential

   ○ **B.** Broadcast

   ○ **C.** Parallel

   ○ **D.** Peer

56. Preparing for an installation of an SBCS system, you learn that the customer has decided to allow employees to connect from home one day per week. Which of the following security features would you use to implement this service?

   ○ **A.** NAT

   ○ **B.** VPN

   ○ **C.** Firewall

   ○ **D.** PAT

57. There are six monitoring graphs displayed by default with the Health monitoring feature. Which of the following statistics are graphed on this screen? (Choose two.)

   ○ **A.** Voice port utilization

   ○ **B.** PoE utilization

   ○ **C.** Flash memory utilization

   ○ **D.** CPU utilization

58. Software upgrades for the UC500 components are highly automated. How many files are required to upgrade all the components?

   ○ **A.** 1

   ○ **B.** 2

   ○ **C.** 27

   ○ **D.** 43

19

Practice Exam 2
Answer Key

1.	A, C	**21.**	C	**41.**	A, B, D
2.	C	**22.**	C	**42.**	A, D, G
3.	D	**23.**	B	**43.**	B
4.	D	**24.**	A	**44.**	C
5.	D	**25.**	E	**45.**	B
6.	A, C	**26.**	B	**46.**	A, E
7.	D	**27.**	B	**47.**	A
8.	A, D	**28.**	C	**48.**	D
9.	B	**29.**	B	**49.**	C, E
10.	C	**30.**	D	**50.**	C
11.	D	**31.**	D	**51.**	C, D
12.	B	**32.**	A	**52.**	B, D
13.	C	**33.**	C	**53.**	A
14.	D	**34.**	D	**54.**	B
15.	A, B	**35.**	A, D	**55.**	A, D
16.	A, B	**36.**	C	**56.**	B
17.	D	**37.**	B	**57.**	B, D
18.	D	**38.**	C	**58.**	A
19.	A, B, C, D	**39.**	D		
20.	C	**40.**	B		

Question 1

A and C. H.232 and SIP are peer-to-peer protocols. Answer B is incorrect because MGCP is a client/server protocol. Answer D is incorrect because it is not a signaling protocol. Answer E is incorrect because SCCP is a client/server protocol.

Question 2

C. Four call legs are required in this example. Answers A, B, and D are incorrect because one inbound and one outbound call leg are required per gateway.

Question 3

D. The maximum number of phones supported by Cisco Unified CME is 240. Answers A, B, and C are incorrect because CME supports 240 phones.

Question 4

D. The command used to define the maximum numbers of ephones is `max-ephone`. Answers A, B, and C are incorrect because they are not valid commands.

Question 5

D. This answer is correct because `noasw` is not a valid keyword for the `call-forward` command. Answer A is incorrect because `noan` is a valid keyword for the `call-forward` command. Answer B is incorrect because `busy` is a valid keyword for the `call-forward` command. Answer C is incorrect because `all` is a valid keyword for the `call-forward` command.

Question 6

A and C. CCA offers the topology and front panel graphical views. Answer B is incorrect because there is no "Current Traffic Volume" in the graphical view. Answer D is incorrect because there is no "Auto Attendant Call Flow" in the graphical view.

Question 7

D. The hunt type does not affect other hunt groups; it pertains only to the hunt group it was configured on. Answers A, B, and C are incorrect because hunt type settings of one group have no effect on the other groups.

Question 8

A and D. H.323 is an open-standard, peer-to-peer protocol and MGCP is an open-standard, client/server protocol. Answer B is incorrect because MGCP is a client/server protocol. Answer C is incorrect because H.323 is a peer-to-peer protocol.

Question 9

B. A VoIP dial peer is used to route a call to an IP destination. Answer A is incorrect because a POTS dial peer is used with a traditional analog or digital voice port. Answers C and D are incorrect because they are not valid dial peer types.

Question 10

C. 720 is the maximum number of directory numbers that are supported by Cisco Unified CME. Answers A, B, and D are incorrect because the maximum number of DNs that CME supports is 720.

Question 11

D. A second line is needed for full-consult transfers to work; if a second line is not a available, a blind transfer occurs. This does not mean that two DNs need to be configured; a single DN configured as a dual-line will suffice. Answer A is not correct because while the statement does not contain any incorrect information, it is not as complete as Answer D. Answer B is incorrect because the call will not fail if the second line is not available. Answer C is incorrect because full-consult does not use H.450.12.

Question 12

B. The WAN port is used to connect to an Internet provider. Answer A is incorrect because the Expansion port is used to connect a switch to the UC500. Answers C and D are incorrect because there are no such ports.

Question 13

C. Most phones are configured the same in keysystem mode. Answer A is incorrect because PBX mode is the default, not keysystem. Answer B is incorrect; calls are routed to an operator or Auto Attendant in PBX mode, not keysystem. Answer D is incorrect because keysystem mode has nothing to do with traditional keysystem integration.

Question 14

D. The Media Gateway Control Protocol (MGCP) is an IETF-standard client/server protocol. Answer A is incorrect because MGCP is a client/server protocol. Answer B is incorrect because MGCP does need a server. Answer C is incorrect because H.323 is a peer-to-peer protocol and does not operate like MGCP.

Question 15

A and B. The session target of a VoIP dial peer is an IP address, and a POTS dial peer uses the `port` command to determine where a call is routed. Answer C is not correct because the tag does not have to be between 100 and 1024. Answer D is incorrect because dial peer 0 only matches calls that do not match any other dial peer.

Question 16

A and B. The license and hardware platform determine how many phones can register to a Cisco Unified CME. Answer C is incorrect because the type of phone does not impact how many can register to CME. Answer D is incorrect because answer C is incorrect.

Question 17

D. The m separator of the `button` command configures the line as a monitor line. Answer A is incorrect because calls cannot be placed or received from ephone-dn 101. Answer B is incorrect because not only will ephone-dn not be able to receive multiple calls, but it will also not be able to receive any calls. Answer C is incorrect because the m separator of the `button` command makes the button a monitor-only button.

Question 18

D. The last line in the configuration defines that the call will be transferred to 2010 after the limit count is reached. If 2010 is busy, the call is sent to 2012. Answer A is incorrect because the call park number is 5510 and 121 is the tag number. Answer B is incorrect because the reminder is sent every 12 seconds and is the number of times the reminder will occur. Answer C is incorrect because the number that parks the call and 2002 receive the reminder.

Question 19

A, B, C, and D. All answers are correct. Dial plan, VLANs, PBX configuration, and autodiscovery are all supported by CCA.

Question 20

C. The internal pilot number for voicemail is configured in the Voicemail Access Extension field. Answer A is incorrect because the internal pilot number for the Auto Attendant is entered in this field. Answer B is incorrect because the number dialed from the PSTN to reach the Auto Attendant is entered in this field. Answer D is incorrect because the number dialed from the PSTN to reach voicemail is entered in this field.

Question 21

C. H.323 is an open-standard signaling protocol that supports voice, video, and data. Answer A is incorrect because PIMG is not a signaling protocol. Answer B is incorrect because DTMF does not support data. Answer D, MGCP, is incorrect because it does not support data. Answer E is incorrect because SMDI is a voicemail protocol.

Question 22

C. The session target command is part of a VoIP dial peer, not a POTS dial peer. Answers A, B, and D are incorrect because they are all valid POTS dial peer commands.

Question 23

B. A BRI has two B channels and one D channel. Answers A, C, and D are incorrect. PRI supplies 23B+D, and T1 and E1 are each 24 and 32 digital channels, respectively.

Question 24

A. Before an audio file can be selected in CCA, it must be uploaded to flash. Answer B is incorrect because the audio file is not uploaded when selected from CCA. Answers C and D are not correct because the file format is .wav or .au, a-law or mu-law.

Question 25

E. Network Address Translation, Standard IEEE 802.1X on switch, Cisco IOS Firewall, and Cisco Easy VPN Remote and Server support are all security features of SBCS.

Question 26

B. SS7 is used for call setup between COs. Answers A, C, and D are incorrect because they are CPE components.

Question 27

B. Answer A is incorrect because there is no international organization that mandates numbering plans. Answer C is incorrect because PBXs are controlled within an organization. Answer D is incorrect because the NANP manages only the United States and Canada.

Question 28

C. Answers A and B are incorrect; H.323 and SIP are call control protocols. Answers D and E are incorrect because they are variations of CCS call setup protocols for digital circuits.

Question 29

B. Humans can detect sounds in the 0–4000Hz range. Answer A would provide a very poor reproduction of the original signal. Answers C and D reference specific frequencies; a theorem is generic. Therefore, answers A, C, and D are incorrect.

Question 30

D. RTP helps VoIP endpoints identify sequence and missing packet issues by providing a sequence number and a time stamp with every voice sample group. Answers A (IP), B (TCP), C (UDP), and E (FTP) are incorrect.

Question 31

D. The Annex B variant applies to both G.729 and G.729a and is used to implement voice activity detection service with comfort noise generation. VAD and CNG go together and cannot be configured individually. Annex B does not impact the DSP processing power required or the codec complexity. Answers A and B are the two different companding methods for PCM encoding, and answer C, Annex C, is a fragmentation technique for Voice over Frame Relay. Therefore, answers A, B, and C are incorrect.

Question 32

A. G.711 uses 64Kbps and G.729 uses 8Kbps, respectively, so answers B, C, and D are incorrect.

Question 33

C. Compressed Real Time Protocol (cRTP) identifies the fields that are unchanged during a voice call, and after the first packet of a voice stream has traversed the link, only the changed header values are forwarded with the payload. cRTP requires only 2 bytes to convey the IP+UDP+RTP header changes for subsequent packets to the destination, after the first full 40-byte IP+UDP+RTP header has been transmitted. Answers A (RTCP), B (RTP), and D (secure RTP [sRTP]) are incorrect.

Question 34

D. TFTP requires a `tftp-server` command for each image file required by the IP phone to become operational. HTTP, DHCP, and FTP are not used during the automatic provisioning and registration process, so answers A, B, and C are incorrect.

Question 35

A and D. Poke a hole in the firewall, set up an NTP server in the DMZ (if present), or purchase an atomic or radio clock as your source. Answers B and C are incorrect because the internal clock on the router platform can drift over time.

Question 36

C. Answer A is incorrect; the default language is U.S. English and other options are configured globally or per phone. Answer B is incorrect because the time is derived from the router platform. Answer D is incorrect because ring tones are determined with the `RingList.xml` and `DistinctiveRingList.xml` files.

Question 37

B. The `tftp-server` command references the full URL, and the `telephony-service load` command references the filename without the extension. FTP service is not supported for IP phone firmware image upgrades, so answers A and D are incorrect. The complete filename including extension must be referenced by the `tftp-server` command, so answer C is incorrect.

Question 38

C. Before configuring anything, prepare a QoS policy based on information gathered prior to the installation. Answers A, B, and D are incorrect because they are configuration steps used to implant the QoS policy.

Question 39

D. The DSCP field is 6 bits long and contains a maximum of 64 different values, 0–63. The DSCP field is 6 bits long with 64 values, so answers A, B, and C are incorrect.

Question 40

B. QoS is enabled on this interface only when the phone is connected. Answers A and C are in the wrong configuration mode and are incorrect. Answer D provides static QoS and is active at all times.

Question 41

A, B, and D. AutoQoS will generate additional commands to implement PPP, cRTP, and LFI on circuits that are 768Kbps or slower, and not on higher-speed circuits. Answer C is incorrect; there is no conversion for PPPoE because Ethernet and higher (Fast and Gigabit) circuits have a bandwidth of at least 10000Kbps.

Question 42

A, D, and G. Per-line costs are less expensive, ITSPs use H.323 or SIP VoIP connections, and PSTN connections can be incremented in units of one line. Answers B and C apply to a direct ISDN PRI circuit and are incorrect. Answer E is incorrect because each ITSP connection has a negotiated service-level agreement for a maximum number of phone calls. Answer F is incorrect just because it uses the word *never*. Even if there are no billed long-distance charges, the charges are built into the circuit termination fee.

Question 43

B. Wildcard digits represent the digits starting with the leftmost wildcard in the destination pattern to the end of the dialed digits. Answer A has some truth to it, answer C could be true if no other digit manipulation occurs before the call is placed, and answer D is just a distracter, so answers A, C, and D are incorrect.

Question 44

C. The `numexp` global command can expand or replace the digits dialed prior to the outgoing dial peer match process. Answer A, the `prefix` command, prepends digits to the called party as the last dial peer digit manipulation and is incorrect. Answer B, `forward-digits`, modifies the default digit consumption rules for VoIP and POTS dial peers and is incorrect. Answer D sounds like a hoax but it is a hidden Cisco IOS command, just not for voice calls (just kidding) and is not correct.

Question 45

B. Answers A, C, and D are incorrect. Hardware conferencing uses SCCP, and the ITSP and VPIM locations are not local Cisco Unified Communications Express components.

Question 46

A and E. MWI on and off dial peers require an activation code followed by a wildcard period (.) for each digit in the dial plan extension length. Answers B, C, and D are incorrect because call park, group paging, and group call pickup features require a specific dialable number.

Question 47

A. The IP address and web administrator credentials are required to use the integrated Cisco Unified Communications Manager Express and Cisco Unity Express GUI. Answer B is incorrect; Cisco Unity Connection is a server-based product. Answer C is incorrect because the administrator password is set during the initial configuration script. Answer D, IPCCX, is a server-based platform.

Question 48

D. Answers A, B, and C are incorrect. There is no Telnet access to Cisco Unity Express, external ports cannot be used, and there is no external console port.

Question 49

C and E. Call-in numbers and Cisco Unified Communications Manager Express credentials are entered. Answer A is incorrect; host name is entered after an installation or factory default restore. Answer B is incorrect; the IP address is entered on the host router. Answer D is incorrect; users are imported from Cisco Unified Communications Manager Express or entered manually using the Cisco Unity Express CLI or GUI.

Question 50

C. In enabled exec CLI mode, the `service-module service-engine` `mod/port status` command returns the operating status and latest installed version. Answers B, D, and E cannot be operated as shown from configuration mode, even though B is the correct syntax. Answer A is incorrect due to keyword sequence, and answer F is incorrect because of missing keywords.

Question 51

C and D. The `debug ephone mwi` and `debug voip dialpeer all` commands can be used together to solve MWI outcall problems. Answer A is incorrect because there is no voicemail option, and answer B is incorrect because this command is used for integrating PSTN access to legacy voicemail systems.

Question 52

B and D. These answers show the two options used to turn off all `debug` commands. Answer A is incorrect; it displays the active `debug` commands. Answer C is incorrect because it is an incomplete command.

Question 53

A. The no console logging command disables all console messages. Answer B is an invalid command; answer C activates console message output for Telnet sessions, and answer D is used to store console messages in a local buffer.

Question 54

B. This command displays the Cisco IOS version and feature set. Answer A is incorrect; it displays the current active debug options. Answer C is incorrect; it displays the status of the currently configured ephones. Answer D is incorrect; it displays the version of Cisco Unified Communications Manager Express. Answer E is incorrect because it displays the information for all configured ephone-dns.

Question 55

A and D. The sequential option searches through the hunt group starting with the first extension in the group, and peer starts the search with the extension after the last selected extension. Answer B is an invalid option and is incorrect. Answer C is a correct option for voice hunt groups and is incorrect.

Question 56

B. The VPN service provides secure remote access. Answer A, NAT, is used to translate private internal IP addresses to public Internet addresses and is incorrect. Answer C is incorrect because it refers to protecting the platform from external or public security threats. Answer D, PAT, is another way to translate private internal IP addresses to public Internet addresses and is incorrect.

Question 57

B and D. Answers A and C are not default health graphs in CCA; therefore, these answers are incorrect.

Question 58

A. There is a single .zip file that contains all the software required to upgrade all components of the UC500 installation. Answers B, C, and D are not correct.

PART VI

Appendixes

APPENDIX A

Cisco Unified Communications Overview

Cisco Unified Communications represents an innovative way of delivering unified communications to customers. Rather than patching together voice, video, and messaging components from various vendors, Cisco Unified Communications presents the first coordinated release of a set of products that are tested, documented, and supported as an integrated system.

The topics covered in this appendix have been added to this book in anticipation of future Cisco exam updates. Cisco lists these topics as potential exam topics that could appear on the exam.

Describe the Function of the Infrastructure in a Cisco Unified Communications Environment

The infrastructure lays the foundation with network components based on Cisco routers and switches that use a common management interface. The infrastructure consists of routers, switches, and voice gateways and is used to carry quality of service (QoS)–enabled voice, video, messaging, and data between all the network devices, end devices, and applications.

Describe the Function of Endpoints in a Cisco Unified Communications Environment

The telephone is the most visible component of the voice communications network. Cisco Unified IP phones are next-generation, intelligent communication devices that deliver essential business communications. Fully programmable, the growing family of Cisco Unified IP phones provides the most frequently used business features in phones.

Most Cisco Unified IP phones provide the following enhancements:

- Display-based user interface
- Straightforward user customization
- Inline Power over Ethernet (PoE)
- Support for the G.711 and G.729 audio coder-decoders (codecs)
- Support for Internet Low Bit-rate Codec (iLBC) on the newest phones such as the Cisco Unified IP Phone 7942G, 7945G, 7962G, 7965G, and 7975G

Each Cisco Unified IP phone provides toll-quality audio and does not require a companion PC. Because it is an IP-based phone, you can install it on any LAN segment in the enterprise, regardless of whether it connects to Cisco Communications Manager over the LAN or WAN.

Describe the Function of the Call Processing Agent in a Cisco Unified Communications Environment

Cisco offers four different product options for call processing:

- **Cisco Smart Business Communications System:** This option runs on the Cisco Unified Communications 500 Series for Small Business platform and provides entry-level wired and wireless data transport, firewall security, remote secure access, phone service using PSTN or SIP service providers, and integrated voicemail.

▶ **Cisco Unified Communications Manager Express:** This option runs on the Cisco Integrated Services Routers and provides small to medium businesses with advanced phone features and phone service using PSTN or SIP service providers. Cisco Unified CallConnector Mobility provides advanced features such as Presence, Single Number Reach, and Direct Inward Service Access.

▶ **Cisco Unified Communications Manager Business Edition:** This option runs on a Cisco 7800 Series Media Convergence Server. This product targets small to medium organizations and provides call agent, mobility, presence, and voicemail with integrated messaging in a single integrated package.

▶ **Cisco Unified Communications Manager:** This option runs on the Cisco 7800 Series Media Convergence Servers. This solution targets larger organizations and includes features such as mobility and presence.

These products offer the ability to set up and tear down phone calls and provide additional call features such as call park, conferencing, call waiting, call pickup, and many others.

Describe the Function of Messaging in a Cisco Unified Communications Environment

A Cisco Unified Communications system has several options to provide end-user messaging services for voice, email, calendaring, and faxes. The products described in the following sections provide these messaging services.

Cisco Unity Express for up to 250 Users

Cisco Unity Express helps reduce the total cost of ownership (TCO) for small- and medium-sized business (SMBs) and branch offices by providing integrated voicemail, greeting, fax, and IVR services.

Cisco Unity Express is available on selected voice-enabled Cisco Integrated Services Routers and provides the following features:

▶ Affordable messaging and greeting services for increased customer service and rich employee communications

- ▶ Intuitive telephone prompts and a web-based interface for fast, convenient voicemail and Auto Attendant administration

- ▶ Rich features and functionality, including the ability to view, sort, search, and play back voice messages using the display of a Cisco Unified IP phone or your email client, and Internet Message Access Protocol (IMAP)–compliant email integration

- ▶ Centrally managed voice services at branch locations

Cisco Unity Connection for up to 3,000 Users

Cisco Unity Connection is a full-featured voice and integrated messaging solution with a broad range of productivity-enhancing features, including advanced call-routing rules and speech recognition capabilities. Cisco Unity Connection scales to meet the needs of organizations with up to 3,000 users.

For organizations with up to 500 users, Cisco Unity Connection is available as a single-server solution with Cisco Unified Communications Manager Business Edition, further simplifying installation, support, and maintenance. Large, multisite organizations can network Cisco Unity Connection with up to 10 Cisco Unity, Cisco Unity Connection, or Cisco Unity Express messaging products, allowing users from one location to transparently reply, forward, and exchange voice messages with users in other locations.

Cisco Unity Connection enables you to do the following:

- ▶ Manage your messages in hands-free mode with natural voice commands

- ▶ View, prioritize, and listen to voice messages with Cisco Unified Personal Communicator, an email client, or a web browser

- ▶ Use the Cisco Unity Connection Phone View to use the display of a Cisco Unified IP phone to view, sort, search, and play back voice messages

- ▶ Use voice commands to list and attend Cisco Unified MeetingPlace Express meetings

Cisco Unity for up to 7,500 Users

Cisco Unity delivers powerful voicemail, integrated messaging, and unified messaging options that transparently integrate with Microsoft Exchange, Lotus Domino, and Novell GroupWise. It scales to meet the needs of large, multisite organizations and offers extensive personalization options, a broad range of productivity-enhancing features, and powerful migration tools, which include the following:

▶ Interoperability with existing voice messaging and telephony systems

▶ Custom keypad mapping of the telephony interfaces

▶ Integrated context-sensitive help

▶ Desktop voice message access using Cisco Unified Personal Communicator

▶ Mobile voice message access across a variety of handsets and operating systems using Cisco Unified Mobile Communicator

▶ Alternative device recognition, which automatically recognizes alternate devices, such as mobile phones, when accessing the system to streamline access

▶ Secure messaging, which allows only authorized clients connected to the network to retrieve encrypted voice messages

▶ Message monitor, which listens to and picks up calls while a message is being recorded

▶ Interrupted session recovery, which allows you to automatically return to in-progress message composition or playback if you ended a session prematurely

▶ Cisco Unity Phone View, which allows you to view, sort, search, and play back voice messages

▶ Speech access, which allows you to press or say commands to deliver hands-free operation

Describe the Function of Auto Attendants and IVRs in a Cisco Unified Communications Environment

For many enterprises, it is useful to "front-end" calls to an Auto Attendant. An Auto Attendant effectively replaces the human operator and allows the caller to self-direct his or her call. The following are some common functions that an Auto Attendant provides:

▶ Callers can spell out the name of the user they are trying to reach, and the Auto Attendant will use a corporate directory to try to find a match.

▶ The option to reach a user by dialing his name.

▶ Basic menus that allow a user to navigate by pressing phone keys or using spoken requests.

▶ Informational applications for calls that are not destined for a person, such as a movie hotline.

Cisco Unity and Cisco Unity Connection both have a highly functional and robust Auto Attendant in addition to voicemail. You configure the Auto Attendant logic and functions using the web-based administrative pages.

Cisco Unity Express is a Linux-based appliance that implements an optional Auto Attendant and has IVR capabilities.

Cisco Unified IP IVR is an integral component of the Cisco Unified Communications system that provides an open, extensible, and feature-rich foundation for the creation and delivery of self-service voice applications. The Cisco Unified IP IVR provides the following features:

▶ Is an IP-based IVR application

▶ Provides self-service applications, such as prompt and collect, as well as more advanced applications that can include database functions, Java integrations with third-party applications, speech recognition, and text-to-speech (TTS)

▶ Can provide call treatment for call center calls that are waiting for agents

▶ Integrates with Cisco Unified Communications Manager, Cisco Unified Contact Center Express, Cisco Unified Contact Center Enterprise, and Cisco Unified Contact Center Hosted

▶ Supports multiple languages

▶ Has built-in historical and real-time reporting

Describe the Function of Contact Center in a Cisco Unified Communications Environment

Cisco Unified Contact Center Express helps you improve operational efficiency, reduce business costs, and improve your customer response. It is a contact center solution that is designed for mid-market, enterprise branch, or corporate departments that require a customer interaction management solution for 10 to 300 agents. Cisco Unified Contact Center Express is easy to deploy, easy to use, secure, virtual, and highly available and has the following characteristics:

- Contains a fully integrated automatic call distributor (ACD) that allows calls to be routed to agents based on skills

- Provides an integrated IVR function that allows complex and full-featured call treatment

- Contains computer telephony integration (CTI) that allows an agent to receive data about the caller that is being routed to her

- Provides outbound dialing capabilities that allow calls to be initiated from the call center

Cisco Unified Contact Center Express is intended for both formal and informal contact centers, and offers the following:

- Sophisticated call routing

- Comprehensive contact management

- Robust email management

- Chat and web collaboration

- Outbound dialing capabilities

- Easy-to-use administration features

- Simplified installation, configuration, and application hosting

Cisco Unified Contact Center Express is available in three versions—standard, enhanced, and premium—to better match product function to your customer contact center requirements. You can easily upgrade from one version to the next.

Describe the Applications Available in the Cisco Unified Communications Environment: MeetingPlace, Emergency Responder, Mobility, Presence, and TelePresence

Cisco Unified MeetingPlace is a large-scale conferencing server that also supports video integration. It is a full-featured product that integrates lecture-style conferences and full collaboration. For small- to medium-sized enterprises, you should use Cisco Unified MeetingPlace Express.

Cisco Emergency Responder enhances the existing emergency functionality offered by Cisco Unified Communications Manager. It ensures that Cisco Unified Communications Manager sends emergency calls to the public safety answering point (PSAP) that is appropriate for the location of the caller, and that the PSAP can identify the caller location and return the call if necessary. In addition, the system automatically tracks and updates equipment moves and changes. Deploying this capability helps ensure more effective compliance with legal or regulatory obligations, thereby reducing the risk of liability related to emergency calls.

Cisco Unified Mobility, commonly known as Single Number Reach, gives users the ability to redirect incoming IP calls from the Cisco Unified Communications Manager to up to four different designated client devices such as cellular phones or IP phones.

Cisco Unified Presence collects information about the availability status and communications capabilities of a user, including whether the user is using a communications device, such as a phone, and whether the user has web collaboration or videoconferencing enabled on his system.

Cisco TelePresence provides the "Star Trek" experience for videoconferencing. The conference rooms used for Cisco TelePresence are built to detailed specifications to provide conference attendees with the experience of sitting across the table with attendees at distant geographic locations.

The Cisco TelePresence Multipoint Switch extends the Cisco TelePresence experience by enabling you to include three or more locations in a single meeting. This solution delivers an exceptional Cisco TelePresence experience by enabling all participants to be seen in life-size, high-definition (1080p) images and heard in CD-quality, spatial audio with near-zero latency.

The Cisco TelePresence Multipoint Switch is an affordable, purpose-built appliance that is easy to install and offers superior scalability with up to 36 locations in a single meeting. Both point-to-point and multipoint meetings are easily set up directly from the groupware calendar of a user (such as Microsoft Outlook), and meetings are initiated with the push of a button.

Describe how the Cisco Unified Communications Components Work Together to Create the Cisco Unified Communications Architecture

Cisco Unified Communications products deliver voice, video, fax, email, and voicemail services. These products are integrated over Cisco networking products and are developed with a common architecture using standards-based communications protocols.

What's on the CD-ROM

The CD-ROM features an innovative practice test engine powered by MeasureUp, giving you yet another effective tool to assess your readiness for the exam.

Multiple Test Modes

MeasureUp practice tests can be used in Study, Certification, or Custom Modes.

Study Mode

Tests administered in Study mode enable you to request the correct answer(s) and the explanation for each question during the test. These tests are not timed. You can modify the testing environment during the test by selecting the Options button.

You may also specify the objectives or missed questions you want to include in your test, the timer length, and other test properties. You can also modify the testing environment during the test by selecting the Options button.

In Study mode, you receive automatic feedback on all correct and incorrect answers. The detailed answer explanations are a superb learning tool in their own right.

Certification Mode

Tests administered in Certification mode closely simulate the actual testing environment you will encounter when taking a certification exam and are timed. These tests do not allow you to request the answer(s) and/or explanation for each question until after the exam.

Custom Mode

Custom mode enables you to specify your preferred testing environment. Use this mode to specify the objectives you want to include in your test, the timer length, number of questions, and other test properties. You can also modify the testing environment during the test by selecting the Options button.

Attention to Exam Objectives

MeasureUp practice tests are designed to appropriately balance the questions over each technical area covered by a specific exam. All concepts from the actual exam are covered thoroughly to ensure you're prepared for the exam.

Installing the CD

System Requirements:

- ▶ Windows 95, 98, ME, NT4, 2000, or XP
- ▶ 7MB disk space for the testing engine
- ▶ An average of 1MB disk space for each individual test
- ▶ Control Panel Regional Settings must be set to English (United States)
- ▶ PC only

To install the CD-ROM, follow these instructions:

1. Close all applications before beginning this installation.
2. Insert the CD into your CD-ROM drive. If the setup starts automatically, go to step 6. If the setup does not start automatically, continue with step 3.
3. From the Start menu, select Run.
4. Click Browse to locate the MeasureUp CD. In the Browse dialog box, from the Look In drop-down list, select the CD-ROM drive.
5. In the Browse dialog box, double-click Setup.exe. In the Run dialog box, click OK to begin the installation.
6. On the Welcome screen, click MeasureUp Practice Questions to begin installation.

7. Follow the Certification Prep Wizard by clicking Next.

8. To agree to the Software License Agreement, click Yes.

9. On the Choose Destination Location screen, click Next to install the software to C:\Program Files\Certification Preparation. If you cannot locate MeasureUp Practice Tests through the Start menu, see the section titled "Creating a Shortcut to the MeasureUp Practice Tests," later in this appendix.

10. On the Setup Type screen, select Typical Setup. Click Next to continue.

11. In the Select Program Folder screen, you can name the program folder where your tests will be located. To select the default, simply click Next and the installation continues.

12. After the installation is complete, verify that Yes, I Want to Restart My Computer Now is selected. If you select No, I Will Restart My Computer Later, you cannot use the program until you restart your computer.

13. Click Finish.

14. After restarting your computer, choose Start, Programs, Certification Preparation, Certification Preparation, MeasureUp Practice Tests.

15. On the MeasureUp Welcome Screen, click Create User Profile.

16. In the User Profile dialog box, complete the mandatory fields and click Create Profile.

17. Select the practice test you want to access and click Start Test.

Creating a Shortcut to the MeasureUp Practice Tests

To create a shortcut to the MeasureUp Practice Tests, follow these steps:

1. Right-click on your Desktop.

2. From the shortcut menu, select New, Shortcut.

3. Browse to C:\Program Files\MeasureUp Practice Tests and select the `MeasureUpCertification.exe` or `Localware.exe` file.

4. Click OK.

5. Click Next.

6. Rename the shortcut MeasureUp.

7. Click Finish.

After you complete step 7, use the MeasureUp shortcut on your Desktop to access the MeasureUp products you ordered.

Technical Support

If you encounter problems with the MeasureUp test engine on the CD-ROM, please contact MeasureUp at (800) 649-1687 or email support@measureup.com. Support hours of operation are 7:30 a.m. to 4:30 p.m., EST. Additionally, you can find Frequently Asked Questions (FAQ) in the "Support" area at www. measureup.com. If you would like to purchase additional MeasureUp products, call 678-356-5050 or 800-649-1687 or visit www.measureup.com.

Glossary

A

Advanced Integration Module (AIM)
A daughter card plugged into the motherboard to provide ancillary services for the host router.

analog voice port A physical port in a router or gateway that an analog device or line is plugged into.

Answer and Disconnect Supervision Monitors and controls circuit connect and disconnect operation.

Asynchronous Transfer Mode (ATM) A dedicated-connection switching technology that organizes digital data into units and transmits them over a physical medium using digital signal technology.

attenuation The reduction in strength of a signal. Attenuation occurs with any type of signal, whether digital or analog. Sometimes referred to as *signal loss*.

auto-assign A command used to automatically assign a DN to button 1 of a phone when is registered.

auto-reg-ephone A command used to enable or disable autoregistration.

B

bandwidth The available capacity of a network link over a physical medium.

Basic Rate Interface (BRI) This service uses frequencies higher than 4000Hz to transport two DS0 channels across a local loop.

bridge A device used to segment a LAN into multiple physical segments. A bridge uses a forwarding table to determine which frames need to be forwarded to specific segments. Bridges isolate local traffic to the originating physical segment but forward all nonlocal and broadcast traffic.

bridge protocol data unit (BPDU) A data message that is exchanged across the switches within an extended LAN that uses a Spanning Tree Protocol topology.

broadcast A data frame sent to every node on a local segment.

button A command used to assign an ephone-dn to a button on an ephone.

C

call blocking The ability to block certain phone numbers from being reached.

call forwarding A command used to activate the forwarding state and indicate where calls are forwarded.

call park A command used to configure a call park slot. Call park allows a call to be placed on hold and retrieved from another dn.

call pickup A command used to configure call pickup groups. Call pickup allows an incoming call to be answered on a phone other than the one that is ringing.

call transfer A command used to determine the call-transferring method.

central office (CO) The local telephone company office where all local loops in an area connect.

channel A single communications path on a system. In some situations, channels can be multiplexed over a single connection.

channel-associated signaling (CAS) The reserved bits in the digital frames for T1 and E1 that provide basic end-station status such as on-hook and off-hook.

Cisco Configuration Assistant (CCA) A graphical user interface application used to manage UC500 SBCS implementations.

Cisco Discovery Protocol (CDP) A Cisco-proprietary protocol that operates at the data link layer. CDP enables network administrators to view a summary protocol and address information about other directly connected Cisco routers (and some Cisco switches).

Cisco Unified Communications Manager Express (CME) A Cisco IOS router-based telephony system.

class of service (CoS) Used to identify Layer 2 trunk priority tags 0 through 7.

class-based weighted fair queuing (CBWFQ) An administrator-defined bandwidth allocation for up to 14 Layer 3 QoS classifications.

client/server The relationship between two devices. One acts as the client, the other as server.

codec (coder-decoder) A technique used to compress and uncompress audio and visual signals.

command-line interface (CLI) A text-based router, switch, and Cisco Unity Express interface.

common channel signaling (CCS) One DS0 channel is reserved for call setup and teardown for all bearer DS0s.

compression A technique used to reduce bandwidth requirements.

console A terminal attached directly to the router for configuring and monitoring the router.

convergence The process by which all routers within an internetwork route information and eventually agree on optimal routes through the internetwork.

D

default dial peer 0 A dial peer used for arriving calls that do not match a configured dial peer.

default mask A binary or decimal representation of the number of bits used to identify an IP network. The class of the IP address defines the default mask. A default mask is represented by four octets of binary digits. The mask can also be presented in dotted decimal notation.

default route A network route (that usually points to another router) established to receive and attempt to process all packets for which no route appears in the route table.

Delay Dial Supervision Supervision in which E&M circuits seize an analog circuit and, when the far side acknowledges the connection, the originator waits for a fixed interval and then sends the dialed digits.

destination pattern The patterns of digits used by a dial peer to match outbound calls.

DHCP relay A router function that relays a local broadcast DHCP request to a remote DHCP server.

dial peer A set of commands that instructs CME how to handle incoming and outgoing calls. The information contained in these commands can include codec, protocol, and phone number.

`dialplan-pattern` A command used to expand a number to a fully qualified E1.64 number.

Differentiated Services Code Point (DSCP) An IETF standard that defines up to 64 QoS priority levels for the ToS field in the IP packet header.

digital signal processor (DSP) A computer chip used to process analog and digital signals in real time.

digital voice port A physical port in a router or gateway that a digital circuit is plugged into.

Domain Name System (DNS) A system used to translate fully qualified host names or computer names into IP addresses and vice versa.

dual tone multifrequency (DTMF) The tone played when a button is pressed on the telephone keypad.

Dynamic Host Configuration Protocol (DHCP) A protocol that is used to dynamically assign IP addresses to endpoints.

E

E&M An Ear and Mouth analog circuit with bidirectional circuit control to prevent glare.

E1 A digital circuit with 32 DS0s used outside North America.

encoding The process of transforming information from one format into another.

endpoints User communication devices: phones, faxes, and videoconferencing.

Ephone An Ethernet phone; an IP phone.

Ephone-dn An extension number.

European Telephony Numbering Space (ETNS) The European numbering scheme.

EXEC The user interface for executing Cisco router commands.

Extensible Markup Language (XML) A technique used to send user-defined data using HTTP. See *XML*.

F

File Transfer Protocol (FTP) A protocol used to copy a file from one host to another host, regardless of the physical hardware or operating system of each device. FTP identifies a client and server during the file-transfer process. In addition, it provides a guaranteed transfer by using the services of the Transmission Control Protocol (TCP).

Foreign Exchange Office (FXO) An analog port into which a phone line is plugged.

Foreign Exchange Station (FXS) An analog port into which a phone or other endpoint is plugged.

Frame Relay A switched data link layer protocol that supports multiple virtual circuits using High-Level Data Link Control (HDLC) encapsulation between connected devices.

frame tagging A method of tagging a frame with a unique user-defined virtual local-area network (VLAN). The process of tagging frames allows VLANs to span multiple switches.

full duplex The physical transmission process on a network device by which one pair of wires transmits data while another pair of wires receives data. Full-duplex transmission is achieved by eliminating the possibility of collisions on an Ethernet segment, thereby eliminating the need for a device to sense collisions.

G

global configuration mode A router mode that enables simple router configuration commands—such as router names, banners, and passwords—to be executed. Global configuration commands affect the whole router rather than a single interface or component.

graphical user interface (GUI) An interface with fill-in fields, drop-down menus, and check boxes that replaces text-only configuration.

ground start A local loop circuit type used to reduce glare.

H

H.323 An ITU standard used widely among many vendors. It is often referred to as an umbrella protocol under which a number of other protocols sit. This protocol is based on the ISDN q.931 protocol and allows traditional telephony features to function within an IP network.

half duplex The physical transmission process whereby one pair of wires is used to transmit information and the other pair of wires is used to receive information or to sense collisions on the physical media. Half-duplex transmission is required on Ethernet segments with multiple devices.

High-Level Data Link Control (HDLC) A bit-oriented, synchronous data link layer protocol that specifies data encapsulation methods on serial links.

header Control information placed before the data during the encapsulation process.

host name A logical name given to a router.

hunt group A group of DNs that a call cycles through until answered.

I

IEEE (Institute of Electrical and Electronics Engineers) An organization whose primary function is to define standards for networks LANs.

IEEE 802.3af A standard for delivering Power over Ethernet (PoE).

IEEE 802.1p A standard for providing quality of service marking on Layer 2 networks.

IEEE 802.1Q A standard for providing VLAN identification.

immediate start The originator of a call on an E&M circuit waits for connection acknowledgment from the far end and immediately sends the dialed digits.

intercom A feature that allows a call between two Cisco Unified Communications Manager Express endpoints to be initiated with the press of a single button.

interface A router component that provides a network connection through which data packets move in and out of the router. Depending on the model of router, interfaces exist either on the motherboard or on separate, modular interface cards.

Internet Control Message Protocol (ICMP) A protocol that communicates error messages and controls messages between devices. Thirteen types of ICMP messages are defined. ICMP enables devices to check the status of other devices, to query the current time, and to perform other functions such as ping and traceroute.

Internet telephony service provider (ITSP) An entity that provides PSTN connectivity over VoIP connections.

Inter-Switch Link (ISL) A protocol used to enable virtual local-area networks (VLANs) to span multiple switches. ISL is used between switches to communicate common VLANs between devices.

IP (Internet Protocol) One of the many protocols maintained in the TCP/IP suite of protocols. IP is the transport mechanism for Transmission Control Protocol (TCP), User Datagram Protocol (UDP), and Internet Control Message Protocol (ICMP) data. It also provides the logical addressing necessary for complex routing activity.

IP Precedence A method used to prioritize packets.

IP source address The IP address of the interface on the CME that is servicing SCCP requests.

IPSec A suite of security protocols that is used to provide a secure VPN. IPSec can operate in tunnel mode, where a new IP header is added, or transport mode, where the original IP header is used.

K

keepalive frame A protocol data unit (PDU) transmitted at the data link layer that indicates whether the proper frame type is configured.

keysystem mode A configuration of the CME in which most phones are configured the same and incoming calls can be answered on any phone.

L

LAN protocol A protocol that identifies a Layer 2 protocol used for the transmission of data within a local-area network (LAN). The three most popular LAN protocols used today are Ethernet, token ring, and Fiber Distributed Data Interface (FDDI).

load A command used to associate a firmware file with a phone model.

local loop The line from the customer's premises to the telephone company's central office (CO).

loop start A basic CO local loop used for residential phone service.

M

MAC (Media Access Control) address A physical address used to define a device uniquely.

Management Information Base (MIB) A database that maintains statistics on certain data items. The Simple Network Management Protocol (SNMP) uses MIBs to query information about devices.

max-dns A command that defines the maximum number of ephone-dns that can be configured in the system.

max-ephones A command that defines the maximum number of ephones that can be configured in the system.

Media Gateway Control Protocol (MGCP) An IETF client/server protocol used in Cisco VoIP to control PSTN gateways.

Message Waiting Indicator (MWI) Typically a light on the phone that is illuminated when there is new voicemail. A stutter dial tone is often used on phones that do not have an MWI.

multicasting A process of using one IP address to represent a group of IP addresses. Multicasting is used to send messages to a subset of IP addresses in a network or networks.

multiplexing A method of flow control used by the transport layer in which application conversations are combined over a single channel by interleaving packets from different segments and transmitting them.

Music on Hold (MOH) A feature that plays an audio steam when calls are placed on hold.

N

Network Address Translation (NAT) The process of translating multiple internal IP addresses to a single registered IP address on the outside of your network.

network interface card (NIC) A circuit board that provides network communication capabilities to and from a network host.

Network Module (NM) A router plug-in component that provides extended services for Cisco ISR routers.

Network Time Protocol (NTP) A protocol used to set the time on network devices.

network-based application recognition (NBAR) A method of data recognition that analyzes the data packets by examining the header and payload to identify the data type for QoS marking and queuing strategies.

network-locale Defines the locale for a phone.

nonvolatile random-access memory (NVRAM) A memory area of the router that stores permanent information, such as the router's backup configuration file. The contents of NVRAM are retained when the router is powered down or restarted.

North American Numbering Plan (NANP) Defines the characteristics of the dialing plan when calling to or from North America.

O

Open Systems Interconnection (OSI) model A layered networking framework developed by the International Organization for Standardization. The OSI model describes seven layers that correspond to specific networking functions.

P

packet switching A process by which a router moves a packet from one interface to another.

paging A one-way audio stream to multiple phones.

PBX mode A configuration of the CME in which incoming calls are routed to an Auto Attendant or operator and then routed to the desired party.

peer-to-peer communication A form of communication that occurs between the same layers of two different network hosts.

ping A tool for testing IP connectivity between two devices. Ping is used to send multiple IP packets between a sending and a receiving device. The destination device responds with an Internet Control Message Protocol (ICMP) packet to notify the source device of its existence.

plain old telephone service (POTS) The voice service provided by traditional telephone companies.

Point-to-Point Protocol (PPP) A standard protocol that enables router-to-router and host-to-network connectivity over synchronous and asynchronous circuits such as telephone lines.

port A physical interface on the router or gateway that is used to connect to another device or system.

Power over Ethernet (PoE) A means of providing power to endpoints over the Ethernet cable. Typically refers to the 802.3af power standard.

preference A command used to determine the priority of an ephone-dn or regular dial peer.

Primary Rate Interface (PRI) These types of circuits use ISDN protocols Q.921 and Q.931 to send and receive call flow messages to establish phone calls through the PSTN.

private branch exchange (PBX) A phone system that connects internal phones to the PSTN through a shared group of circuits. Each user has his or her own extension number and dials an access code to reach outside numbers.

privileged mode An extensive administrative and management mode on a Cisco router. This router mode permits testing, debugging, and commands to modify the router's configuration.

propagation The time taken to transmit electrons, traveling at the speed of light, across a length of wire or fiber.

protocol A formal description of a set of rules and conventions that define how devices on a network must exchange information.

protocol data unit (PDU) A unit of measure that refers to data that is transmitted between two peer layers within different network devices. Segments, packets, and frames are examples of PDUs.

public switched telephone network (PSTN) The circuit-switching facilities maintained for voice analog communication.

Q

quality of service (QoS) The means of prioritizing traffic on the network.

quantization The measurement of an analog signal converted to a digital value.

R

router mode A mode that enables the execution of specific router commands and functions. User, privileged, and setup are examples of router modes that allow you to perform certain tasks.

Real-Time Transport Control Protocol (RTCP) The control protocol for RTP.

Real-Time Transport Protocol (RTP) The protocol used for voice traffic on an IP telephony system.

running configuration file The current configuration file that is active on a router.

S

sampling The measurement of analog signals that starts the conversion to digital signals.

Secure Shell (SSH) A protocol that allows secure communication between a client and a router. It is a secure alternative to Telnet.

serialization The process of placing packets on the network for transmission.

service set identifier (SSID) A 32-bit unique identifier that is used to name a wireless network.

Session Initiation Protocol (SIP) An IETF-standard protocol that handles signaling for a number of IP communication formats. This includes voice, video, instant messaging, and presence.

session target The destination IP address configured on a VoIP dial peer to reach the destination pattern.

Signaling System 7 (SS7) A protocol used in the PSTN.

Simple Mail Transfer Protocol (SMTP) A protocol used to pass mail messages between devices; SMTP uses Transmission Control Protocol (TCP) connections to pass email between hosts.

Skinny Client Control Protocol (SCCP) A Cisco-proprietary signaling protocol used by Cisco IP voice devices.

Smart Business Communications System (SBCS) The Cisco PBX-in-a-box solution for small- to medium-sized organizations.

Spanning Tree Protocol A protocol used to eliminate all circular routes in a bridged or switched environment while maintaining redundancy. Circular routes are not desirable in Layer 2 networks because of the forwarding mechanism used at this layer.

startup configuration file The backup configuration file on a router that is used when the router first boots up.

subinterface One of possibly many virtual interfaces on a single physical interface.

switch A device that provides increased port density and forwarding capabilities as compared to bridges. The increased port densities of switches enable LANs to be microsegmented, thereby increasing the amount of bandwidth delivered to each device.

switch hook A physical device in an analog phone that closes the circuit on a local loop start residential circuit to indicate that the handset is off-hook.

T

T1 A digital circuit that includes 24 DS0 analog circuits using TDM.

Telnet A standard protocol that provides a virtual terminal. Telnet enables a network administrator to connect to a router remotely.

TFTP server A server that serves files through the TFTP protocol.

Trivial File Transfer Protocol (TFTP) A protocol used to copy files from one device to another. TFTP is a stripped-down version of FTP.

Transmission Control Protocol (TCP) One of the many protocols maintained in the TCP/IP suite of protocols. TCP provides a connection-oriented and reliable service to the applications that use it.

transport layer Layer 4 of the OSI model. It is concerned with segmenting upper-layer applications, establishing end-to-end connectivity through the network, sending segments from one host to another, and ensuring the reliable transport of data.

trunk A switch port that connects to another switch to enable virtual local-area networks (VLANs) to span multiple switches.

U

User Datagram Protocol (UDP) One of the many protocols maintained in the TCP/IP suite of protocols. UDP is a Layer 4, best-effort delivery protocol and therefore maintains connectionless network services.

user-locale Defines the locale for a user on CME.

user mode A display-only mode on a Cisco router. Only limited information about the router can be viewed within this router mode; no configuration changes are permitted.

V

virtual LAN (VLAN) A technique of assigning devices to specific LANs based on the port to which they attach on a switch rather than the physical location. VLANs extend the flexibility of LANs by allowing devices to be assigned to specific LANs on a port-by-port basis versus a device basis.

VLAN Trunking Protocol (VTP) A protocol for configuring and administering VLANs on Cisco network devices. With VTP, an administrator can make configuration changes centrally on a single Catalyst series switch and have those changes automatically communicated to all the other switches in the network.

voice activity detection (VAD) A method used to detect when there is voice on the line to ensure that traffic is only being sent when there is voice. This saves bandwidth by not sending silence.

Voice Profile for Internet Mail (VPIM) A protocol used to send voicemail messages over an IP network.

W

WAN (wide-area network) A network that uses data communications equipment (DCE) to connect multiple LANs. Examples of WAN protocols include Frame Relay, Point-to-Point Protocol (PPP), and High-Level Data Link Control (HDLC).

weighted fair queuing (WFQ) A method of delivering QoS based on TCP header IP precedence and average packet length for data networks. This is a flow-based algorithm that schedules interactive low-volume traffic ahead of bulk high-volume traffic.

wink start An E&M circuit seizes a circuit, and the far end sends wink start to the originator to signal that it is ready to receive dialed digits.

Wired Equivalent Privacy (WEP) A security protocol used in Wi-Fi networks that encrypts packets over radio waves. It offers 40-bit and 104-bit encryption (often referred to as 64- and 128-bit encryption because of the added initialization vector in the algorithm).

Wi-Fi Protected Access (WPA)/Wi-Fi Protected Access 2 (WPA2) Security protocols for Wi-Fi networks that provide greater security than WEP.

X

XML (Extensible Markup Language) A language that is similar to HTML but is not limited to webpages. It is used to create data exchange applications to provision Cisco IP phones.

Index

telephony services
commands, 197-200
configuring, 197-205
endpoint reboot, 205
endpoint verification, 204-205
firmware provisioning, 201-203
registration configuration, 203-204
users, importing, 222-223
version number, verifying, 269
Cisco Unified Communications, 371
architecture, 379
Auto Attendants, 375-376
call processing agent, 372-373
Cisco Unity, 374-375
Cisco Unity Connection, 374
Cisco Unity Express, 373-374
Contact Center, 377
Emergency Responder, 378
endpoints, 372
infrastructure, 371
IVRs, 375-376
MeetingPlace, 378
messaging services, 373-375
Mobility, 378
Presence, 378
TelePresence, 378
TelePresence Multipoint Switch, 378-379
Cisco Unified Communications 500 (UC500) series devices, SBCS (Smart Business Communications System), 276-278
Cisco Unified Communications Manager (CM). *See* CM (Cisco Unified Communications Manager)
Cisco Unified Communications Manager Business Edition call processing (CUC), 373
Cisco Unified Communications Manager call processing (CUC), 373
Cisco Unified Communications Manager Express (CME). *See* CME (Cisco Unified Communications Manager Express)

Cisco Unified Communications Manager Express call processing (CUC), 373
Cisco Unified Contact Center Express, 377
Cisco Unified Meeting Place, 378
Cisco Unified Mobility, 378
Cisco Unified Presence, 378
Cisco Unity, 374-375
Cisco Unity Connection, 374
Cisco Unity Express, 212, 373-374
AA (Auto Attendant), 227
activating, 227
Edit screen, 228-229
main screen, 227
managing prompts, 229-231
call handling parameters, setting, 224-225
capacities, 212-213
Cisco Unified CME
importing users, 222-223
integration, 220-226
configuring, 212-226
GUI initiation wizard, 220-226
preintegration CLI configuration, 214-217
service module interface, 214
factory defaults, resetting, 219
features, 213-214
functionality, 213-214
host router CLI tools, 231-233
IMAP (Internet Message Access Protocol), 212
installing, 217-220
integrated messaging, 214
logging into, 220-221
platforms, 212-213
troubleshooting, 231-233
upgrading, 217-220
user mailboxes, setting defaults, 223-224
VoiceView Express, 214
***Cisco Voice Gateways and Gatekeepers*, 48**
***Cisco Voice over IP (CVoice) (Authorized Self-Study Guide)*, 102, 121**

F

S

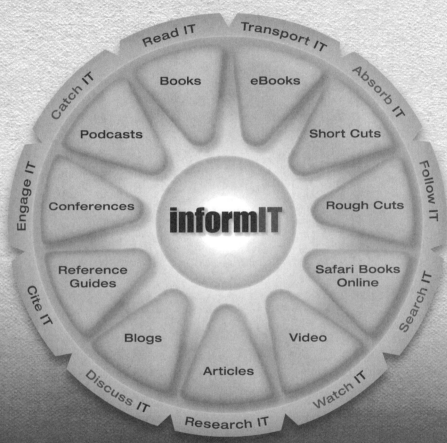

FREE Online Edition

Your purchase of **CCNA Voice Exam Cram** includes access to a free online edition for 45 days through the Safari Books Online subscription service. Nearly every Que book is available online through Safari Books Online, along with more than 5,000 other technical books and videos from publishers such as Addison-Wesley Professional, Cisco Press, Exam Cram, IBM Press, O'Reilly, Prentice Hall, and Sams.

SAFARI BOOKS ONLINE allows you to search for a specific answer, cut and paste code, download chapters, and stay current with emerging technologies.

Activate your FREE Online Edition at
www.informit.com/safarifree

> **STEP 1:** Enter the coupon code: WGRYSAA.

> **STEP 2:** New Safari users, complete the brief registration form.
> Safari subscribers, just log in.

If you have difficulty registering on Safari or accessing the online edition, please e-mail customer-service@safaribooksonline.com

  Addison Wesley

  AdobePress

 ALPHA

Cisco Press

  FT Press

   IBM Press

lynda.com

  Microsoft Press

New Riders

O'REILLY

Peachpit Press

 PRENTICE HALL

que

 Redbooks

SAMS

 SAS Publishing

Sun

  WILEY